In the writing [...] Durrani worked [...] of *Midnight Ex[...]* [...] Mahmoody's *Not Without My Daughter*.

www.booksattransworld.co.uk

MY
FEUDAL
LORD

Tehmina Durrani

with William and Marilyn Hoffer

CORGI BOOKS

MY FEUDAL LORD
A CORGI BOOK : 9780552142397

Originally published in Great Britain by Bantam Press,
a division of Transworld Publishers

PRINTING HISTORY
Bantam Press edition published 1994
Corgi edition published 1995

23

Set in 10/11pt Monotype Plantin
by Kestrel Data, Exeter, Devon.

Corgi Books are published by Transworld Publishers,
61–63 Uxbridge Road, London W5 5SA,
a division of The Random House Group Ltd.

Addresses for Random House Group Ltd companies outside the
UK can be found at: www.randomhouse.co.uk
The Random House Group Ltd Reg. No. 954009.

The Random House Group Limited supports The Forest Stewardship
Council® (FSC®), the leading international forest-certification organisation.
Our books carrying the FSC label are printed on FSC®-certified paper.
FSC is the only forest-certification scheme supported by the leading
environmental organisations, including Greenpeace. Our
paper procurement policy can be found at
www.randomhouse.co.uk/environment

Printed and bound in Great Britain by Clays Ltd, St Ives plc

Author's Note

There is a fantasy of a feudal lord as an exotic, tall, dark and handsome man, with flashing eyes and traces of quick-tempered gypsy blood. Images of him parrying thrusts with the fiercest of swordsmen and riding off into the sunset on his black steed set the pubescent heart aflutter. He is seen as a passionate ladies' man and something of a rough diamond, the archetypal male chauvinist who forces a woman to love him despite his treatment of her.

But the fantasy is far from reality, and my country of Pakistan must face up to reality if it is ever to grow and prosper.

When I decided to write this book, I was aware of the perils of exposing the details of my private life to a male-dominated Muslim society. But I had to cast aside my personal considerations in favour of the greater good. There is a deep-rooted deficiency in the feudal value system; it must be diagnosed before it is treated.

T.D.

Dedication

I dedicate this book:

To the people of Pakistan, who have repeatedly trusted and supported their leaders – leaders who have, in return, used the hungry, oppressed, miserable multitudes to further their personal interests. I want the people of my country to know the truth behind the rhetoric, so that they might learn to look beyond the façade.

To the five other ex-wives of Mustafa Khar, who have silently suffered pain and dishonour while he walked away with impunity. As his sixth wife, I am holding him accountable.

To Mustafa Khar himself. I wish that this book might serve as a mirror, so that he may see in it reflections of the man, the husband, the father, the leader and the friend he is.

To my beloved children, who, in our closed society, shall have to suffer the trials of a family exposed. I trust that this book will help them muster strength and courage to face continuing trauma. I want them to reject wrong and endorse right. I hope and pray that their values may be based on true Islamic principles, rather than a distorted, self-serving interpretation. May their love and respect for their motherland cause them to reject any compromise. May my sons never oppress the weak; may my daughters learn to fight oppression.

Finally, to my grandmother. No-one could have understood my story better. May her soul, wherever it may be, know that I survived.

Acknowledgements

Four special people helped me through the nearly impossible task of writing this book. They understood the risks of speaking out, of breaking the taboos of a closed society, yet bravely saw the project through. One remarkable man and two women have encouraged and helped me relive the traumas of the past. A fourth person, under similar restrictions of security, typed the manuscript. I cannot take the responsibility of naming them, but I am indebted to them all.

I offer special appreciation to Bernard Fixot and Antoine Audouard for carrying the story to the world.

Thanks to Jean Souza for producing the map.

Contents

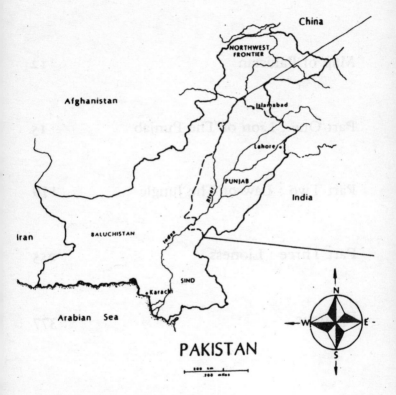

PAKISTAN

200 km
200 miles

Murree

Islamabad

Rawalpindi

River

Chenab

Lahore

Ravi

River

Kot Addu

River

Multan

District of
Muzzafargarh

River

Indus

Sutlej

Punjab

Detail

200 km

200 miles

Part One

LION OF
THE PUNJAB

1

My pale-green chiffon sari rustled softly as I moved, and my braided plait of auburn hair fell all the way to my knees. Around my neck a row of diamonds matched my earrings. As I checked my appearance in a full-length mirror my face flushed with self-conscious pleasure.

It was spring 1974, in Lahore, the second-largest city of Pakistan. The reception was being held in the main hall of the Punjab Club. Summoned by the honorary consul of Spain, Lahore's beautiful people were celebrating Spain's National Day. My uncle had invited my husband Anees and me to accompany him. Having arrived in Lahore only the week before, it was our first opportunity to meet the city's élite. Anees felt flattered and pleased to be included. He was only a junior executive in the state-owned National Shipping Corporation – these were people he felt he should know. As for me – could any sense of foreboding have told me that I was about to have the most crucial meeting of my life?

Anees wandered off on his own, making contacts, and I was suddenly alone – a twenty-one-year-old woman feeling very self-conscious among this older crowd, who seemed so self-assured. Around me, in the spacious halls and shaded patios of the Punjab Club, I could sense the atmosphere of the British Raj that had ended twenty-seven years earlier with independence and the splitting up of British India into two separate states. This was Pakistan, my country; beyond the border-crossing just outside Lahore lay India, our overpowering neighbour. Sharing, to a large extent, a common heritage of culture,

17

language, and family ties, the two countries are locked in a fateful, and at times bloody, relationship of love and hate. I found a seat and took a glass offered by a bearer, as waiters are called here. They are trained to attend, at a mere wink, to the needs of the former colonial, and now indigenous, members of this distinguished club. With their long white coats, buttoned all the way down over baggy trousers, their stiffly starched turbans arranged in peacock shapes, they were figures from our Imperial past. Looking around, I exchanged a formal smile with my neighbour. She made an effort to talk, and I was pleased to realize that I had a friend for the evening. Her name was Dr Shahida Amjad. She was a physician and well-versed in the game of who's who. I told her that I was new to Lahore, and feeling rather lost. Too well-mannered to point, she gestured with her eyes towards various people in the crowd as she delivered quiet potted biographies.

Lahore proudly calls itself the cultural capital of Pakistan. Twenty years ago it could still live up to this reputation with splendour. At its heart, the centuries-old walled city, with its overflowing bazaars and its splendid, though dilapidated family mansions, broad canals lined by old trees, and shady avenues were not yet polluted by an ever-increasing flow of traffic. Formal gardens created by Mogul emperors centuries ago had become public parks, but were not yet crowded at all hours with thousands of visitors. Along the Mall, the city's main avenue, lay the stately buildings from its colonial past: the Governor's House, Aitchison College, the High Court, the Punjab Club. This was where the well-mannered and highly educated members of Lahore's élite had congregated this evening. The gentlemen were wearing western suits or the traditional *achkans*, buttoned coats in black or white, made of silk or the finest wool. Alcoholic drinks such as whisky-and-soda and gin-and-tonic were freely offered and accepted (nowadays they have been banned as sinful signs of western decadence). Politely chattering in separate, but not segregated, groups the ladies were most elegantly draped in saris, each requiring a six-metre length of colourful, and often gold-embroidered silk or chiffon (today, these graceful garments have become quite rare, discarded as being 'Indian').

With Shahida talking on, my gaze settled upon a tall, dark, handsome man in a black suit. His starched white shirt was set off by a burgundy tie and a matching handkerchief. My mind classified him as a rake, a bit devilish in an appealing sort of way. He had attracted a group of women around him, who seemed to hang on his every word. But the buzz of gentle conversation, the tinkle of ice cubes and well-manicured laughter made it impossible for me to hear. I asked my new friend who he was.

'Him? You mean you don't know who he is?' Shahida sounded surprised.

My face must have registered curiosity because she quickly explained, 'That is Mustafa Khar.' The two words were spoken as one: 'Mus-sta-fa-khar.'

'Oh,' I replied.

The ash on his Davidoff cigar was about to flake and fall on the expensive carpet, but he did not seem to care. Slowly and stylishly, he raised a glass of Scotch to his mouth. Instead of taking a drink he merely touched the vessel to his lips below his well-groomed moustache. His eyes glittered, like those of a cobra ready to strike. He obviously relished his ability to mesmerize this élite female company.

An attractive young woman in an orange chiffon sari glided past us. She, too, carried herself with an important, self-confident air. I asked Shahida who she was.

'That's Shahrazad,' my friend replied. 'Sherry. Mustafa Khar's wife.'

'Oh.' I thought: Mus-sta-fa-khar's wife is very beautiful.

I asked Shahida to tell me more about this man, and

I learned that he had just resigned as chief minister of the Punjab. This told me a great deal. The Punjab is the largest province of the country, ruled more or less by the whims of the feudal lords who controlled vast land holdings and whose vassals voted as instructed. The Punjab wielded great political power in the federal government; therefore, its chief minister would be a man of consequence.

Shahida said that this Mustafa Khar was extremely popular here, having earned the nickname 'Lion of the Punjab', and some said that he had been the second most powerful politician in the whole of Pakistan – second only to Prime Minister Zulfikar Ali Bhutto. But that situation had changed. He had annoyed Bhutto, his mentor, by becoming an obvious threat. Mustafa Khar was committed to a political platform that offered real reform for the myriad of social problems that beset the common millions of the Punjab, who lived their lives in poverty and illiteracy. In the history of Pakistan's politics, it had always been necessary for the national leader to quash the leader of the Punjab, lest the sheer number of his supporters assure his superiority.

Shahida knew that my curiosity was piqued. 'Come,' she suggested, 'I'll introduce you to Sherry. You'll like her.'

We made our way through the rich throng. Shahida presented me to Sherry and our conversation turned naturally toward our families. When Sherry learned that my father was Shakirullah Durrani she jokingly asked if I would like to meet her husband. I would. Mustafa Khar had been Bhutto's right-hand man when Bhutto had sent my father to prison. I told Sherry that I hated Bhutto for this injustice, but certainly held no resentment towards her husband.

Within moments Sherry was introducing me to the Lion himself, mentioning my father.

'I hope your parents are well,' Mustafa said graciously. 'Politics can be unfair. There was nothing personal in what happened to your father. Where are they now?'

'They're doing well,' I said. I detailed how, after he was freed from prison and exonerated, Father had taken a banking job in New York City and had, a year later, accepted another banking post in London. My parents, younger brother and three younger sisters lived there now (an older sister was married).

Anees suddenly appeared at my side, and he too was introduced. Anees indicated to me that he had apparently made a favourable impression upon our host, who had extended an invitation for us to remain for dinner.

Mustafa Khar was the kind of man who could choose his place at the dinner table, and he chose to sit directly across from me. We made small talk across the salt-cellars. He asked about my parents again – how they were, where they were, what they were doing. His words did not hold me, but his eyes had me riveted.

They grew lustrous; they glittered and blinked rather frequently; they peered across the table at me hyp-notically. Their message was far from subtle. Perhaps I should have been frightened; instead I was drawn like a moth to a flame.

After dinner, we adjourned to a sitting-room for cognac and liqueurs. The men smoked and so did some of the women. Mustafa was clearly the chief of this group, and all the rest of us were merely rank and file. As he drained the last of his Napoleon brandy, three men moved at once to replenish it. He rolled his cigar in practised fingers and, the very moment he lifted it toward his lips, a cigar-cutter appeared. When it was snipped and ready, six lighters flicked open.

Mustafa took this deference in his stride.

I drank it in.

I was the perfect victim.

A painting hangs on the wall of my home in Lahore, depicting a breathtakingly beautiful woman draped in an emerald green sari. Every feature is exquisite, as if an artist hallucinated and then painted an imaginary ideal. Her translucent, ivory complexion is complemented by enormous almond-shaped brown eyes with heavy lids and long lashes. She has a tiny waist even after six children, and her face remains soft and innocent, masking her dominant personality. Yet the painting does not do full justice to the subject. I should know, for she is my mother, Samina.

She came from the Hayat family of the Khattar tribe, which had settled in Wah, on the northern edge of the Punjab near the border with the Northwest Frontier Province. As a result of loyal service to the Crown, British colonial masters had given vast tracts of lands to the family. The Hayats had fought alongside the Moors in Spain, and claimed that the family's renowned good looks were the result of intermarriages with Spanish women.

My mother's Anglicized family had been actively involved in the politics of the princely states that were scattered throughout India prior to independence. Before partition her father, Nawab Sir Liaqat Hayat Khan, had been prime minister of Patiala State and her uncle, Sir Sikander Hayat Khan, governor of a then undivided Punjab. Both her brothers had been knighted. In my mother's childhood home, the British way of life was slavishly aped. The Hayat men pursued the pastimes of the idle rich. They strove for sartorial elegance with their classic, tailored clothes, played polo, learned all the latest dances, went on *shikar* (hunting expeditions) and threw lavish parties. The beautiful women of the family, who wore exotic Eastern dress, nevertheless spoke and behaved in an Anglicized way and were thus considered, by the 'natives', to be 'advanced' or 'fast'. They had 'come out of the veil'.

Only over time would I come to understand what a shock I was to my mother. She was a light-skinned beauty – and proud of it; her family was fair-skinned and considered itself to be superior by that fact. A dark child was condemned to neglect. And yet there I was, arriving in the world in 1953 with a dark skin. It seemed evident by my mother's attitude that she regarded me as ugly and was embarrassed to present me to friends and relatives. Even as a baby I felt my inadequacy. My surroundings seemed hostile to the way I looked, and very early I withdrew into an isolated, 'condemned-by-nature' cell. I never remember my mother hugging or kissing me when I was little.

Regardless of my growing, deep-rooted, internal complexes, my childhood must have appeared extremely comfortable to an outsider. Our home was impeccable and always orderly, as though waiting to be photographed. We were a model family, the sort of offspring who are pointed out as examples of decorum to other, naughtier, children. We were lavished with comforts and privileges and travelled the world.

My father is a Pathan, descended from the family of Ahmed Shah Durrani of Afghanistan. He had met my mother after her divorce from the Nawab of Tank's eldest son. He was a captain in the army and aide to the governor of West Pakistan at the time they met. After he left the army, during Field Marshal Ayub's presidency, he had initiated and developed the first Investment Corporation of Pakistan (ICP). Then, in 1967, he was appointed Managing Director of PIA, our national airline. Later, when General Yahya Khan declared martial law and became President, my father was appointed Governor of the State Bank of Pakistan.

I loved my father. Six foot tall, he had the presence of a film star. He was as handsome as my mother was beautiful. They made a very glamorous couple, though my mother was the dominant partner and seemed to have the final say in everything. To me he was a rather distant figure: he controlled his affection. Whenever he had the chance he would tell me he loved me most of his children, but chances were rare. I never really understood why he could not show his love or express

23

it. I believe now that my mother did not approve of him displaying any affection towards me, because I was his eldest child and she felt insecure about Rubina, my half-sister through her first marriage.

My father would return home from work each day cheerful and full of life. In fact, to a small daughter he was larger than life in his conservative suits and pinstripe shirts. But despite the important offices he held, the instant he entered our home he seemed to wilt. His demeanour turned serious as he reported the details of his day to Mother in clipped, crisp English, as if looking for approval. If he ventured a joke, her lips tightened. Father had to live by my mother's rules. He interfered with nothing in the house; my mother took all the decisions regarding our home.

In our social circle in the giant metropolis of Karachi, in the southern tip of Pakistan, Mother was renowned for her fashionable soirées, which featured recitations from poets and readings from other intellectuals. She was very shrewd in anticipating who was about to become 'In'. The guests were gleaned from Pakistan's version of the Social Register. As children, of course, we did not participate in these events, except as a home-grown set of helpers, along with the retinue of servants. We learned how to lay the silver cutlery for a formal dinner party. We were told how to serve a five-course meal using the appropriate Rosenthal or Wedgwood crockery. We knew the proper way to sprinkle rose petals into the lukewarm water of a finger bowl – and never to forget the lemon. We knew how to arrange the individual salt and pepper shakers and assortment of condiments.

My mother demanded total obedience and, although I always complied, she discerned early signs of rebellion in both my expression and my body language. I obeyed, but my crime was that I did not look obedient. I was sullen, and she resented my resentment. We never spoke openly about this, however. Her disapproval was communicated through pursed lips and a deep, icy stare that crumbled me – or anyone – into instant submission. When my mother spoke it was a command, and we were to carry out orders in silence.

We rarely ate with our parents in the evening – either they were going out to dinner or entertaining, and we were not included. But lunchtimes, when my father was away at his office, were occasions for another command performance. Mother, immaculately groomed and perfectly dressed, lectured from the head of the table with soft-spoken formality. When she grew silent, the meal became a muted symphony of silver cutlery tinkling against fine bone china; the tempo was set by the ticking of the grandfather clock. There was no play and very little laughter in the household and a childhood burst of enthusiasm was frowned upon. Untidiness was a crime.

Mother accomplished her objectives without ever raising a hand to us. When we did misbehave, we were subjected to a stern lecture which we could neither react to nor counter. She was masterly at playing one of us against another, and we all became tiny spies. 'I can find everything out,' she boasted. She never read Machiavelli's *The Prince*, but she crafted a careful divide-and-conquer strategy that kept us all off-balance.

The lesson was clear and I learned it well: blind acquiescence was necessary to gain approval; being yourself earned only condemnation. I was acceptable only when I was unlike myself – whoever that was – because I wore a mask of submission. I developed a personality that was against my true nature, but compatible with mother's. Inwardly I became confused and sometimes ashamed that what I must really be was incorrect and unacceptable.

Mother was not subtle in playing favourites. Almost every word and action indicated her preference for her white-skinned children, her son Asim and her daughters Minoo and especially the baby Adila. Rubina, Zarmina and I – the darker daughters – never seemed able to please her. This was especially difficult to comprehend in the case of Zarmina, who was the sweetest, most considerate and lovable child one could imagine.

My maternal grandmother, Shamshad, was well aware of the stigma that a dark complexion assured. She had blatantly favoured my mother over her darker sister, Samar. Yet my grandmother loved Zarmina and me so much that she constantly sought to rid us of the dark curse. Cucumber juice, lemons, fresh cream and a pungent-smelling bleaching agent called Amex were rubbed into our mud-coloured faces.

As we grew older nature bestowed the benefit – necessary if one is to be acceptable to the Hayat family – of lightening the pigment of our skins. It was as if I shed the chrysalis of my dark skin and emerged as a socially acceptable butterfly. Sometimes I wondered whether my grandmother had been able to work the transformation through her potions, or her prayers. But Mother did not notice, or if she did, the development did not affect her attitude.

Our elder half-sister Rubina was placed in charge of the younger three girls, as a training exercise in preparation for her own marriage and motherhood. At the age of twelve I was given the position of wardrobe mistress. I was expected to maintain my mother's bedroom, and to make sure that her lavish wardrobe was always in order. Despite our modern lifestyle, Mother disdained the western manner of dressing and demanded that our entire family conform to eastern fashion. Each day before school, I laid out the appropriate outfit for my mother's morning, complete with the correct shoes and accessories. She favoured cotton saris or delicate drapes of chiffon across her bosom. I had to select the jewellery with care from her exquisite and expensive collection, so that it did not clash with her ensemble. Once her toilette was completed, I was free to leave for school.

After school, we repeated the ritual for her dinner outfit. Mother never retrieved anything from cupboards or dressers. She simply put out her hand, and I was to have the necessary item ready, leaving her concentration free to attend to braiding her long hair, rimming her eyes with kohl and brushing her cheeks with colour. I stood in silence behind her. When she finally left her bedroom for the evening, I would sigh with relief and lay out her nightclothes on the bed, place her slippers exactly where she expected them to be, and tidy up the bath and dressing-rooms. The servant would turn the sheets over and switch on the bedside lamps, place the water jug and glasses, and draw up the curtains.

The muscles in my neck and shoulders still relive the tension created by the ever-present fear that I would misplace something or be unable to locate the keys to her armoire or jewellery box. To do so would render me inadequate in her eyes and create such wrath that I became obsessed with the seemingly simple task. Panic would overtake me and the location of the keys took precedence in my mind over everything else. Schoolwork and other responsibilities paled in comparison.

All the maternal love I remember came from my mother's mother. She pampered me so much that we ended up squabbling – because I was so skinny she constantly tried to force-feed me. Her emphasis on my appearance brought out the worst reactions in me. 'Parents like pretty children,' she would say. 'Your mother will love you more if you are looking nice.' Waving her hands in despair at my rejection of her plans for my beautification, she would suggest, 'Put your hair over your ears. It looks nicer.' Or, 'Put some *kajal* [kohl] over your eyes; they stand out more.' Poor grandmother never realized how deeply the complex of being ugly was setting in – how much it would affect my life.

Grandmother had another paranoia, because I loved to paint. She was convinced that artists are usually eccentric and end up becoming mad. She would hide my paints, so that I would avoid indulging in what might take me further into a mad world.

At the age of thirteen I was stricken with meningitis,

27

which, it was whispered, Grandmother and my father attributed to the strain brought on by the chore of caring for Mother's wardrobe. I was not expected to survive. Doctors ventured the opinion that if I did pull through, I might suffer paralysis or brain damage. My father hired round-the-clock nurses and converted our guest room into a hospital ward. For six months a strange aura of life and death pervaded the household. Even after my survival was assured, my parents considered me sickly and somewhat unstable.

It was during this time that my baby sister Adila was born.

Apart from my father, brother and a few close relatives, men were alien creatures, and from my earliest moments I was trained to avoid them. My childhood was encumbered by a lengthy list of don'ts, all designed to maintain an inviolate distance between myself and the masculine world: Never wear make-up or nail polish. Do not look at boys. Avoid modern girlfriends and avoid any girl who has an older brother. Never visit a friend without special permission and without your nanny. Never pick up the telephone. Never go out alone with the driver. Never stand around in the kitchen with the male servants.

And yet, clearly, a man was the only future available to a Pakistani girl. My role in life was to marry and to marry well. Mother had an ideal man in mind for each of us. Our husbands were to be the only males to whom we would ever be exposed. Not surprisingly, they would exhibit a combination of eastern and western traits. They would come from good and noble families and be well educated, preferably at Oxford or Cambridge. Our marriages were supposed to add to our parents' social standing; personal happiness would be an added bonus. To ensure that we kept no secrets from her and that she knew our every move, Mother had us convinced that she would not oppose anyone whom we wished to marry – as long as we informed her immediately of our

intention. Despite the fact that our mother had divorced
her first husband, we were taught that marriage was a
sacred and irrevocable institution. If a husband turned
out to be a brute, it was the wife's duty to persevere until
she changed his character. A broken marriage was a
reflection of a woman's failure.

My mother had been married by arrangement when
she was only fifteen years old to the Nawab of Tank's
eldest son and heir, Hebat Khan. Tank was situated in
the remote tribal belt, and the women were kept in strict
purdah. My mother hardly saw her husband – he only
came indoors at night. The Nawab's seven sons had been
educated abroad, played croquet and flew their own
small planes. However, when my mother became pregnant, the convent nuns who looked after her told her
that it was believed that the family practised infanticide
– the Nawab had no living female offspring, which was,
in those days, not uncommon amongst remote tribes.
My mother left for Lahore to give birth at her own family
home (this was quite normal – the wife stayed away from
her husband for forty days so that she could be well
cared for and healthy enough to return to him).

After her baby, my half-sister Rubina, was born, my
mother demanded a divorce; her father had died and
her mother realized the pressure on her. Although the
divorce was shocking, it was accepted by my mother's
family who had virtually lost her to the very backward family of Tank. She was branded as a divorcée,
which was apparent by the reaction of my father's family
to his decision to marry her: she was divorced, had a
daughter and was Punjabi. Although my father's family
could not match my mother's family in their affluence
and social status, they were still very unhappy at his
decision.

Looking back, I realize that we were being raised to
be schizophrenic; an appearance of perfection was more
important than genuine feelings. There was no question
of discovering oneself. Identity and individuality were

crushed. Personality failed to develop. My mind became a sanctuary for secret thoughts of escaping from this household. But for that, there was no other goal in life but marriage.

In 1968 my sister Rubina, only seventeen and still at school, married a commercial airline pilot with the consent of her father, my mother's first husband. Although Mother was appalled and very disturbed, everybody compromised swiftly and silently to avoid a scandal.

By the time I was sixteen, nature had allowed me to evolve into a pretty young lady. I was thrilled to hear people say that I was beautiful, but in our household this was a two-edged sword. Almost always a compliment was couched in the statement, 'You look so much like your mother.' The comparison only partially pleased me. My mother was stunning, yet I wanted to be beautiful in my own right and not compared to her. A comparison with her always left me in second place. I was convinced that I would fail any competition with her; therefore, the comparison always diluted the compliment: 'She looks so much like her mother – but, no, she is not a patch on her!' Mother, too, silently resented the comparison; she remembered me as an ugly duckling and wished to remain as the family's standard-bearer of beauty.

Nevertheless, I attracted increasing attention. Weddings or any social gatherings were glorified marriage marts where women bartered their daughters' futures. Mother, like any Pakistani woman with five daughters to marry off, was an active player in this game. My sisters and I were allowed to converse only with our eyes.

We flew north to Lahore to attend a wedding and it was there that I met twenty-seven-year-old Anees Khan. His mother scrutinized me first and must have granted her approval, because he approached and asked, 'Are you still studying?'

'Yes,' I replied.

'Where?'

'In Murree. At the convent.'

'Oh.'

He asked, 'Which class are you in?'

'I'm doing my Senior Cambridge,' I said.

I thought little more of Anees when I returned to the Roman Catholic boarding school I attended in the hillside summer resort town of Murree until one Sunday my classmates and I were allowed the treat of walking through the shopping mall. We were on guard. We knew that the mall was filled with romeos on the prowl, strutting about for our benefit. We watched them discreetly, and giggled amongst ourselves. I was surprised when I saw Anees among this crowd, and even more shocked when he approached.

Anees invited me and my friends to have tea with him at 'Sam's', Murree's famous restaurant. My friends and I shared nervous glances. A boarding-school girl's dreams are fashioned of Sam's cakes and pastries, and we voted with our stomachs. As we ate the glorious chocolate éclairs, we glanced nervously at the clock and soon fled in undignified haste. Anees waved goodbye, and told me that he was leaving for Karachi the next day.

But he did not go. I was shocked once more to see him, the following day, loitering outside the school gate. All I could think was: he must know that we are not allowed to converse with boys. He did not attempt to speak to me directly; rather, he smuggled in a note, via one of the day students. He wrote: 'I am not going back to Karachi to my job because I want to be close to you. I will stay on in Murree. At least here I can catch a glimpse of you.'

I was in love.

Each of the next fifteen days Anees managed to have a letter smuggled in to me, and I treasured them. When it was time to fly home for the summer holidays, I was armed with these letters, and with my resolve to tell my mother that he was the man I wished to marry. Anees and I travelled on the same plane, but we dared not sit together or speak to one another.

Once home in Karachi, my resolve wavered. I could not muster the courage to confront my mother face to face, so I penned a note, declaring that I had met a man who wanted to marry me, and left it underneath her pillow. Then I prayed to Allah (Catholic schooling never altered a student's commitment to Islam). On the prayer mat, I had a personal relationship with God. I confided in Allah and asked him to soften my mother's heart.

That day Mother disrupted my prayers, storming into my room livid, waving my note, demanding to know all the 'lurid' details. I told her there were no details, only letters. She requisitioned the notes and I handed them over. As she read, I sat before her with my head bowed, blushing with shame.

Mother informed me curtly that Anees's mother had already proposed the marriage – and she had turned down the proposal on grounds of my youth. But the real reason was that she felt that Anees was not good enough for me – or her. His family was not very well-to-do or well known, and he was a mere junior executive, earning the paltry wage of 800 rupees (about £618) per month. On the basis of this information, Mother classified him as a loafer.

After a few moments Mother informed me menacingly that she would speak to Anees and his mother, telling them once more that the marriage was out of the question.

I was left in a void of embarrassment, disillusionment and hopelessness. My one ray of freedom had faded all too quickly. During the month's vacation I was a prisoner at home, forbidden to go out, forbidden to approach the telephone. Mother said few words to me, and when she did she made me feel unclean.

Mother accompanied me back to school and spoke to the nuns, instructing them to do a better job of watching me, coercing them into censoring my mail. Deeply depressed, I tried to concentrate on my studies for the final exams, but I lived for the clandestine notes that Anees still, somehow, managed to smuggle in. I was also panic-stricken at the thought of losing a man whom love had blinded, so that now he perceived me as some great beauty. My low self-esteem convinced me and made me fearful that this error might never occur again. No other man would find it possible to love me.

My mind turned to romance and I began to look for signs of Anees in the smell of pines and in the sound of rain on the tin roof on a chilly night. I saw myself with him in the mountains, walking down narrow, winding dirt roads. Murree was like Switzerland, and I would rather be here honeymooning than sitting for exams.

He did not give up the struggle. His mother spoke to my mother on numerous occasions. Then he, too, began to call on her. She made them wait for endless hours and, when she did receive them, did so with arrogance. They took the treatment with patience and grace.

I passed my final exams and returned home qualified with the requisite education for a fashionable marriage. By now Anees was twenty-eight and I was seventeen. We were virtual strangers, but were convinced that we were deeply in love. There were other suitors – several more acceptable to Mother – but I grew quietly stubborn and visibly rebellious for the first time. Anees was the first man to fall in love with me, and I felt somehow that he was my only chance for happiness and a speedy escape. I told my mother that, if I could not marry Anees, I would marry no-one. For a time the stand-off was bitter.

But Mother was in a bind. My father's conservative family worried that I would be left a spinster. At seventeen, I should have been engaged. This was the worst humiliation for a Pakistani woman. My father's family was even more averse to my colouring than my mother's family. The Pathans are a very fair race – a dark Pathan like myself was quite rare and, in fact, terribly noticeable – and although I had 'lightened', I was still not quite the conventional beauty. But someone would surely marry me because of my father's position as airline chief, and that had to be made use of quickly, while he still held the position.

Visions of a scandal flashed through Mother's mind and she could not cope with the prospect of a stigma of this nature. As I tidied her dressing table, I overheard a conversation between my mother and her best friend, who said, 'Samina, she's not your best-looking daughter. It won't be so easy for her to find a boy who'll love her as Anees does. I suggest you agree to the proposal. You still have three daughters for whom your position will be stronger.' I did not hear my mother's answer; Anees's love and gushing compliments had allowed a little idea of beauty to creep into my mind, and it suddenly evaporated. I had heard the verdict. It was cruel but I was sure that it was true. When I looked into the mirror over my mother's dressing table, there were no signs of a swan emerging.

And so Mother agreed to my marriage with Anees and, having made the decision, she became the beaming mother of the bride-tobe. The engagement reception of S. U. Durrani's daughter was a great event. Baskets of sweetmeats were sent off to friends and relatives. Mother had a decorator flown in from Lebanon.

My father was appointed Governor of the State Bank of Pakistan, a position he valued highly in that it took him to the most prestigious point of his banking career. But then Pakistani politics intervened in our lives. In 1971, when the country was in the midst of up-heaval and on the brink of war with India, Bhutto had approached my father with a proposition. At the time, Pakistan was divided into the two regions of East and West Pakistan, separated by a thousand miles of India, and East Pakistan was attempting to secede and form the independent nation of Bangladesh. As Governor of the State Bank, my father was a key sideline-player.

Bhutto, who was the leader of the People's Party, was now committed to fighting for the supremacy of West Pakistan. He asked my father surreptitiously to withdraw state assets from the east. Although my father was sympathetic, he refused to undertake such an unethical action, and Bhutto took the rebuff poorly. In December of that year India finally invaded East Pakistan. General Yahya Khan accepted responsibility for the defeat and break-up of Pakistan and resigned; and Bhutto became the undisputed leader of all that remained of our country – what had formerly been West Pakistan.

When the dust settled and Bhutto became President, one of his first actions was to dismiss my father as Governor of the State Bank. He had him arrested and thrown into a cockroach-infested prison cell on a trumped-up charge that he was in league with the CIA.

My father's imprisonment was traumatic for the family. My mother endured the 'trauma' with great dignity, although it broke her inwardly. She was shamed by the charges, in fact she was quite unable to cope with the idea that her husband was blemished or marked professionally. (This was always in private – publicly she feigned courage and strength.) My father's family and her own family were very supportive, as were some friends, like BCCI's Agha Hasan Abidi, whose car was at Mother's disposal.

We moved out of the official residence to Rubina and Kemal's house. Mother was in mourning when alone or with the family. There were constant prayers, and women relatives and friends would read the Koran. Almost everybody in the house said their 'Ramaz' prayers five times over for father's exoneration and health.

I remember often crying at night for my father. Daytime was solemn and tense: there was no question of laughter or fun. My parents were humiliated: the perfect image of success, beauty and refinement seemed shattered by bad luck, we believed.

35

I knew nothing about their financial worries, except that we no longer had the official residence and its ample facilities. The fact that we lived at Rubina's or in Lahore with Uncle Asad or Auntie Samar did bring home the truth that we had 'fallen' from grace.

I knew it would be difficult for my parents to restart a life without official power, and that they would have to live as ordinary people. Our own home had been rented out to a Japanese company, so they would have to rent a house. But the comforting feeling that I was engaged to be married detached me somewhat from their future plans.

Only my mother, Rubina and my father's brothers visited him in prison. We children were not taken, perhaps because we could not contribute to the serious matters that were being discussed. I missed my father a lot, and so did my little sisters and Assim.

Six months passed, and then the trial exonerated my father and he was released from prison. Although Bhutto attempted to make amends, my father, disgusted and humiliated, decided to leave the country. He accepted a post as vice-president of the First National City Bank – in the United States. I was relieved that he was still valued and could begin to continue his career without having to compromise further in Pakistan.

My parents prepared to move to a suite in New York's Waldorf Astoria, but what were they to do with me? Mother concluded that the convenient course of action was to marry me off quickly in a simple ceremony. At first I was relieved that Mother would not be in the same town, or indeed the same country, as myself. The prospect of her leaving made me feel free. Until now she had been paramount in my life, although I had never felt the affection for her that I had felt for my father. The pain of parting from the rest of my family was diffused.

Then reality dawned. Three days prior to the wedding, it occurred to me that, despite our limited contact, I was

36

already bored with Anees. I did not love him enough and most definitely did not want to marry him. I suddenly saw an alternative. If I travelled to the States with my parents, I might have more freedom and more opportunities to find whatever it was I sought. I locked myself inside my room and howled in distress. My grandmother stood outside my door, begging me to eat.

Gradually I composed myself and resolved to face up to what had to be done. I spoke to Anees on the telephone and confided in him, 'I probably do not love you. I was only in love with the idea of love. I wanted to escape from my family.'

He was disturbed but attempted to convince me that I was suffering from bridal jitters. 'Everything will be all right,' he counselled. 'You're just nervous.'

My father offered similar reassurance. As I hugged him and wept on his shoulder, he lectured quietly: daughters have to leave their homes and enter alien surroundings. A marriage, he said, was a confluence of grief and happiness. He understood my pain and ambivalence at the thought of leaving him, but I had to embark upon my future.

I realized it was too late. No-one believed that I did not want to marry. They were all ascribing this to last-minute nerves.

Three days later I became a most confused bride.

Two and a half years passed. My marriage to Anees reached a bland plateau. I knew that something was amiss, but did not have a clue as to what it was. Although I was now showered with compliments and loved dearly by my in-laws, my mind remained troubled by a childhood with which I did not know how to come to terms – I did not even know with what it was that I had to come to terms. I was haunted by feelings of being a non-person and by extremely low self-esteem. If Mother did not approve of me and love me, Anees's weak opinion – and those of his lower-positioned family – was of little consequence.

When my daughter Tanya was born I was not only bewildered but puzzled at having become a mother, understanding little of the woman into which I was developing. Emotionally I was hopelessly immature, as I struggled to cope with what should have been the most rewarding of relationships between mother and daughter. I loved Tanya dearly, and yet I still felt so unfulfilled as a child and daughter myself. My own craving to be mothered still remained, and weighed heavily upon me. I tried to compensate through Tanya, playing with her, dressing her and loving her, as if she might be me and I my mother.

I knitted and embroidered clothes for her. She had a nanny but I always took her with me, even though it was only ever to my inlaws. I worried constantly about her food, spoon-feeding her with mashed bananas and mashed potatoes – the fatter she became the happier I was.

I still did not love Anees. If I had, perhaps I would have found Mustafa Khar less intriguing, and less troubling.

2

That Mustafa was authoritarian, conservative and overpowering I knew from the start – but that was precisely what attracted me so much. Psychologically I had suffered from my father's weak role in our family. Now here was someone who presented a quite different personality.

The men of the Kharral tribe are known to be taller than average, with marked features and legendary energy and endurance. One scholar described them as 'wasteful in marriage expenditure, hospitable to travellers, thievish and with little taste for agriculture'. A Persian proverb holds that they are 'rebellious and ought to be slain'.

Their roots go back to the Neli Bar region of India, near Kamalia, but they fell into a dispute with the British rulers when they refused to pay tribute. After several lethal encounters, they decided to move west. They slaughtered their women and children, so as not to impede their journey, then packed their vast stores of gold and migrated to the Punjab, settling along the banks of the Indus river.

There are various versions as to why, in modern times, one branch of the family shortened its name to Khar. One of those holds that the name was bestowed by an angry victim of their plunder, who dubbed them with the name Khar because it means 'ass' in Persian. But the more likely explanation is that their religious beliefs made them refrain from using the full name, out of respect for their mystical leader, Pir Chishtian Sharif, who was himself a Kharral. Whatever the truth of the

39

matter, it is certain that the Khars consider themselves superior to those who cling to the old name.

By systematically marrying the daughters of tribal chieftains, Mustafa's grandfather, Malik Ghulam, eventually became one of the largest landowners in the Muzaffargarh district of the Punjab. In the feudal system wealth equates with honour and power; thus in 1940 Mustafa's father, Mohammad Yar Khar, was granted the title Khan Sahib by the British crown.

Mohammad Yar Khar was sixty-four years old when he married his third wife, a sixteen-year-old girl from Multan, who became Mustafa's mother. All told, Khan Sahib had sixteen children; Mustafa's mother bore him seven sons and a daughter. The seven sons grew up in their isolated village of Kot Addu with little discipline from their ageing father and submissive mother. Like his brothers, Mustafa was raised by a pair of nannies, who breast-fed him for the first six years of his life. The women's diet was carefully monitored and, during their wet-nurse years, the nannies were allowed to visit their husbands only in the presence of a supervisor, to guard against pregnancy. The Khar brothers attribute their vigour to this childhood nurturing.

As young feudal lords, Mustafa and his brothers had few worries concerning legal and societal proscriptions. The feudal system is a carry-over from the time when the British ruled the whole of south central Asia. By bestowing land and absolute power upon certain 'loyal' individuals, the 'white masters' were able to control the country's multitudes with relatively little effort. With the passage of time, the privileged few multiplied their wealth by exploiting the feudal practices of tenant farming and arbitrary taxation. Feudalism was a licence to plunder, rape and even murder. The rich got richer; the poor despaired.

In the areas that were later to become Pakistan, some feudal families utilized Islam as a weapon of control. The patriarchs were venerated as holy men, who spoke with

Allah. And, indeed, at some earlier time many were pious and righteous. But gradually power passed to elder sons who were neither pious nor particularly moral, yet were revered by the illiterate people of the area and perceived as 'envoys of Allah'. They had the authority to justify their every deed on the basis of their own, quite convenient, interpretation of the Koran. A feudal lord was an absolute ruler who could justify any action.

When British rule ended in 1947, the stage was set for at least a half-century of turmoil. The vast holdings of the Commonwealth were divided along religious lines. The Hindu stronghold became India. Muslim Pakistan was a country like no other in the world, divided into two slabs of land by the immense impediment of India.

Democracy took hold in India and the feudal system collapsed. But in Pakistan, although lip-service was paid to democratic principles, feudal lords remained in control. It was they who decided who would sit in the National Assembly and who would reside in the prime minister's house.

The Khar family elders were not interested in politics. Mustafa and his brothers lived for *shikar*, the hunt. They stayed away from home for days at a time, tracking their prey, mostly on horseback, sometimes on foot. Once they achieved success, they could not wait to taste its delights. They enjoyed cooking the food themselves and ate the meat rare. *Shikar* taught Mustafa courage, endurance and patience. And through hunting he grasped the importance of strategy and tactical manoeuvring. He learned how to lure, entice and entrap.

When he was barely seventeen, at the decision of his father, Mustafa told me later, he had married his illiterate cousin, Wazir, who was many years older than him. She immediately became pregnant. Mustafa ran away from his village and his fate, fleeing first to Multan and then to the great city of Lahore. Here he was fascinated by such mysteries as the sight of a woman with a stylish hair-do sitting cool and poised behind the steering wheel of a shiny car. He lacked the social graces necessary to approach such an ice-maiden; at the moment, he could only lust from a distance.

At the hillside resort of Murree, Mustafa met women who purveyed their charms for a price, and he discovered that he was comfortable with professional sex. He scoured the market, inspected the wares and hired the services. For their part, the women were fascinated by this wealthy young feudal chieftain who bemoaned his enforced marriage.

Back home, Wazir suffered in silence. Her humiliation was compounded when the elders dissolved her marriage to Mustafa and gave her to her much younger brother-in-law. But at least she was spared the indignity of returning to her parents' home as a divorcée – which, in the feudal system, is a dismal destiny. She bore Mustafa's first son, Abdur Rehman.

Meanwhile, in Murree Mustafa befriended a man who had an attractive and somewhat educated sweetheart Firdaus. When Firdaus discovered that she was pregnant, the man fled and Mustafa provided a comfortable crying shoulder. To Mustafa, the fallen Firdaus was a victim of society. He married her on impulse, and in the course of time Firdaus gave birth to a son, bearing Mustafa's surname. And within a year a second son, Billoo, was born. All this responsibility proved too much for Mustafa, who now decided that he had confused sympathy with love. Even as Firdaus was in the hospital recuperating from Billoo's birth, Mustafa sent her divorce papers.

Somewhat chastened, Mustafa returned to his village and – in typical feudal fashion – was forgiven by his elders.

The men of the Khar family were content with their isolated domain, and saw no reason to expand the scope of their vision, until the time-old pattern of power-worship gave them a jolt. Mushtaq Ahmed Gurmani became governor of the Punjab. The Gurmani clan lived in an adjoining area and, suddenly having become so important, began to make its presence felt. Over time, in bureaucratic fashion, the loyalties of local officials were deflected. The police turned a blind eye to crimes committed by Gurmani clansmen against the Khars. The precious water supply was diverted. Perhaps worse, the peasants began to pay more attention to the new political leaders than to their traditional lords. It was in 1962 when the Khars realized that their feudal world could no longer function without political clout. Only politics could bring legitimacy, power and protection.

Mustafa was twenty-four years old when he stood for a seat in the National Assembly. He was a novice, but an energetic one. Patiently he travelled from family to family within the region, explaining his concern for the erosion of their traditional power in the area. He was pleased to discover that another powerful feudal clan, the Legharis, were equally concerned by the political encroachment of the rival Gurmani clan, and he was able to form a strong coalition that resulted in victory. Mustafa would be the first of the Khars to travel to the prestigious National Assembly.

Ecstatic over his win, Mustafa's father presented his son with a substantial sum of money. This he squandered on several shiny new American cars. At times, as he drove one of his new toys to Parliament, he instructed drivers to follow with his other vehicles, producing a showy cavalcade.

Inside the National Assembly, Mustafa remained silent, very conscious of his status as a country neophyte. But he listened carefully and absorbed everything. Fortuitously, seated next to him was Ghulam Mustafa Khan Jatoi, a distinguished-looking, slightly older man who came from one of the largest and wealthiest feudal families in the Sind province in the southern half of West Pakistan. Mustafa Jatoi was a valuable new friend for Mustafa – a relationship that was to last for twenty-six

43

years and with whom his political fortunes were to remain closely linked.

Jatoi introduced Mustafa to the dynamic foreign minister, Zulfikar Ali Bhutto, and the two men began a complex relationship that was to vacillate between the extremes of love and hate. Like many young men at that time, Mustafa fell under the magnetic spell of Bhutto, a hard-working leftist politician who cried out for social justice. For his part, Bhutto was impressed with Mustafa's potential as a true son of the soil, a man who understood the aspirations of the people and had the ability to address their issues.

Following the Tashkent Agreement in 1966, which ended the second India–Pakistan War, Bhutto, believing that President Ayub Khan had won the war on the battlefield but lost it across the negotiating table, resigned his post as foreign minister. He was an immediate political pariah, and as he prepared to board a train to return home to Karachi no-one came to bid him farewell – except for Mustafa Khar. The younger man did so in direct defiance of the establishment and of the sympathies of the Nawab of Kalabagh, the feudal governor of the Punjab, and this was an indication of the anti-establishment course of Mustafa's political career. Bhutto, who was a shrewd and cunning politician, immediately saw that there was more to Mustafa than a silly twenty-four-year-old who arrived at Parliament in a parade of American-made automobiles. He commented on Mustafa's show of courage, and Mustafa responded with his favourite, enigmatic phrase: 'Time will tell.'

Women entered Mustafa's life speedily and left just as quickly. The young member of the National Assembly was still searching for the nebulous ideal, but he lacked the self-confidence necessary to court women of society, and for a time continued to settle for low-life companionship.

During one of his numerous flights to attend Parliament sessions in East Pakistan, Mustafa was smitten by an apparition in green, the flight attendant who served him his meal. Her name was Safia and she was from a lower middle-class background, working to help support her family. A feudal lord rarely met such a 'liberated' woman elsewhere; Safia exuded an aura of adventure. They spent the next two days together and married.

Mustafa immediately reverted to the dictates of his feudal heritage. He plucked Safia from the sky and locked her in a cage. His formerly modern bride went behind the veil, banished to the oblivion of his home village of Kot Addu, where her mission was to live in anticipation of his infrequent visits. At the time, there was no electricity or plumbing in Kot Addu. The women of the family were completely isolated from the outside world – the only sky Safia saw here was the patch above the compound of her new home. The walls were built high and no males other than her father-in-law and brothers-in-law could enter. She grew reconciled to a desert life, the area being renowned for its barrenness and dry heat, and became part of the *zannana* (women's chambers) where in every sense the male was king and the female slave.

Here, Safia bore Mustafa a son, named Bilal, and a daughter who, owing to a lack of medical facilities, died of diarrhoea.

It was at this time that Mustafa was called upon to perform a special duty under the Jirga system, whereby the feudal lord acts as judge and jury to settle disputes among his vassals out of court. Sentences are passed by consensus or merely on the lord's authority. The case of two lovers was brought before him and he listened attentively to the allegations against them. The woman, Ayesha, was in her mid-twenties, a beauty who resembled the American film actress Ava Gardner. She was tall and regal-looking, with glowing brown skin and deep black eyes. Ayesha was known in Kot Addu for her mischievous and lively nature, and this earned her a reputation for being 'fast'. Apparently she 'made eyes' at the young village men and constantly tried to attract attention. Her case was weak. She was a married woman who had fallen in love with another man – also married. Throwing convention and religion to the winds they had impulsively eloped, and now it was Mustafa's duty to decide the punishment. For Mustafa this was an easy decision; he recognized that Ayesha was the legal property of her husband, and ordered her to be returned to him.

The lovers had fled for sanctuary to a holy shrine near Multan, but they were caught and brought before Mustafa. Ayesha pleaded not to be forced to return to her husband and begged, instead, to be allowed to work for Mustafa and his family. For daring to disobey him, Mustafa committed Ayesha's lover to an asylum, where he soon grew truly mad and died. But Ayesha was installed as Bilal's *dai* (nanny). Mustafa agreed to give her family a small portion of wheat each year, but other than that she received no wages. Henceforth she became known by the name of Dai Ayesha and was, like numerous others, a household slave.

Mustafa became Bhutto's protégé and, leaving Safia in the village, he moved into Bhutto's residence at 70 Clifton in Karachi, where he was to live for many years, and where his political and social education began in earnest.

The curriculum included the intricate tactics of how to mesh an elegant lifestyle with political ambitions. One of Bhutto's heroes was the Indonesian President, Sukarno, who understood that Third World peoples are emotional and illiterate, and require simple oratorical slogans to keep them loyal to their politicians. In this view, the masses are attracted to colourful leaders

46

whose romantic liaisons are not so much overlooked as expected. This philosophy allowed Sukarno to live a private life filled with romantic intrigue. Bhutto viewed moral licence as one of the privileges of power, and his disciple learned the lesson well. Citing Sukarno, Bhutto often said that exceptional men needed extraordinary wives who were understanding and able to cope with their husbands' eccentricities. As an example, he referred to Adolf Hitler's liaison with Eva Braun.

Bhutto did, indeed, have an extraordinary wife, the Iranian-born Nusrat. For years she was forced to live with the open secret that her husband was carrying on an affair with the beautiful and vivacious divorcée, Husna Shaikh. Bhutto was passionately in love, but at the time Husna played hard to get, sceptical of her suitor's playboy reputation. Mustafa now became his confidant and often drove Bhutto to his clandestine meetings with Husna.

Bhutto also had a passion for Persian and Chinese carpets, and would pay lavishly for any piece that caught his fancy. If he coveted a friend's carpet, he would not leave the house until they had struck a bargain. And like India's Prime Minister Nehru, Bhutto loved roses, and grew specimen plants in his gardens. The teacher nurtured his student as carefully as his prize roses, tutoring him in both political and personal behaviour. The elder coached the younger on the importance of clothes which, in Bhutto's case, tended to be rather rakish. Soon, Mustafa was sporting the same style of Savile Row suits and Turnbull & Asser shirts as his mentor. Bhutto's library was one of the best in Asia, and here his most prized possession was his collection of books on Napoleon Bonaparte; he was fascinated by the little Corsican who had the audacity to crown himself Emperor of France. Bhutto presented Mustafa with a recommended reading list and later questioned him on what he had read of it.

Mustafa did not totally succumb, but tried to preserve

his identity and earthiness. They made an odd couple. At breakfast, for example, Bhutto ate his fried eggs and baked beans as Mustafa – proud of his culinary heritage – insisted on the traditional foods of the rural Punjab – *lassi* (a yogurt drink), *paratha* (a thin, flat bread cooked in butter) and an omelette with green peppers and tomatoes.

This was a mutually beneficial friendship. Bhutto discerned intelligence and native cunning in Mustafa, although it was unschooled. The younger man understood the plight of the illiterate, impoverished masses. Both men, even as they enjoyed the trappings of power and prestige, ached to move Pakistan into the twentieth century. Mustafa came to see the irony in their political quest, for in order to bring true democracy and equality – and thus progress – to the country, they had to find some way to destroy the archaic feudal system. If they were to realize their political ambitions they had to annihilate their very own power base.

Mustafa continued to live the good life, and this revolved around Bhutto's spectacular dinner parties. Each was a major event for Pakistan's social and cultural élite. Bhutto was expert at the finer points of cuisine, and he dictated every detail of the menu. He loved French food and was a connoisseur of fine wines and selected with great care. He personally chose the china and cutlery. He inspected the attire and procedures of the retinue of servants. He even supervised the floral arrangements.

In 1967 Mustafa became one of the founding members of Bhutto's Pakistan People's Party, committed to fighting for the liberal cause. For the common man its message was powerful, but for several years the new socialist party had to struggle. Its leaders toured the remotest areas of the country, reaching out to the people who, they believed, were the real power. Bhutto's zeal and energy filtered almost everywhere, and very soon his hard work established the People's Party as a major voice of reform. Mustafa waited for the moment when events would pave his way to power.

Pakistan was a nation in transition, and its political life was tumultuous. In the 1970 elections the People's Party swept to victory in West Pakistan, but the Awami League, which had raised a six-point programme that had separatist undertones, captured all but two seats in East Pakistan: this plunged the nation into a deep and divisive crisis. East Pakistan exploded into riots, aimed at winning independence from West Pakistan.

The People's Party's regional triumph thrust Mustafa into prominence. He was suddenly courted by power-seekers, some of whom threw lavish but sleazy parties where women were part of the menu. At one of these events Mustafa met Naubahar, a professional dancing girl who used her face and her body to ensnare the young politician. Mustafa rented a house in Lahore and installed Naubahar there as his mistress. Then he married her, despite the fact that he had a wife waiting for him in Kot Addu. (The Koran allows a man to have as many as four wives, but tempers this with the almost impossible requirement that he love them equally.) He made Naubahar promise to keep the marriage a secret.

Within a year, fuelled by a hostile press, mainly in India and Britain, the battle for the liberation of Bangladesh had begun. The West seemed to have misread the plight of the East Pakistani people. West Pakistan was attempting to stop the Indian government's dismemberment of their country, but it was projected as though we were the villains by not allowing autonomy to a people demanding their rights and freedom. In December 1971 Indian troops exploited the situation, moving into East Pakistan under the pretext of protecting refugees. The previous two wars between India and Pakistan, in 1948–9 and 1965, had been inconclusive, but this time Indian armed forces (benefiting from a shared border with East Pakistan and the allegiance of the local populace) prevailed. The Pakistani army and air force were severely crippled. Bangladesh secured its independence.

By the end of 1971 West Pakistan was simply and humbly Pakistan. It would be a while before we recognized Bangladesh as a country. In the meantime a coalition of military men determined that it was time for new leadership to overcome this setback and installed Bhutto as president and chief administrator of martial law. Operating from his centre of power in Islamabad, the capital of the new Pakistan, he proved his acumen with a series of swift, effective strokes that settled tensions between Pakistan and Bangladesh, and won the release of 93,000 Pakistani POWs held by the Indians. Then, knowing that he owed his new-found power to the military and would continue to be subject to the demands of the generals who had installed him, he coerced them into resigning and replaced them with men more loyal to him.

Bhutto appointed his young protégé as Governor and Administrator of Martial Law in the Punjab, the most powerful of the remaining provinces in Pakistan, and ironically this great moment of triumph brought Mustafa's secret marriage to Naubahar into the open. Word of Mustafa's new prominence encouraged the dancing girls of Punjab to cavort joyously in the narrow old city streets, publicly celebrating the fact that one of them was the new governor's wife! After the swearing-in ceremony, Mustafa drove to meet Naubahar at her family home in an official limousine. As the garish car wound its way into the red light district, Mustafa was mobbed by fans.

Hearing of this, Bhutto summoned Mustafa and warned that he must not flaunt his position with impunity. The governor of the Punjab could not have a common dancer as his wife. Mustafa was told to correct the situation immediately. He divorced Naubahar. Safia was rescued from the exile of Kot Addu and installed in the Governor's House as the legitimate and respectable wife, but this illusion was shattered almost immediately. Mustafa's brothers came to him: 'Now you are governor, your honour is at stake. Your wife has had an illicit relationship with your younger brother, Ghulam Murtaza. We cannot hide this fact from you any longer.'

It did not matter that Mustafa had ruined Safia's life, that he had also married Naubahar and ruined her life, that he had visited Safia for mere hours in the course of their seven-year marriage, that he did not love her. Feudal law allows a man to act in such a manner, but for a wife to betray a husband is the supreme sin. Mustafa's world tumbled about him. He was the cuckold, the object of sniggling whispers.

He flew to Islamabad to seek solace from his mentor. The president of Pakistan and the governor of the Punjab drank late into the night, and their conversation took on a philosophical tone. Mustafa indulged in self-pity and pathos. He told Bhutto that he wished to resign; he could not concentrate on affairs of state. Because of this great betrayal, his self-esteem was shattered; he had lost confidence in himself.

Bhutto placed an arm around Mustafa's shoulder and proposed drunkenly: 'I think we should both resign. We should give up this government. There is nothing but pain and betrayal in life. If you resign, I will too. I cannot work alone. I've suffered your pain too. Let's just go away somewhere, dammit – away from all this.'

But in the sober light of morning, Bhutto chastized Mustafa and told him not to be so stupid and give way to emotions. They had a great destiny. They were the chosen ones. They had to bring about change in Pakistan. History would not forgive them if they showed weakness, especially for a mere woman. Bhutto's expression turned serious and he suggested, with sincerity, 'I say, why don't you bump her off?'

Mustafa let the suggestion pass. In his feudal moral scheme, Islamic law allows a man to kill his unfaithful wife in a fit of passion, but does not allow for premeditated vengeance. So he simply divorced Safia and banished his offending younger brother to Britain. (It was at this time that I married Anees.)

Bhutto wanted Mustafa to marry again, and the search was soon on for a modern woman who could serve as the ideal hostess for the Governor's House. Bhutto was ready to embark on his first trip to the US as president of Pakistan when Mustafa met Shahrazad, the niece by marriage of Bhutto's education minister. Sherry was extremely beautiful, and westernized. As was his pattern in these matters, Mustafa acted compulsively. He was to accompany Bhutto to the US, and he was in a hurry to have a charming, well-bred and – best of all – stunning woman on his arm as he walked into the White House.

Bhutto was against the union. Sherry was from an upwardly mobile, anglicized, middle-class background, and Bhutto reasoned that she would not find Mustafa's feudal background compatible. But Mustafa indicated categorically that he would not blindly follow Bhutto. It was a further signal that he would not – now or later – take any instruction concerning his private life. This was to become the great contradiction in his character. He ignored Bhutto's objection and proposed. Sherry accepted and, nine days later, with the president attending, she became his fifth wife.

Mustafa served as governor for a year. When a new constitution was adopted in 1973, Bhutto became Prime Minister and Mustafa's title was changed to Chief Minister of the Punjab. He developed a reputation as an effective administrator. His close relationship with Bhutto provided him with both the real and assumed power to crush any opposition. The euphoria of a new, people's government hung in the air. Mustafa genuinely believed in the party slogan: 'The fountainhead of power is the people.' When the police force went on strike,

Mustafa labelled the action a mutiny and appealed to the people to take charge of law and order, to man the police posts and even direct traffic. This worked, and backed up Mustafa's ultimatum to the police that anyone who did not return to work within twenty-four hours would be fired. They returned.

It was during this period that Bhutto sent Mustafa to Washington as his most trusted emissary, to meet President Nixon and deliver a special message.

Exhibiting a native canniness, Mustafa used the power of his office to re-establish his financial position. Over the years he had sold off much of his land holdings in order to finance his political aspirations. When he took over as governor, he owned only a paltry area of Kot Addu. But now those who had bought from him found themselves hauled in by the police on trumped-up charges and coerced into returning his land. Before long, Mustafa had recouped almost all of his holdings.

Mustafa crushed opposition with the fierce hand of a feudal lord. When the students of Punjab University went on strike, closing down the institution and resorting to hooliganism, Mustafa was alleged to have had them stripped naked and marched in the street. Some political leaders and opponents were said to have been sodomized in prison. Mustafa was compared to the Nawab of Kalabagh, the previous governor, favourably for his administrative abilities and negatively for his cruel tactics. On the other hand, the gates of the Governor's House and, later, the Chief Minister's House, were opened to the people of his constituency every Friday. He gave priority to the people he represented and precedence to their problems.

However, gradually the relationship between Bhutto and Mustafa grew strained. The Chief Minister of the Punjab was now a politician in his own right, emerging from the shadow of his mentor. Bhutto knew that the Punjab, being the largest province, was the vote bank of

Pakistan, and thus the backbone of the People's Party; he could not afford to lose it to his own Frankenstein monster. Everywhere Mustafa went he was greeted with the slogan *Sher e Punjab* ('Lion of the Punjab'), and he acted the part of the number two man in Pakistan, which he was. Bhutto worried that Mustafa's inflated ego might persuade him to go his own way in politics – and, if he believed himself to be the number two man, there was only one job to which he could aspire.

Indeed, there was reason to worry. Bhutto had many enemies. People with vested interests regarded his theories of Islamic socialism as anathema. They realized that if the Punjab could be extricated from Bhutto's control he would fall, and they started to form a wedge between the two men. Mustafa also began to undertake crucial initiatives without first clearing them with the prime minister. Disagreements sprang up both on policy matters and personnel appointments. If Bhutto rejected Mustafa's nominees, Mustafa sulked and turned down the alternatives presented by Bhutto. He developed a strong political personality of his own. Islamabad was abuzz with stories of his megalomania: he was rumoured to have said that he would be the next prime minister; the people of the Punjab would catapult him into power. Bhutto's advisers suggested to him that two swords could not be accommodated in one scabbard.

Bhutto loved Mustafa like his own son and tried to admonish him like a father. In return Mustafa pleaded his case. He argued that his emergence as a leader in his own right would enhance Bhutto's rule. A prime minister could not be expected to oversee everything; the People's Party needed a strong second-line leadership. On several occasions Mustafa reaffirmed his loyalty and support to Bhutto as well as to the party, but his pledges did not hold water. He referred to himself as Bhutto's shock-absorber. 'I take the flak and criticism upon myself,' he proclaimed. 'I do not direct it towards you.' But Bhutto knew that Mustafa was chipping away at his power base.

It was not long after Mustafa became chief minister that he and Bhutto began to disagree. At a Cabinet meeting in Karachi the tension finally erupted. At Mustafa's instruction, a Punjabi bureaucrat presented a paper that argued in favour of protecting the Punjab's water resources. Bhutto interrupted and raged, 'Nobody can tell me how to allocate resources between the provinces of the country. If I wish I can divert everything to Larkana [a village near the River Indus in the south]. I have the mandate of the people.'

'That Sir, is not correct,' Mustafa responded. 'You have a mandate to serve the people of this country as a whole. Not only your village of Larkana. As long as I am Chief Minister of the Punjab, I will protect the interests of the Punjab.'

Bhutto threw his papers on to the table and stormed out of the room, muttering, 'Either I stay Prime Minister of Pakistan or you become Prime Minister.'

Mustafa's colleagues gathered around him and warned that he had overstepped the bounds of his authority and urged him to apologize. Mustafa immediately sought out Bhutto in his chambers and did so. Bhutto accepted the apology, but noted, 'You're getting out of hand. I won't tolerate such insolence in public again. Talk to me privately next time.'

Following this episode, the tension grew to intolerable proportions. Mustafa had many colleagues who were jealous of his very trusted and comfortable position with Bhutto; on the other hand Bhutto was paranoid about a Punjabi leader wresting power from him. In 1974, an Islamic summit was held in the Punjab, attended by King Faisal of Saudi Arabia, Libya's Colonel Gaddafi, the PLO's Yasser Arafat, Idi Amin, and many other important Arab leaders. Mustafa presided over the summit at Bhutto's side. Sheikh Mujibur Rahman, now President of Bangladesh, was also there. It was at this summit that Pakistan at last accepted the independence of East Pakistan. Following the meeting, Mustafa tendered his resignation and moved from the Chief Minister's residence into a rented house.

And soon after that, I met him at the Punjab Club in Lahore.

3

The morning after we attended the reception at the Punjab Club, Anees and I received a call from one of Mustafa Khar's friends, inviting us to lunch. Anees had a previous commitment and was desperately disappointed. 'No problem,' said the persistent voice on the phone. 'We'll have dinner together.'

That evening, Anees and I became part of the charmed circle. Our new group of friends had one thing in common – Mustafa Khar. The Lion of the Punjab had entered our lives, and we were now two of the many satellites in orbit about him. Almost every day our group met for lunch or dinner.

Mustafa was at his most passionate whenever the conversation turned to politics. He was a socialist who wanted to do away with the feudal system that impeded progress in Pakistan – even though he was part of it himself.

'I feel disgust for the upper classes,' he raged. 'I have no time for them. I'm not interested in their acceptance. They are merely the litter of the British stooges.' He preached that Pakistan was made for people who wanted to get on in this world, people who expected to gain now that the power structure had been freed from the Hindus and the feudal élite. 'The people who should have power are the rickshaw drivers, the peasants, the factory workers.' He could smell the sweat of the poor and underprivileged in his nostrils and he had styled himself as their leader.

He argued that the unchecked accumulation of wealth must not be permitted. He wanted to take from the rich and give to the poor in a system where opportunities were more equal and where resources were more equitably distributed. He supported trade unions and other countervailing forces to curb the capitalists. He was eloquent when he proclaimed, 'The proletariat is the responsibility of the industrialist. Their children must be educated by the industrialist. There must be job security, welfare provisions, medical facilities and child-care centres for working mothers. Low-cost housing schemes must be initiated. The big industrial houses must contribute to society by setting up schools, colleges, hospitals and orphanages. They must repay their debt to Pakistan instead of feathering their own nests all the time.'

I found this deliciously exciting. This was the sort of man considered very dangerous by people like my parents. Such radicals were regarded as preachers of hatred who traded in false hopes and widened the already vast chasm between the affluent and the indigent. They allowed the genie of rising expectations to escape from the bottle. Mustafa articulated thoughts that had buzzed in my brain since childhood. I was a product of the powerful, privileged class, but I had been a misfit, an underdog in my own surroundings. I understood the zeal, for I was a rebel in search of a cause. Mustafa Khar defined the cause for me. For the first time in my life, I felt a purpose beyond mere existence. He noted my interest, and from then on made a point of steering the conversation toward politics. He could sense that I was hooked.

He was a perfect gentleman to the women in our group, treating them with respect, courtesy and even veneration. Whenever a woman entered the room, he stood and offered her a chair. His impeccable manners seemed to come naturally. I had heard whispered accusations that he was coarse and vulgar, but I saw no trace of these traits; I saw, instead, the epitome of good breeding.

Powerless to prevent it, I felt pulled by an under-current: I was magnetically attracted to him. All at once my marriage to Anees seemed very dull – I no longer loved him. I longed for excitement. Yet Mustafa was married to a beautiful woman who appeared to be devoted to him. He was forty-two, twenty years older than I was. He was mature; I felt like an incorrigibly romantic schoolgirl.

As one dinner party merged with another, dreadful, tempting thoughts plagued me. I knew that illicit liaisons were endemic in our social milieu – although one *never* admitted to them in public – but the combination of my Catholic schooling and Muslim faith produced a strong taboo.

I believed that there was safety in numbers. Everyone who attended the social functions in our new crowd of friends did so with his or her spouse. There were no bachelors and no girlfriends.

The male conversation, when it strayed from politics, often revolved around hunting – planning expeditions or recounting favourite stories of the great hunts. The women listened with pride and no traces of boredom. Anees was not a hunter. To my surprise I discovered loneliness amidst the crowd. Anees and I could not participate in these discussions, so we tried our best to become avid listeners.

At times, the conversational tone deteriorated to a very low level. Quite oblivious to the presence of their wives, the men spoke ecstatically about the sensual dances known as *mujras*. The custom came from the days of the Mogul emperors, when the courtesans were very well-bred and refined women, trained to dance, sing and please men. Nawabs and noblemen sent their teenage sons to them for entertainment and etiquette training. Virgins always commanded the premium price. By modern times, the custom still existed but had deteri-orated. The women were now lowly, uneducated peasant girls who merely danced sensuously. The tinkle of their ankle bells enticed men to throw rupee notes at their feet. The men in our new social circle took delight in discussing the intricacies of the dancers' movements – on the floor and in bed – and spoke openly of the rates they charged for the night. The wives suppressed their feelings and pretended to treat these discussions as harmless male fantasies. It was all very alien to me, and I decided that the élite were sophisticated enough to deal openly with risqué topics; it did not occur to me at the time that, for these men, this was simply another version of discussing the hunt.

Some of our old friends warned Anees about Mustafa's reputation: 'He's a womanizer, a compulsive Casanova. The man is evil. He'll damage you.' But Anees was unmoved. Mustafa was his new and powerful friend, and Anees believed that the social relationship would pay personal and professional dividends. He was too charmed by Mustafa, too busy enjoying his new-found status, to worry about his young wife.

Mustafa made no direct overtures. He said nothing to me that could be remotely construed as flirting, yet his eyes continued to cast an unmistakable message. He was formal without being stiff, friendly, but at a carefully cultivated distance. He did not contrive to get me alone. It was as if he were taking extra care to wash away the blots on his reputation. His actions broadcast the message: I'm not a lecher; I'm merely misunderstood.

A more sensitive husband might have noticed the signs, but Anees never suspected. His placid and complacent nature began to irritate me. I prayed that he would notice. That he would stop me before I went over the brink.

I understood the danger, but the abyss enticed me, inexorably. I knew that I would most certainly fall.

Mustafa's shabby, greasy and unkempt home was my first indication about the state of his marriage. Some of the chairs on the veranda were broken, their paint peeling, their upholstery threadbare. Everything in the living-room matched the turquoise-coloured sofas: the lamps, paintings, rugs and ashtrays – even a wastepaper basket – were turquoise! Thank god, the wall-to-wall carpeting and the walls were white. It seemed like a furniture showroom selected as a complete setting.

The rest of the house was a mess. It smelled of food cooking in the kitchen and old fruit. Sherry walked through the chaos unfazed as my mind presumptuously redecorated the house to suit my taste. I thought: I would not save food with the threat of flies falling into it. How can she allow this? Where are the flowers? Has she not heard of house plants? Where is the woman's touch?

Mustafa did not mind living this way. It was not his priority. But if he had hoped that Sherry would bring some comfort and class into his home, she had disappointed him. Mustafa may have been only vaguely aware of what he expected in a home, but this could not even be a mild approximation of his ideal. His eyes searched me out and silently complained. Mine responded.

On one occasion, Anees and I happened to be visiting Mustafa and Sherry as they packed for a trip to Murree. I found Sherry bending over an enormous shipping trunk, stowing Mustafa's clothes: a muslin *kurta* (loose shirt), a greatcoat more in keeping with the First World War, T-shirts, safari suits, starched dress shirts, striped shirts, checked shirts, footwear that ranged from Wellingtons to crocodile shoes, every conceivable style of trousers, every conceivable style of suit.

I asked, 'Are you going away for long?'

'No,' Sherry answered casually, without looking up. Then she turned her attention to a second large wooden chest. She inventoried its contents: Pharmaton, multi-vitamins, cough syrups, cod-liver capsules, Listerine, throat paint, iodine, Litrosen, Alka-Seltzer, blood-pressure pills, varieties of aspirin, bandages, band-aids, scissors, eye drops, nose drops, a thermo-meter.

'Is Mustafa that ill?' I asked in bewilderment.

Sherry glanced up and remarked cryptically, 'No. But you never know what he may want.'

The more I learned, the more I came to understand his inability to maintain a stable marriage. I rationalized that, had he found the right woman at the right time, he would have settled down as a good husband. But his reasons for marriage were always wrong, based on expediency rather than love. He seemed to marry women in transit. His political life exposed him to a high-powered world; he was changing and evolving all the time and he tended to outgrow his women.

I became curious about his relationship with Sherry: it seemed to be in a state of disequilibrium. Her position as his wife should have given her stature, yet his condescending treatment made her servile. Mustafa was the boss, the brain, the soul. Sherry was in awe of him, and rarely made a remark that was not drenched in his thoughts. She dared not differ from his views. She looked to him for constant approval. The strength of his personality diminished her to the point where she existed only in the reflection of his light. Sherry had surrendered her will to Mustafa and I saw this as her failure.

Since Sherry was powerless in her relationship with her husband, she often flexed her muscles in other directions, with inappropriate and hostile treatment of the servants, and especially her seven-year-old stepson Bilal. At times it seemed that she went out of her way to make trouble for the boy, perhaps in an effort to deflect Mustafa's aggression away from her and on to a surrogate target. The dynamics of the family fascinated me, yet I remained convinced that the failure was with Sherry, not Mustafa. She was simply not woman enough for this charismatic, powerful man.

On one occasion, Anees and I drove Sherry to a

furniture shop. On the way home I wanted to stop and pick up some food, but Sherry was nervous. She glanced sidelong at her companion, the ever-present Dai Ayesha, who functioned more as a stool pigeon than a servant, and said, 'We can't stop here.'

'Why not?' I asked.

'Because I didn't tell Mustafa that we'd be stopping here to pick up food.'

'So what?'

'I can't,' Sherry said adamantly. 'I don't have his permission. He'll be very angry.'

I suggested, 'Just tell him I decided to do so on the spur of the moment.'

'No. He'll be very angry. He'll beat me. He beats me if I do anything without his permission.'

'Don't tell him,' I said.

'That's impossible,' she countered, pointing toward Dai. 'She will.'

We did not stop for food.

In public, Mustafa treated Sherry with contempt. In conversation – with her there at his side – he constantly declared that Sherry was the wrong woman for him, and he made no secret of the fact that he was in the market for the perfect wife. 'I've made another mistake,' he would say. 'I'll have to marry again.' She laughed off the insults, pretending – and obviously hoping – that he was speaking in jest. But deep down she knew that his eye had begun to rove, and she did not believe that she had the charm or guile to keep him riveted to her.

As she grew to trust me more, Sherry revealed other facets of Mustafa's character. She was not allowed to visit her parents. Sherry's mother smuggled clothes, through mutual friends, for her granddaughter, Amna. When I asked her why she was banned from meeting her parents, Sherry replied, 'He says that my family abuses its relationship with him. They get things done by telling people that their son-in-law was the Governor.'

This type of behaviour was common in Pakistan.

Powerful men spawn opportunistic relatives and Sherry came from a family that could never aspire to the heights that her husband had achieved. But Sherry's stories sounded too fantastic to believe and I wondered if she was exaggerating. The Mustafa I was coming to know was a gracious and rational man. I could speak my mind in front of him. I could tell him what I thought about a given issue and, to my pleasure, he carefully considered and often accepted my views. I believed that Mustafa was desperately searching for a companion who could challenge him, rather than indulge his whims. I found myself thinking more and more about this misunderstood man who had become entangled with all the wrong women. I came to view myself as the elusive companion whom he was so desperately seeking.

The force of my mother's legacy was surfacing in my daily life. Without actually being aware of it, I was emulating much of what I had learned under her rule. I dressed like her. I styled my hair in the same fashion as she had done. Even my relationship with Anees echoed her voice.

The misgivings I had experienced prior to my marriage had proved correct. I now viewed my husband as inconsequential. Try as I might, I had no faith in his abilities and little respect for his intellect. I felt that he lacked the necessary drive and ambition to enhance his career and I was constantly badgering him and questioning his decisions. And yet I did not want a marriage like my parents. I needed a strong man who could manage his own professional life without my interference. I was also thinking of how inadequate a person I had become in my mother's eyes – eyes that represented the entire world to me. I was weakened by my attachment to Anees, because he carried no weight to strengthen me. Mother treated *us* with the same contempt that she had treated *me*.

My mind was in a turmoil: I began to imagine that Anees would be far more suited to a woman like Sherry, and that the chemistry that Mustafa and I could combine would be unstoppable.

No words were spoken, yet there was obvious electricity between us. Mustafa was observing me, making sure that this time his choice was right. Sometimes the lack of an overt advance upset and confused me. I felt nervous and a trifle guilty. How could I countenance such a situation? Had anyone else noticed what I was feeling? Did Anees know? Did *Mustafa* even know?

The women in our circle did not seem to look beyond their raised noses. They chattered endlessly about disobedient servants, clothes, jewellery and interior decorations. Occasionally they spoke about their children – about the horrible state of the schools in Pakistan and of their dreams to send their sons and daughters abroad for a 'proper' education. Many a day in the lives of these women was almost completely devoted to the topic of what to wear that evening.

I was no different. I now dressed for Mustafa. I had been raised to operate on the principle that appearances are paramount. I sampled all the clothes that had been gathering dust in my wardrobe, exploiting, in particular, the French chiffon saris from my trousseau. I was flattered when Mustafa noticed, and upset when he did not.

Picnics and *shikar* became a part of our lives. On the outskirts of Lahore, near the Indian border, is a fertile hunting preserve. We would pile into jeeps with lots of snacks for the journey, then find a flat, clear spot to pitch our tents and light fires. We women sat around the fires as the men hunted, assisted by local beaters, who made loud bird noises to flush out the partridge from the long grass along the bank of the Ravi River. Mosquitoes, flies and a variety of other insects added to the mêlée. The area was rich with migratory duck, water fowl, quail, partridge – and also wild boar, the eating of which is prohibited by Islam. These would be left to the locals to sell. The night fires kept away the winged predators and the cold. Local *marasis* ('professional singers') sang to the beat of the *dholki*. The men exchanged stories of the day's shoot as the women concentrated on the music.

Against this backdrop, Mustafa seemed always to be trying to impress me, but the seduction was subtle. When he returned from the hunt he sought my approval by showing off his bag. He looked very attractive with his khaki trousers tucked into his Wellingtons, with his rifle in one hand and a Mao cap on his head. I happened upon him early one morning, just as he was bending down to the waters of a lake to retrieve a wild duck that he had shot. The sun's first rays etched his profile. He looked up, and straight at me. My heart skipped a beat.

Mustafa was an excellent chef. The meat had to be young, and it could not be overcooked lest it lose its flavour and nutritional value. He was a perfectionist in his art; he prepared a partridge with meticulous care.

Amid this motley crowd, I mused, Mustafa and I were two intermeshing spirits. We were both loners, who felt misunderstood. Ours, I decided, were artistic souls, struggling to find a cause to which we could commit ourselves. Both of us were searching for someone who could understand the turmoil in our hearts and minds. Something told me that we were fated for one another. I wanted to help him dismantle the façade of ruthlessness and callousness that had been erected by the superficial perceptions of people who did not know the real Mustafa Khar.

What amazed me and what I admired most about him was his total disregard for public opinion – especially so since images and public opinions had always been important to my family. He had the courage to be outrageous if he felt that his position was right. Mustafa did not give a damn about conventions, and I believed that only extraordinary men possessed such a trait. He was a natural leader who, having decided upon a course of action, blazed a new trail in that direction. As a rule, politicians are circumspect, especially in their private lives. Yet Mustafa's marriages and divorces were known in the bazaars and alleys of the countryside, and he did not care. Whatever mud was flung at him slithered off. The people seemed to have balanced his political acumen against his romantic interludes and concluded that the former was more significant.

We fell in love under a million stars. We both sensed it, but Mustafa postponed the moment and prolonged the foreplay. When would he make his move? I wondered. *Would* he make his move?

It was an *Eid* dinner, the feast celebrating the end of Ramadan, the holy month of fasting. The setting was an old mansion, built during British rule; it had a marvellous ballroom with sprung floors and old cut-glass chandeliers. The ball was hosted by the Khan Bahadur of Badrasha's son. Anees and I attended as part of Mustafa's entourage. I dressed for the evening with particular care.

Mustafa approached me with measured, determined steps. He believed in body language. He understood that a masculine bearing exuding confidence can make most people crumble; he had perfected the art. He could achieve his will by the sheer force of his posture. That night, he appeared very dapper in a steel-grey suit, light blue shirt and black crocodile shoes. He asked me to dance. My eyes demurred: what would Anees think? Suddenly Mustafa imperiously ordered Sherry to dance with Anees. Anees was flattered by the supreme compliment that a feudal lord would allow his wife to dance with another man. He escorted Sherry to the floor and indicated that I should not refuse Mustafa.

I had waited eight months for this moment. Anticipation quietly merged with a tingling uncertainty. I was sure that the diamond *tikka* dangling on my forehead took on an extra measure of sparkle.

The band was playing 'Strangers in the Night'. Mustafa trespassed with great confidence, and I found myself unable and unwilling to resist. After only a few moments he led me toward the edge of the dance floor and whispered bluntly, 'Will you marry me?'

Stunned by the suddenness of the advance, I mumbled, 'But – but – I'm already married.'

'Leave it to God,' he said.

All too soon I became aware of the other couples in the room and imagined that everyone had heard this exchange. I felt myself blushing. I broke away from Mustafa's grasp, in the midst of the dance, to catch my breath. He walked me back to my chair, appearing nervous, but also quite relieved that he had finally unburdened himself.

Now, try as I might, I was totally under Mustafa's spell. He would telephone me, and we would talk for hours over the phone. I became convinced that my future was with Mustafa, and that my marriage to Anees was over. We met as frequently as we could, often at a prefabricated cabin within the compound of the large house that he was having built. Mustafa used the cabin as his den, his den of iniquity. Common sense vanished along with caution, morality and decency: my emotions overwhelmed me.

Theoretically, under the Hadood ordinance, a woman could be stoned for adultery in Pakistan. But that is not the reality. The Koran states that four witnesses to the actual penetration must be present, or that one of the participants must publicly confess. At any rate, I was not concerned for my life; in my heightened emotional state, I felt it had only just begun.

Bhutto and Mustafa kept up an appearance of friendship, although their relationship was marked by cool formality. Astute observers noticed the gulf between them, but many others believed that Bhutto's apparent hostility toward Mustafa was an act. The term *noora kushti*, 'fixed wrestling match', was bandied about. As a result Mustafa's followers remained loyal to him, and

68

Hanif Ramey, the new Chief Minister, found it difficult to win support in the Punjab.

Ramey went on the attack against Mustafa, feeding the press trumped-up stories of the ex-Governor's escapades. For example, they distorted Mustafa's role in intervening in an abduction case, and used the incident to portray him as a *badmaash* (sex fiend). Wives and daughters of the Punjab were told 'to fear the time that Mustafa Khar would return'.

And, indeed, he did return. After a sojourn in the political wilderness, Mustafa was reinstated as Governor of the Punjab in 1975, but Ramey retained the more powerful post of Chief Minister – at least for the time being. Bhutto placed Mustafa on three months' probation; if Mustafa acceded to Bhutto's wishes, he would again become Chief Minister. Mustafa was back in power, proclaiming that Bhutto would never have reinstated him had the slanders against him been true.

Anees and I drove to the huge gates of the Governor's House where Mustafa was to be sworn in. They were manned by white uniformed armed guards, their high, starched turbans bearing testimony to the everlasting influence of the British Raj. After confirmation of our identities and much checking of our invitation card, we were motioned inside.

The car turned into a sweeping driveway, in front of which stood one of the most impressive architectural relics of colonial rule. The white building had been conceived by a former governor, Sir Robert Montgomery, as if possessed by a desire to impose the architectural will of the Raj on Lahore. It lay amid 300 acres of gardens, with a lake, weeping willows, aviaries, tennis courts and cyprus-lined walks laid out for the private delectation of India's masters. The house had dozens of teak-panelled, high-ceilinged guest suites.

Anees and I walked into the famous banquet room known as *Darbar* ('Court') Hall. This grand room – the central feature of the mansion – could seat more than 500 guests. On the walls hung portraits of the lords and masters of the Punjab, on whose smallest gesture the destiny of millions depended.

All around the building were balconies where a Scottish piper strutted up and down playing tunes from the faraway Scottish highlands. Throngs of people offered congratulations to Sherry before we were silenced by the entry of the new Governor and Chief Justice of the Supreme Court. I was emotionally distraught. As Mustafa placed his hand on the Koran to take the oath of office, his eyes met mine. He noticed my discomfort and my insecurity. Later in the day, he told me that no government position could take precedence over his love for me.

He proved this statement with his actions. Mustafa was an indiscreet lover – it was almost as if he wanted Sherry, Anees, indeed the world, to find out about us. He called one day and said he wanted to see me at once, and was coming over. 'But how?' I asked. 'Anees is at home.'

'Don't worry,' he assured me.

Two minutes later the phone rang again. Anees took the call and listened carefully. After he hung up, he smiled at me and announced, 'I have to go to the Governor's House. Mustafa wants to see me. The Governor needs to talk to me!' He left immediately.

When Anees arrived at the Governor's House, Mustafa met him with the news that he had to rush off on urgent business, and told him to swim in the pool and await his return. Mustafa's friend Rauf Khan provided a pair of bathing trunks and stayed with Anees in the pool, guarding the unsuspecting prey.

Mustafa and I were still together, when Rauf Khan called from the Governor's House and reported, 'Sir, we can't keep him in the water any longer. He'll pass out with exhaustion. He looks cold and bothered.'

'Let him out in five minutes,' Mustafa said. 'Tell him

I've just called. I'll be there in fifteen minutes.' Musi
hung up the phone and we collapsed in mirth.

Of course I felt an underlying guilt. Cheating on
man was an unnatural situation for me. Anees wa
good-natured and innocent – I often felt torn and sorr
for him. However, on this occasion I was entering a new
phase, and Anees was becoming distanced from the way
I saw my future.

Matters of state beckoned. Mustafa was off with Bhutto
on a tour of the Punjab, and I was left in limbo with
Anees in Lahore.

Wherever they travelled, the two politicians were met
with banners such as *Mustafa Khar Zindabad* ('Long
Live Mustafa Khar') and *Sher-e-Punjab Zindabad*
('Long Live the Lion of the Punjab'). At an appear-
ance at the holy shrine of the saint Data Gangh
Buksh, Mustafa noticed how Bhutto's face paled as the
huge crowds thronged about the governor. The Prime
Minister was clearly chagrined.

Meanwhile, I seized the opportunity to reassess my
turbulent, double life. I decided to take my daughter
Tanya on a visit to a relative in Kasowal, in the interior
of the Punjab, to get away from the intrigue. I wanted
a place that would be inaccessible to Mustafa, to see if
I could live without him, and Kasowal was ideal. There
were no telephones and no electricity. A part of me also
wanted to challenge Mustafa and his stated commitment
to me. Would he miss me? Would he follow?

When Mustafa returned to Lahore, he was frustrated
to learn that I had left. Acting quickly, he ordered a
driver to take his official Mercedes 500SEL to Okara
and await the arrival of his aeroplane there. He assigned
Rauf Khan to a covert task: he was to send Anees on a
'top secret mission' to Peshawar, to take delivery of
a fictitious 'for your eyes only' letter. Rauf was to take
Anees to the airport and make certain that he boarded
the flight to Peshawar and that the plane took off. Anees

was told to remain in Peshawar until the letter was ready. Mustafa then instructed his pilot to fly him to Okara. There, he took command of the Mercedes and sped towards me in Kasowal.

The poor inhabitants of this godforsaken hamlet were amazed and impressed when the Governor of the Punjab arrived unannounced. Wide-eyed people crowded the alleys and narrow lanes. I was inside my relative's house when I heard the sounds of a siren and an approaching car. Moments later, the cane blind covering the front door of this little farmhouse lifted to reveal Mustafa in his safari suit and Mao cap, silhouetted in the light. He grinned mischievously.

He stepped into the house and proclaimed, 'You have to come back to Lahore. Now. I can't live without you.'

I was shocked by his arrival – though secretly I had longed for it. I made the excuses necessary to cover up an extra-marital relationship – in retrospect they seemed unbelievable. The Governor of the Punjab was a friend of my husband, I said, and Anees had requested that he come to bring me home. It was a transparent ruse, but my relatives were basking in the glow of a visit from the Governor, and showed no sign of suspicion.

I could not just run from the house. This was the countryside, where respectable women cover themselves. I fashioned a makeshift *chader* (face and body covering) from a white bedsheet and wrapped it around my head and face, leaving only my eyes visible. Mustafa, my baby, her nanny and I left together in the Mercedes. Mustafa drove expertly, at speeds approaching 100 miles per hour, until we reached Okara. Then we flew back to Lahore.

There, as we had discussed on the plane, Mustafa entered an official car and Tanya, the nanny and I stepped into another, with darkly tinted windows. We drove to the Governor's House escorted by a phalanx of motorcycles, with their sirens blaring.

The national press picked up the story of Mustafa's

surprise visit to Kasowal and portrayed the Governor as a benevolent public servant, eager to show his concern for the hinterlands. No-one knew that he was simply after a woman.

Tanya, her nanny and I were installed in the Presidential Suite of the Governor's House. Mustafa joined me for dinner, with an impish smile on his face. But I was nervous. Anees was away in Peshawar, cooling his heels, but what if Sherry found out that I was under her very own roof? Mustafa told me not to worry. He had told Sherry that he was downstairs entertaining the *ulema* (a group of religious men). There was no question of a female being present, so Sherry would remain in the private wing of the official residence.

Late that evening, after Mustafa left me to return to his wife, I found it difficult to sleep.

I woke early. The nanny dressed Tanya and we left for home.

Shortly after we left, Sherry noticed that an inordinate amount of milk had been used the day before, and she accused the servants of pilfering it. They pleaded innocence, and explained that the little baby had consumed it.

'Whose baby?' Sherry asked.

The servants did not know my name, but with one sentence they changed the course of my life. 'The begum Sahib with the long brown hair.'

Now Sherry knew.

She confronted Mustafa, who coolly admitted that he was in love with me.

4

Nothing changed.

Everything changed.

Mustafa and Sherry continued as Governor and first lady of the Punjab. Our trysts became more frequent and very brazen. Passionate emotions encourage total recklessness, I was carried along on their wave. At the same time I hated being an unfaithful wife to a decent man. But Mustafa's romance and personality blotted out the wrongness of it all, and coloured everything with expectations of a perfect relationship. It was terribly traumatic because I was a one-man woman and felt unclean. Mustafa called me three or four times daily, and professed misery if he did not see me at least once a day. I learned to trot out excuses for being away from home.

Mustafa was an incurable romantic. Once, at 3 a.m., the ring of the telephone awakened me. Anees was sleeping soundly at my side. Sensing whom it might be, I quickly slid out of bed and picked up the phone that was just outside the bedroom.

'Tina, I'm dying to see you,' Mustafa's voice pleaded.

'But you can't,' I whispered. 'I can't see you now.'

'I can't live without you. I want to give up everything and be with you.'

'Mustafa, it's late. I can't speak to you. Anees—'

'Don't put down the phone,' he interrupted. 'I'm going to drive past your house in ten minutes. Go to your window and stand there. Just for one minute. I want to see you.'

Quietly I replaced the receiver and tiptoed back into

the bedroom. Anees stirred and I told him that the call was a wrong number. Moments later, he drifted back to sleep and I slipped out of the room.

I stood at the window in my nightdress and soon the headlights of the Mercedes came into view. I smiled into the darkness, then drew the curtains.

A certain bitterness crept into our relationship, caused by my status as a married woman. Mustafa began to cringe at any mention of Anees. Without actually mentioning the word, he was pushing me towards divorce. He wanted me to make the decision – as proof of my love for him. I wavered, reluctant to hurt Anees, and worried about the social consequences for my parents and unmarried sisters, my brother's honour, Anees and his family's disgrace.

At social functions, Mustafa's provocative looks, and his comments, became bolder and very obvious. Anees avoided the signals, but the women in our group stared daggers at me. I felt as if a sudden chill had descended. I tried not to break down and thus confirm the gossip. I was very glad that my parents were living in London, so that my mother would not hear the rumours that her daughter had become an adulteress.

Led by Sherry, the women decided that silence did not hurt enough, so they began to taunt me. They spoke loudly to one another – aware that I was listening – about a hypothetical married woman involved with a married man. With their looks and their acid tongues they enforced the Hadood ordinance, symbolically stoning me.

For a time, Anees and I stopped attending the banquets. Anees knew that our friendship was now established and accepted the various excuses I gave for not wanting to go. But soon our disappearance from the social scene was noted. Mustafa called me and asked, 'What's the problem? Why are you staying away?'

I told him that the gossip and mockery had become too humiliating and that my conscience could not justify my position as 'the other woman'. I said that I no longer felt able to cope with the situation.

Mustafa was incensed. He demanded total loyalty from these people. They had no right to champion Sherry; he expected them to respect his choices and decisions without question. 'I'll take care of it,' he said. 'Everything will be fine.'

The very next day I was startled to find Sherry at my door, with her friend Kukkoo at her side. I invited them into the privacy of my bedroom, but all three of us were visibly uncomfortable. Eye contact was difficult. Sherry was upset, but she delivered her rehearsed lines. 'I know about you,' she said. 'I accept it. I know my husband and you are in love. He wants you to come to our dinners. I will not resent your presence. Nor will the other women.' Kukkoo nodded to confirm this.

I was very embarrassed and could think of no response. I felt like a slut.

Sherry had delivered the message as Mustafa commanded, but now she launched into an impassioned speech. 'Listen,' she stressed, 'I'm here because Mustafa sent me but I've come under duress. I want to save my marriage. I don't want you to see him again. If you do I'll – I'll have no choice but to commit suicide.' She pleaded with me: 'Get out of my life! Get out of his life! He's a very difficult man. I know him. You don't know him. He's no good for you. He'll ruin your life as he's ruined mine.' She tried to convince me that Mustafa was a violent and dangerous man. She claimed that he beat her savagely for trivial reasons: if she forgot to tell the servants to switch on the hot water; if she misplaced something; if she delayed having his clothes pressed.

The stories were bizarre – quite simply, I could not believe them – and Sherry could surely see the doubt in my eyes. I looked beyond the stories at a very extraordinary, charming but misunderstood man. Perhaps I chose to bury my head in the sand. I rationalized his countless marriages. To me, Mustafa was loving, gentle and, above all, reasonable. And yet I knew that such things did occur in our society far more frequently than anyone wished to admit. I knew that this was the *routine* manner in which most feudal lords treated their women. The most unsettling part of the conversation was that I sympathized with Sherry's position, and could understand the pain that these disclosures – whether real or imagined – caused her.

I countered by asking why, if Mustafa was such a demon, she was fighting so hard to hold him.

'I'm determined to keep this marriage,' she vowed. 'I can handle it. I have to survive. If I try to leave, he'll take my daughter away. I can't live without her or leave her to a life with him. I've adjusted to his life now, I want to be settled. There's no meaning to life without him. He has got into my system. You must help me by getting out of his life. Please.'

This statement also rang true. A Pakistani woman will endure almost anything in order to hold a marriage together. In our society, marriage may be purgatory, but divorce is hell. Despite my love for Mustafa, I found myself wavering. Sherry was in love with him, and yet she hated him, I thought.

I struggled with my conscience. I desperately wanted to *want* to do the honourable thing. Late that night I decided: it had to end. I would not see Mustafa any more. I would sacrifice him. But at the same time a quiet, more powerful inner voice was mocking me. A voice that was saying: I want to be the one he chooses.

I called Mustafa and told him that I intended to end the relationship. 'We're going to hurt too many people,' I said. He was involved in political business and his attention was diverted elsewhere, but he said that he would get back to me soon. I spent the next few days vacillating. I had done the right thing. Why was I so unhappy?

Four days passed. Then Mustafa arrived at my door, with Sherry at his side. She must have been broken and beaten, but she spoke her lines with conviction: she pleaded with me to return to their social scene.

Mustafa was using his wife to court his lover! Was this a sign of how deeply he loved me, or was it evidence of the type of perverse behaviour that Sherry tried to warn me about? I pushed the nagging doubts aside and the darker, selfish side of me smiled inwardly at the victory.

Anees and I re-entered the social circuit. The hostility was muted but it was still in evidence, particularly during that inevitable part of the evening when the women separated from the men. Sherry often held court on these occasions. Discussing her 'perfect' relationship with Mustafa, she laced her conversation with barbs, such as: 'Mustafa says women who have affairs with married men are sluts.' Such words were met with sniggers and nudges, all directed at me.

At one dinner, the wives of two of Pakistan's leading industrialists made several sarcastic remarks that reduced me to tears of humiliation. Mustafa was furious when I told him, and promised to teach them a lesson. The following day he summoned the husbands of the two women to the Governor's House and dictated: 'I want your wives to go to Tehmina and apologize. Today. If they don't, I won't take it lightly. You'll pay the price for their insults. You can go now.' Within a matter of hours, the two women appeared at my home and issued the required apologies.

Sherry was made more distraught than ever by these developments, and she decided to go to Mecca for *umra* (the Muslim religious pilgrimage). Mustafa and I used the opportunity to spend much of our time together. I saw him alone during the day; in the evenings, he entertained Anees and me, along with other friends, at dinner. I enjoyed the extra time with Mustafa, but remained frightened by the realization of Sherry's proximity to Allah and my growing disregard for His commands.

Sherry returned, exuding holiness and calm. It was obvious what she had prayed for and I felt unclean and exposed. I worried that God would answer her prayers.

But instead, for His own mysterious reasons, God answered mine. Perhaps it was His way of exacting retribution.

Magazines began to pry. Everyone seemed to know about our illicit relationship, including my in-laws. Poor Anees continued to dismiss the talk as malicious gossip.

News of our romance spread all the way to my mother in London. With the word *scandal* blazing in her mind, she flew to Pakistan for a heart-to-heart talk with Anees, warning him of the rumours. 'Stop meeting this man,' she said. 'If you don't, you'll lose your wife.'

Anees told my mother. 'I'll see whomever I want to see. I'm not afraid.'

My mother was furious. 'What kind of a husband are you?' she asked. 'My daughter met you while still in her school uniform. What she's becoming now is your responsibility. Her father gave her protection. Now you're exposing her to a man as disreputable as Khar.' She shook her head at him and said, 'I knew it would never work. You can't control her.'

Anees was not the last to know; he simply chose not to know. I felt a glimmer of respect for Anees. It was the first time I had seen him demonstrate the backbone necessary to stand up to my mother. It was a paradox. He stood his ground but the ground he was standing on was quicksand.

When Anees left for a week of business in Singapore, Tanya and I accompanied him on the first leg of his journey, to Karachi. Soon after Anees left us, Mustafa arrived on the pretext of official business. He invited me to dinner with his old friend and political ally, Mustafa Jatoi, who was Chief Minister of Sind, the southern province.

On the afternoon prior to the dinner, a friend had

dropped by to see me, and warn me that Mustafa's love was only superficial. 'He just loves you because you look good,' she charged. 'You dress well. You're good for his image. Once he sees you with curlers or with night cream slapped on your face he won't love you. He likes the package – not the reality.'

I was curious to find out if this could be true. I decided to put Mustafa to the test. That night I walked into the official residence of the Chief Minister of Sind looking like Bo-Peep. I wore a light-blue, checked gingham dress with absurd puffed sleeves and three layers of frills trailing at my ankles. A yoke in front had yet more frills. The dress had a plastic sticker on it depicting a pastoral scene of a cottage and a long-tailed cow. Mustafa was in the bedroom when I arrived, and I went to meet him there. He appeared very dashing in a finely tailored black suit. His eyes were lowered as he knotted his tie, but when he looked up at me his face fell. 'What the hell is this?' he said. My self-confidence immediately evaporated. It was too late to turn back; with an expression of disgust and resignation, he escorted me to dinner.

Beautiful older, sophisticated women with enticingly deep cleavages and flashing navels revealed beneath exotic saris stared at me. I felt completely out of my league. The sound of rustling chiffon mocked me.

Mustafa dumped me for the evening. He circulated among the other women, and made a point of flirting with the most attractive of them. A few men came up to me and ventured words of polite conversation, but they moved on quickly, having fulfilled the duties of etiquette.

I stood around with a glass of Coca-Cola held to my chest, trying desperately to hide the cow's tail. No matter which angle I tilted the glass, I could not cover it completely. In my nervousness I spilled the drink all over my Bo Peep dress. Humayun Baig Mohammad – who ironically owned the local Coca-Cola franchise – came to my rescue. He led me to the bathroom, where I washed out the stain. Then I stood in Jatoi's bedroom, alone for what seemed like eternity, hugging the air conditioner, praying for my dress not only to dry, but to evaporate. Cinderella needed a fairy godmother, but she did not appear. Eventually I slipped back into the party, still wet and very embarrrassed.

Mustafa asked one of his friends to drive me home. That night I howled my eyes out. My friend had been right; Mustafa did only love me for my appearance.

He called the next morning. When I told him that my outfit had been a test, he asked, 'Why do you do these things? You embarrassed yourself more than me. I love you as a person. You are a very gracious woman. You look ridiculous when you try to act undignified. Don't go around accepting stupid challenges. I love you for what you are. Why must you change? If you become a completely diffcrent person, I might change my mind. Do you understand?'

I whimpered, 'Yes.'

He cemented his point when he turned the tables. 'Look,' he said, 'if I came to pick you up dressed like a joker or a clown, would you accept it? Never. You'd feel embarrassed. So don't be silly. Be yourself.'

The dinner party was significant for another, more important reason. Everyone had noticed my presence – how could they not? – and Karachi was abuzz with fresh rumours. What was a beautiful young woman of my background doing in the company of Mustafa Khar when her husband was away in Singapore?

Upon his return Anees heard about this, and at last confronted me.

I could not lie to him. I decided that putting him out of his misery was the only way to quash my own. I confessed everything, and asked for a divorce. Marrying Mustafa was not the relevant issue; I could not live with a man whom I had betrayed, whom I did not respect, and who did not hold my interest.

Anees was very civilized, even in this moment of crisis.

He told me that he would grant the divorce. All he wanted from me was custody of Tanya. 'I need her,' he said. 'She's all I have. She will remind me of the woman I love. You can get her by going to the courts (Islamic law allows the mother custody of children prior to puberty), but please leave her with me until I get over your loss. I'll be desolate without both of you. That's all I ask for.'

I was moved by the speech, and remembered what a good person, and devoted father, poor Anees was. At the same time, Anees would have disintegrated with both of us gone. I knew that Tanya would make him feel the loss less. I wished to remove nothing more from him than myself. I also knew that in time he would heal and would be decent enough to return Tanya to me. It was simpler breaking my own heart than breaking his already broken one again. I felt that of the two of us, I was the stronger. I could withstand the loss more easily than he. I agreed.

Mother was livid; Father was furious. Once more Mother flew in from London, determined to prove that my infatuation with Mustafa was due to some form of mental derangement. She arranged for Dr Haroon, Karachi's most eminent psychiatrist, to pay me a visit and more or less demanded that he diagnose me as insane. If she could not convince me that my actions were the result of mental instability, perhaps the good doctor could. This was a variation on an old theme. Ever since my childhood meningitis, Mother had sought to explain away all my rebellion as madness.

Before the consultation she took me aside and warned, 'Don't tell him . . . everything.' Her message was implicit. If there had been a physical relationship with Mustafa, I was not to divulge it.

After one extended session, during which the psychiatrist did, indeed, discern the truth, he declared to my mother that I was disappointingly normal, and he singled out the cause of my 'fall': 'Mustafa Khar is a professional seducer. Your daughter is a victim.'

This only partially appeased her. By this definition I was not a complete slut, but she proclaimed that Mustafa would not have attempted to seduce me unless and until I had transmitted the message that I was available. Thus I was culpable for the misfortune that smeared my – and the family's – reputation. 'You had availability in your eyes,' Mother charged. 'A man with a track record like Mustafa Khar clearly does not approach decent women. The kind of women he is attracted to are the kind who become kept women and mistresses. None of my other daughters would have been approachable.'

Mother now concentrated her efforts on damage control. I found myself passive and acquiescent – guilty. I reverted to the status of a little girl and bowed to parental authority and economic reality, for my parents were my only source of financial support. My mind was too jumbled to make independent plans. Whatever little personality I had developed, I now lost. Mother sent me back to Lahore to live under the surveillance of my grandmother. I was not allowed to go anywhere on my own, nor was I allowed to make or receive telephone calls. I could not meet my friends. Mentally, I felt at a dead end. Mustafa was a more-than-taboo subject and, in any case, he was still married and heavily involved in politics. I became an outcast even in my own eyes. Public perception was obviously different from what I had intended. 'Discarding Tanya' was how the situation was perceived by people who had no idea of my reasons for behaving this way. That and my scandalous reputation and divorce sank my confidence to rock bottom. I fell quite naturally into the old pattern of following Mother's orders. In my more lucid moments, I prayed for divine intervention.

I was moved to my father's family home in the Northwest Frontier – which is truly like America's wild west – and placed under the control of my father's elder brother. Here, I lived amongst my simple Pathan relatives, where speaking of being in love or divorce was completely taboo – even the women avoided letting me indulge. I either slept or listened to music all day in my room.

One day, Anees was allowed to visit me. At first, his presence made me feel very guilty, but when he began to haggle over custody of our possessions, I began to view him in another light. He asked me to sign a document signifying that I had sold all my belongings to him for a specified sum – which he would, of course, never pay. I signed, and found that a portion of my guilt was washed away. I thought how little it took to make some men heal. Before he left, Anees promised to send Tanya to me.

After a suitable period I was released from confinement, but only after my parents were convinced that I was no longer 'reformable' and would carry on relations with Mustafa Khar from their London residence if they took me there, thereby contaminating their home and setting a bad example for my younger sisters, one that would affect their marriage prospects. They decided to withdraw from my life. My mother said, 'She's a black sheep. If she has stooped to Mustafa Khar's level, she cannot rise again to ours.' They broke off contact with me.

I left for Karachi so that Tanya could return to me, start school and be near her father. I rented a tiny apartment, just big enough for Tanya, her nanny and me, and took a job working in the office of a construction company owned by my friend Farooq Hasan. He and his wife were among the few who were very gracious and supportive.

In truth, the job was merely a favour, created to help me during this difficult time. I redecorated the office and spent the morning hours drinking cappuccino and breakfasting on fried eggs and baked beans on toast. I spent hours on the telephone talking to my friends and freely used the services of the office driver to take me wherever I wanted to go. Occasionally Farooq Hasan entered the office and interrupted me on the telephone, reminding me to make a business call. When that was finished, I resumed my routine.

The driver fetched Tanya from school and brought her to join me for lunch. Afterwards, I spent some time shopping or reading magazines until the close of the business day. For this gruelling labour I was paid 1,500 rupees (about £34) a month.

Very quickly I became aware of my new sub-status. A divorcée in Pakistani society is always a prime target for malicious gossip. Wagging tongues and leering glances turned me into a recluse. I spent most of my time either at home or in the office.

Mustafa was never available. A political storm was brewing, with him in its midst. He had grown increasingly agitated with Bhutto. In Mustafa's view, his mentor had strayed from his commitment to the people. He had isolated himself from the source of his power – the common man – and was now surrounded by cronies and quislings. When Mustafa once more resigned as Governor of the Punjab, I concluded that he was truly a man of honour. He had decided to give up all the perks of high office in order to maintain his ideals.

In 1975 Mustafa wished to stand in a by-election for the Provincial Parliament (Pakistan was now divided into five provinces; provincial legislatures had become operative under the 1973 constitution). Bhutto, realizing the problems Mustafa would create in the Punjab assembly, refused to sanction his candidacy. Instead, to get him out of the way, he offered him the ambassadorship to the United States. The break between the two former friends was now in the open. Mustafa resigned from the People's Party, announcing that as many as forty members of Parliament would follow and form the core group of a new party. But only a few members rallied to his cause; known as the Khar loyalists, many of them were arrested and imprisoned at the dreaded Dalai Camp.

Nevertheless, Mustafa persisted in an independent run for the Provincial Assembly, capitalizing upon a slowly rising wave of anti-Bhutto sentiment. The masses were disillusioned by the failure of Bhutto's promises of prosperity, and Mustafa articulated their thoughts for them. His words of criticism rang true; after all, he had once been the Prime Minister's closest associate.

Bhutto panicked and sent a brigade of People's Party functionaries to campaign against Mustafa. He was shaken by Mustafa's opposition, and was heard referring to him as 'Brutus'. As the election neared, Bhutto's people played dirty. During a Mustafa rally in Taj Pura, Bhutto's henchmen released poisonous snakes in the midst of a crowd of 100,000 people. A stampede resulted and many people were trampled. Gunshots were reported.

Mustafa returned from that meeting shaken and disturbed. One of his loyalists, Sajid, a member of the National Assembly, brought the body of a young man to Mustafa's house, cradling in his arms the evidence of Bhutto's ruthlessness. He suggested that if Mustafa led the funeral procession, the entire Punjab would take to the streets in his support. But Mustafa was not interested in seizing the opportunity to publicize the atrocity. Instead, he screamed at Sajid, 'Are you mad? Why have you brought the body here? Don't you know that I could be hauled up for murder?' Sajid turned away sadly.

It was a time of great unrest. Trade unions in various cities were protesting against high prices, low wages and non-existent social security. A popular trade union leader was killed the following day by police, which led to some bloody scenes in the Punjab. When Mustafa went to console the family and to announce that he would, indeed, lead the funeral procession, he was assaulted by militant workers and had to be rescued by the police. He thought it politically unfeasible and sought to back out of his commitment, but realized that it would be difficult to do so without losing face. He and his advisers hatched a scheme.

That evening, Mustafa and Choudry Hanif, a member of the Provincial Parliament, were driven secretly to Sialkot. Meanwhile, Sherry played her role, making frantic telephone calls, finally managing to get through to Bhutto himself. 'Where is my husband?' she screamed at Bhutto. 'You've killed him, I know. Where is he?'

The innocent Bhutto did not know.

From Sialkot, Mustafa and his companion started back to Lahore on foot. They reached a wayside café, where Mustafa was immediately recognized by the proprietor, who rushed to the authorities for help. Thus 'rescued', Mustafa was driven back to Lahore.

The morning newspapers carried the incredible story that Mustafa Khar had been kidnapped, and the clear inference was that Bhutto's people were behind the deed. Mustafa staged a press conference where he declared, 'I am a *shikari* [hunter]. I did not know where I was, but I found my way back home by looking at the stars.'

Mustafa joined the conservative Muslim League so that he would have the protection of a party platform, changing political colours like a chameleon. I thought this was a mistake.

He was now Bhutto's Number One Enemy. He was under constant surveillance by the intelligence agencies, dodging arrest and incarceration. There was no way that he could risk making contact with me.

I had been living in Karachi for five months when I learned that Sherry was pregnant. I also heard that Mustafa had developed a relationship with a singer. Angry and humiliated, I managed to reach Mustafa on the phone. He protested his innocence in both matters, but I did not believe him. The pain was too great to

87

ignore. I told him that I had finally decided to break all contact with him. It was over.

Five more months passed in loneliness, anguish and insecurity. Finally, craving forgiveness, I left for Mecca to perform *umra*, as Sherry had done earlier.

Standing there before the House of God, I half-prayed, half-cried: Oh God, I don't want to be known as a 'fast woman'. I have strayed. I seek Your forgiveness. Give me strength to restore my honour. My relationship with the man was 'cheap'. Please show me the right path. Stop these loose tongues from wagging. Stop these fingers from pointing at me.

The revelation came to me: the only way to restore my mauled reputation was to marry the man. It was the *only* honourable course of action. Mustafa Khar had branded me for the rest of my life: I was condemned to the lowly position of a 'mistress', which is what men like Mustafa had, apart from his respectable wife. If I could even find someone else to marry me, the man would taunt me whenever he was reminded of the stigma on my soul. I had no choice. Society would never accept me unless I became Mustafa's wife. Even my parents would not accept me unless I improved my status. Mustafa was a man who would command my mother's respect. He was not somebody she could push around; his sheer presence did not permit it. My marriage to him was my only salvation now. I prayed to God, asking Him to make this miracle happen.

Sherry's pregnancy disturbed me, yet explained her effort to keep him. Although I understood her situation, I was overwhelmed by my own messed-up life. There seemed no other way to redeem my honour. I also believed that Mustafa would not remain with Sherry, no matter how many pregnancies she had.

Almost at the very moment I returned to Karachi from Mecca, Mustafa called. He said he was flying in to see me.

He arrived at my house hidden in the boot of a car,

so as to shake off surveillance. I found the fact that the mighty Mustafa Khar would fold himself into such a position for me incredibly flattering. He asked me to marry him immediately. He said that he would not take no for an answer. 'I'm going back to Lahore,' he said. 'You get there. I'll be waiting. We'll get married straightaway.'

I left Tanya with Anees, promising to return for her in three days, and flew to Lahore. Mustafa and I travelled to his home village of Kot Addu. On 25 July 1976, in complete secrecy, we were married by a trusted mullah.

Mustafa held my hand and spoke with great sincerity: 'Tehmina, you must never fear me. You must talk to me about everything, whenever you want to. I'll always love you and be kind to you.'

5

I returned to Karachi to pack, and only then realized how disoriented I was. I was relieved that I was no longer just Mustafa's mistress. But what was to happen now? Our marriage was legal according to the laws of Pakistan and moral according to the Koran, but it was not expedient. Was it to remain a secret until the political environment improved? Would I remain sequestered until Mustafa divorced Sherry? I did not know the answers to these questions, and my tangled mind seemed unable to absorb all that had happened. I knew, however, that Bhutto's cronies would love to hear of Mustafa's latest dalliance. The gutter press would devour this story at a time when Mustafa could ill afford a new scandal.

In a panic as to what was to become of me, I made the bitter decision to leave Tanya with Anees until everything was better defined. It was dreadful to have to do this, but I wished to have her with me only when I was sure she would be accepted and loved, and felt she would belong. Over the phone, I arranged the details. Anees was the first to learn of my new marriage, and he was obviously upset. But he agreed to take Tanya back for a time, and return her to me once my life became more settled. I hoped – somewhat misguidedly, as it turned out – that the uncertain situation would last only a few weeks – a month at the most.

Mustafa called, complaining that he could not bear to be separated from me. He asked me to speed up my return to Lahore. I agreed.

Tanya was sensitive to my sadness. Her wide,

dark-brown, three-year-old eyes watched with alarm as I packed *all* her clothes into several suitcases and placed *all* her toys into cardboard boxes. Packing the boxes was traumatic for us both, and something that neither of us has ever forgotten. As my driver carried Tanya's world out to the car, my baby's lips began to quiver. 'You are going to see your father,' I said, trying to keep my tone bright. 'I'll be back in just a few days.'

What was I? An underdeveloped, irresponsible mother? A child? I couldn't say.

Tanya loved her father. She visited him every week. But her innocent mind sensed the different nature of this episode. She clung to me quietly throughout the drive.

The nanny stood outside Anees's home, awaiting us. I opened the car door. As the nanny's arms reached for Tanya, the little girl turned her face away. Her tiny fingers grasped at my clothes. She howled, screaming out her fear with deep despair, such as I had never heard.

Through my tears I cried out, 'I'll be back soon, Tanya. I'll be back soon.'

The nanny pulled at Tanya. She tried desperately to cling to me but I pushed her away.

Within moments it was over. Tanya was gone and the car sped off. I could hear her terrified wails grow more faint with distance.

I could not look back.

As I flew to my second husband in Lahore, the memory of Tanya's cries was heart-wrenching. So were mine. I needed a mother myself. Sitting in the plane, I had no idea just how far I was actually flying from her. I never thought she would have to grow up without me. I stared out at the ground far below, and wondered what was to become of us. The sudden appearance of a cloud obscured my view.

Mustafa's young aide Sajid met me at the airport, and announced that his house was to be my hideout for the evening. The following day Mustafa drove me to the ancient city of Multan, where I was to live in seclusion for several months. About a two-hour drive from Mustafa's village of Kot Addu, Multan is surrounded by sprawling feudal estates, fruit orchards and rich alluvial soil.

The Qurarshi and Gilani clans hold sway in this ancient trading centre. Originally the two clans were satraps of the mighty Mogul emperors; later, most of them found it convenient to transfer their loyalty to the crown, which awarded them vast tracts of land. The city is built around one of the most magnificent Sufi shrines where, every year, the faithful gather and pay millions of rupees in tribute. The Qurarshi and Gilani clans fought for generations for this windfall, and the old feud continues to affect local politics.

In this milieu, I tried to set the house in order. I had to keep busy, lest my ache for Tanya took over.

Mustafa visited frequently, but his impulsiveness kept me unsettled. Sometimes he left for Lahore, telling me that he was going to be away for a week, yet he would return the very same night. He fought ambivalence: he could not risk exposing our marriage; he could not bear to be away from me. He said that the six-hour journey between Lahore and Multan was worth the few moments he could spend with me.

But he soon tired of the drive. Before long, he moved me back to Lahore, installing me in the prefabricated cabin that was the site of so many of our illicit liaisons. The cabin held many memories for me – both sweet and sour – and living here made me feel uncomfortable. I yearned for legitimacy, and the chance to be reunited with Tanya. Mustafa visited me in the cabin during the day, and then spent the night with his other, still unsuspecting, wife at the main house on the same premises.

One evening, after Mustafa had left, I fell asleep. I was startled when he awoke me, and much more startled to see Sherry at his side. He had tried to break the news to his pregnant wife, but Sherry did not believe him, so he had brought her here to prove his confession. The subterfuge was over, and I moved into the big house. Whatever the consequences, our families and associates would now know that Mustafa had two wives, although he was determined to keep the information away from the press.

My new home was a Spanish-style villa, with a sloping, red-brick roof and many arches. The six bedrooms were all occupied by Mustafa's relatives, so I moved upstairs to the den.

The rumour mill reached my parents in London. They were very upset. Once more their rebel daughter had brought disgrace to their household. They announced that I was dead for them.

But our marriage was so easily accepted by the people around Mustafa that I wondered why I had ever been apprehensive. And my grandmother approved. When she came for a visit, I saw fear for my future in her eyes, yet there was also a contentment, a peace brought about by the decent status I had at last achieved.

It was comedy; it was tragedy. I wanted to spend all my time with Mustafa, yet I did not want him to neglect Sherry. I was self-conscious when he showed affection to me in front of her. Sometimes at night I pushed Mustafa out of my room and sent him to her. I did not want to hurt Sherry, but her pain was palpable. I could never forget that she was pregnant and therefore doubly humiliated.

We attended social engagements as a threesome. Mustafa took this in his stride and Sherry did not *seem* to mind, but I felt alienated and acutely embarrassed when we entered a house together. To me, we appeared anachronistic in this modern age.

I noticed an interesting phenomenon when Mustafa went away on a hunt. I was miserable in his absence, but Sherry was happy that he was gone. As the time for his return approached, I grew happy in anticipation, but Sherry was visibly upset.

Sherry opened up to me, more than before, and began to tell me stories that featured Mustafa as a grotesque sadist who derived pleasure from humiliating the ones he professed to love. It was only now that I learned what had happened when Mustafa had divorced Naubahar, and the dreadful way he had treated Safia and her nanny.

Once he had discovered that it was not politically expedient to be married to a dancer, he had sent for Naubahar. She sat in front of him, quietly waiting to administer to his wishes. With his feet on his desk, Mustafa had puffed calmly on a cigar and stared at her through the 'V' of his crossed legs. Very directly, he told her that, as things had turned out, she had become a liability to him and that the marriage had to end. 'In my position, I cannot afford it,' he said. Naubahar screamed out her pain at the new governor of the Punjab, but he accepted this with stoicism. She begged him to reconsider but he refused. Finally, Naubahar stood up, stared directly into her husband's eyes and uttered a curse: 'Mustafa Khar, may you suffer like you have made me suffer. May you know the pain of being scorned. I pray to God that in every street of this country, your children roam. Every stone you pick up will reveal a child of yours. You shall never be at peace.' Her final words burned into his memory: 'A woman will destroy you like you have destroyed me.' Although Naubahar was gone, the curse lingered.

When he had discovered Safia's infidelity, he had, apparently, beaten her without mercy and broken several of her ribs. But, even worse, he had ordered one of the maids to insert red chili powder into the vagina of poor Dai Ayesha, the nanny, for not informing him of the affair.

Sherry theorized that he suffered from an inferiority complex. He resented women from our social background and made it his mission to subjugate them. He disguised his class envy by assuming a feudal air. She claimed that his political idealism was merely an attempt

94

to gain access to our class and that his concern for the poor and downtrodden was a sham. In truth, she said, it was a manifestation of his hatred for the élite. He wanted to demolish the structure that ridiculed his origins and laughed at his lack of breeding and style. Women were his obvious victims. He was out to destroy us.

A part of me wrote off such statements as the ravings of a woman scorned; another part of me filed them carefully in my memory.

I watched the evidence build.

In his dealings with Sherry, Mustafa exhibited extreme impatience. He treated her with contempt and abused her with filthy language that made my ears burn. One morning he asked her for his Pharmaton multivitamins that he ordered specially from London. When she produced a half-empty bottle, Mustafa was furious. 'Where are the rest?' he demanded.

'I took them,' Sherry admitted. 'I needed to – because of my pregnancy.'

Mustafa kicked her in the buttocks. He pulled off his thick rubber-soled shoes and struck her with them. Then he roughly pushed her out of the room. I froze in shock, but could not find the courage to express my revulsion.

My first experience as the target of Mustafa's wrath came soon after, when I had a dental appointment. Sherry was to take me. I knew that Mustafa was still attempting to keep the news of our marriage out of the papers, so I asked him what name I should use. 'Begum Mustafa Khar,' he replied. When we reached the surgery, I decided that I did not want to humiliate Sherry, so I did not register as Mustafa's wife. I simply called myself Tehmina. Sherry reported to Mustafa that I had disobeyed his instructions. Mustafa interpreted my consideration as betrayal and raged: 'Never – ever – disobey me! You have to do what I tell you to do.'

On another occasion, I was in my bedroom when Mustafa sent a message that he wanted to see me on the veranda. I was changing my clothes, so it took me a few minutes to comply with his request. When I strolled casually out on to the veranda, I found Mustafa livid. His eyes were bloodshot and bulging out of their sockets. 'How dare you keep me waiting!' he raged. 'I told you to come immediately. When I send you a message it means that you have to drop everything and obey.' I tried to explain, but my words were angrily dismissed.

Mustafa and I were sitting in our bedroom when Sherry reported that she had caught nineteen-year-old Abdur Rehman, his son from his first marriage, smoking in the bathroom. Immediately Mustafa summoned Abdur Rehman and the servants. Officiously, he asked his son if he had been smoking. The boy lied. Mustafa rose to his feet and ordered the servants to force the lad to the floor and hold him there, spreadeagled. He began to beat his hapless son with a stick. With each blow the boy screamed for mercy. I cringed at the horrible crack of stick against skin, and at the sight of blood. Mustafa swung it so violently that the stick broke across the boy's back. Undaunted, Mustafa called for another stick, and flailed away until that, too, broke. He was on his third stick when I could take it no longer. I tried to intervene, but was pushed out of the way.

I was petrified and shaken by Mustafa's unreasonable and callous violence toward his own son.

That evening we were invited to Taj-ul-Mulk's house. He was an old and trusted friend, and his home held a special feeling. It was here that Mustafa had first proposed marriage. Mustafa asked me to take cash with me. That evening, when the group decided to go out for dinner, Mustafa asked me for money. I explained that I was not used to carrying a bag, and had forgotten. In front of everyone he snapped, 'Get in the car. Go back home. Pick up the money and come back.' I did as he commanded, but I felt very degraded.

One day Sherry asked idly if I would leave my 'foreign clothes' for her when I went away, as she could not buy them in Pakistan. I was confused, and asked what she meant. We had no plans to travel outside Pakistan. Sherry was confused too, and explained why she had accepted my presence in the household with at least a measure of equanimity. Mustafa had told her that he had only married me to save me from all the vicious talk that was going around, and had said that I would only be in the house for a few months – until the muck had settled. After that he would send me abroad and arrange a quiet divorce. Sherry believed him, because she wanted to.

Mustafa had taken me along for a shoot when we received word that Sherry had delivered a son. He was thrilled. He visited the mother and child immediately upon our return to Lahore, then brought the child home for his mother to see. She made the baby lick honey, an old custom that is believed will help the child develop the qualities of the person performing the ritual. She lifted her lips to his tiny ear and called the *azaan* three times: '*Allah ho Akbar*' ('God is Great'). Then she said the *Kalima*: '*La Illaha Il Allah Mohammad ur Rasool Allah*' ('There is no God but God and Mohammad is His Prophet'). Thus was the boy established in the Islamic faith.

Mustafa took the infant back to the hospital, but that night he fell ill with pneumonia and died. Vicious rumours circulated that Mustafa was unhappy at the birth of the baby and had killed him. It was not true; I had seen how shaken he was by the boy's death. Also, it did not seem to matter to Mustafa that his children were not born into stable marriages. Mustafa had children in various pockets of the country and he felt no sense of responsibility for them. In his view, a child was a victim of his own fate. Mustafa would have no reason to dispose of him. But once again Mustafa's reputation preceded him; people were quite willing to believe the worst about him. Not unreasonably, this was especially true of Sherry's family, and their animosity caused a final break. Mustafa served Sherry with divorce papers. '*Talak, Talak, Talak,*' he said, and it was all over.

We left the house for Sherry and her mother to take what they wished. The jewellery was worth a fortune and included some eighty sets given to her when she had married Mustafa: the Shah of Iran had presented her with the most exquisite turquoise set; watches and jewels came from the King of Saudi Arabia; Bhutto's wedding present was a spectacular gift of gold and precious jewels. Sherry packed up everything and moved out.

I felt sad that Sherry had had to leave her own home for me; but I also felt relieved – two wives together is very medieval and 'cowlike' to me. I began to redecorate the house that was mine now. I removed the thick velvet curtains and went about creating a very Americanized interior. The high ceilings were decorated with intricate designs made with vegetable paints in the traditional colours of Multan, Mustafa's area. Bright orange, green, blue and white complemented the pale furnishings perfectly. I began to train the servants: a slice of lemon decorating the Coca-Cola glass; tea served in silver, with a triangular-folded paper napkin between cup and saucer. The house became orderly; my mother's training was evident.

Mustafa thought that I needed government bureaucrats to be our servants. 'These poor, illiterate boys aren't good enough for you.' He laughed when I gave the bowed, unwashed heads a lecture on cleanliness.

I felt that it was now time to include Tanya in my new life. Mustafa granted his reluctant permission for me to call Anees in Karachi to ask him to send our daughter to me, as he had promised. Mustafa stood over me as I dialled, clearly agitated by this reminder of my previous involvement with another man. The conversation was curt and devastating. Anees had heard the rumours of Mustafa's alleged infanticide, and he proclaimed that his daughter would not be allowed to live with such an evil man. Henceforth, he said, I would have no contact with Tanya. He hung up on me.

I turned to Mustafa for solace. 'He won't give her to me!' I wailed.

But Mustafa's expression silenced me. His eyes said: I have granted you this tremendous privilege to ring up your former husband. Now, be done with it. *I* am the important one in your life, not Tanya.

There was no sleep for me that night. I knew that Tanya's school was reopening the next morning, and I was plagued by dark visions of her motherless existence. Who would dress my baby? Who would prepare her lunch?

In the morning, Mustafa found me crying. 'If you loved your daughter so much, why did you marry me?' he asked. 'You should have known the consequences of your action. You can't ruin my life now by crying for Tanya. You have no business crying for her. I never want to see you crying for her again. Never. Ever! Do you hear?' I glanced up sharply and recoiled at the sight of his face. Anger, bitterness and menace were combined in one terrifying expression.

Soon after that, I learned that I was pregnant.

Mustafa insisted that I start my day by consuming buttered *parathas* and eggs. He ordered me to eat all of this and to wash it down with a sixteen fluid ounces glass of fresh cow's milk. I was to drink yet another glass of the creamy beverage in the evening – which always left me nauseous. Mustafa claimed that the regimen was nutritious for the unborn child. The rich food left me bloated and uncomfortable, and I came to believe that he forced it into me to ensure that I became fat, to assure my unattractiveness to other men. Dai Ayesha was assigned the task of serving the milk, morning and evening, and making sure that I drained the glass.

One evening Mustafa came into the bedroom and asked if I had drunk my milk. I had not. He immediately summoned Dai and railed at the frightened woman,

'Why has she not had her milk?' Dai mumbled an explanation: I had not asked for it; she had forgotten to bring it. Mustafa thrust his foot squarely against Dai's backside, sending her flying through the doorway.

The awareness that had been growing slowly now blossomed into full and ghastly flower. I had fallen into the classic trap of the Pakistani woman. The goal is marriage and, once achieved, the future is a life of total subordination. I had no power, no rights, no will of my own.

Early in 1977, after Mustafa and I had been married for little more than half a year, Bhutto called for elections, pitting the People's Party against a patchwork coalition of nine opposition parties calling themselves the Pakistan National Alliance. Mustafa and I left for a month-long 'vacation' in London so that he could avoid a political confrontation with his estranged friend. The People's Party won a large majority, but the opposition refused to accept the results, claiming that Bhutto's henchmen had resorted to large-scale rigging and ballot-stuffing tactics. Mobs took their anger to the streets. A plague of strikes and violence disrupted the country's economy. There was mounting chaos in all the major cities; Pakistan was on the brink of self-destruction.

The opposition leaders smelled a popular victory, and perhaps found a strong ally. Bhutto's independent foreign policy and his pursuit of a controversial nuclear programme made the US nervous; America was afraid that the so-called 'Islamic bomb' would find its way into the hands of countries like Libya and Syria – not to mention terrorist organizations. Rumour held that opposition to Bhutto was fuelled by US dollars. The opposition also knew that Pakistan's military leaders were waiting in the wings: they feared that a nuclear capability would result in massive cuts in conventional forces, thus eroding their personal power. Events snowballed. The strikes and demonstrations became so severe that in three large cities Bhutto had to call out the army.

Mustafa and I returned from London to find Bhutto struggling for political survival. The Prime Minister knew that he had to win back the allegiance of the Punjab, and the only man who could do that for him was Mustafa Khar. Bhutto swallowed a considerable amount of pride and invited Mustafa to Islamabad and back into the People's Party fold.

Mustafa weighed options, negotiating terms for his return. Times were tense and the pressure built within Mustafa until it erupted with irrational fury. He could not vent his wrath in the political arena, so he chose as his victims those who were closest to him.

The servant was five minutes late laying the food for *iftaari*, the sunset meal that breaks the day's fast during the holy month of Ramadan. When he finally arrived, a hungry Mustafa exploded. In the presence of his mother, who lived with us, he thrashed the poor man until he was barely conscious. Then he sat back down at the dinner table and commanded, 'Eat up.' His mother began to eat, but I mumbled that I had lost my appetite. Mustafa turned a hate stare upon me and spouted obscenities. Quickly, I pecked at my food.

For the next four hours, Mustafa's temper grew progressively worse. By the time we retired to our room, violence was thick in the air. In the dressing-room I donned my infamous Bo-Peep frock, which served as a comfortable nightgown for my pregnant body. I walked toward the bed, but found Mustafa blocking my way, standing in the midst of the room, lit only by a crack of light emanating from the dressing-room door. A chill ran up my spine. He instructed me to sit on the edge of the bed, and sat beside me. Then he began to interrogate me about my marriage to Anees. How had we met? Where? I answered these simple queries, but then the questions became more intrusive. With each question his tone grew angrier, his breathing uneven. His eyes reddened. The skin of his face stretched taut with anger.

And with each answer, my own heart beat faster. He wanted to know *all* the details of our wedding night.

'Can't we forget it, Mustafa?' I requested softly. 'It's all over. Must we talk about it now?'

'I've asked you a question,' he responded curtly. 'Answer me.'

I was very scared, and I could only stammer.

'You're hiding things from me,' he charged. 'There's more to it.'

'There isn't. I've told you everything before. I don't think we should discuss this now. It's upsetting you.'

'Who the hell are you to think? I have asked you a question. Answer me!' He grabbed my right wrist and twisted, forcing me to my knees. Even as a shriek escaped from my lips, I told myself to be quiet, lest the servants, or his mother, hear.

He released his grip and I scrambled to my feet, gasping, rubbing my sore arm. He ordered me to sit down again on the bed, and the interrogation continued. He asked: 'When you had sex with Anees, did you respond?'

I whimpered, 'I was only eighteen. I wasn't interested.'

'Liar!' he raged. I could feel his body tighten. I could hear his breathing grow heavier. In the dark, I could sense that his eyes were bulging out of their sockets. I knew that his fists were clenched. With deliberate malice he asked, 'If you did not want sex with Anees, how did Tanya come to be born?'

The answer – whatever I chose to say – would condemn me, but I had no opportunity. Suddenly he threw me down on to the bed and jumped on me. Sitting astride my belly, he slapped me in the face repeatedly with his open palm, forehand and backhand. The sounds of his blows seemed too loud to remain confined to the four walls of the room. I fought to stifle my screams as he pulled at my hair, thrusting my head from side to side. Like lightning, he leaped off me. One hand clutched my long, braided hair and jerked me off the bed and on to the floor. I felt a wetness run down my legs, but had no time to realize that my bladder lacked the strength to face this kind of fear. He threw me against a wall, picked me up and threw me against another one – again, and again, and again. I no longer knew what was happening. Something burst in my ears. I felt an agonizing pain in my eyes. Something split. Something swelled. Then the pain merged into one deep, enthralling sense of agony.

I did not know how long the beating lasted. It could have been ten minutes; it could have been two hours. The intensity made it an eternity. Then, quite suddenly, it was over. His fury was sated.

I begged in a weak voice, 'Please, God! I need to go – I need to go – to the bathroom.' He allowed me to stagger off.

I leaned heavily against the sink top and struggled to catch my breath. Slowly I raised my eyes to the mirror. I gasped in fresh fright at the monster who gazed back at me. A shiver ran through me. My teeth chattered. My body shook. My braid had opened and my long hair was wild and strewn, like a witch's. The right side of my nose had disappeared, merging into a swollen cheek. My lips protruded in an exaggerated and grotesque pout. My eyes were deeply sunk into huge, purple patches; one of them hurt badly and was bloodshot. A piercing pain screamed in one ear. The left side of my scalp was matted with blood. I pulled at it and tufts of hair came out in my hands. I rinsed my mouth and tasted blood.

Suddenly I was terrified that I had remained too long in the bathroom. I stumbled back into the bedroom, shaken, drained and near collapse. My back ached severely. Mustafa sat on the bed with his head bowed and his palms placed over his temples. He looked up at me, shattered, transformed from a wild, vengeful beast into a meek and frightened little child. He fell at my feet and wept. 'I'm sorry! I'm sorry! I'm sorry!' he wailed. 'What have I done to you?' He begged forgiveness. He said that he must have been possessed by an evil spirit. He had not meant to hurt me. He could not understand his actions – perhaps the jealousy over another man in my life was insufferable because his love for me was overwhelming. He had no control over his behaviour – he could not bear the idea of his wife with another man – even if it was a past husband.

I was very confused by the unaccountable pity I felt for this man who had his forehead on my feet, anointing them with his tears. I tried to forgive him, but the pain would not allow me to forget. All night long I twisted in agony. All night Mustafa sat up, doing his best to ease my discomfort.

We both knew that I needed medical attention, and Mustafa was very nervous about arranging for it. It was obvious that I had been assaulted and cruelly battered, and he begged me to endure the pain in order to keep up appearances. The timing was critical because he was scheduled to go to Islamabad to meet Bhutto and was worried that the servants – or his mother – would see the extent of my injuries and talk. 'If this leaks out people will not give our marriage a chance,' he warned. 'Your position will be reduced to the lowly one that all my other wives had. I don't want you to be humiliated. Nobody should ever say that I dared or wished to lift my hand to you. I want people to respect you – if they thought that I didn't, why should they?'

He had touched the effective spot. My humiliation at his hands was relatively less than if I exposed it to others. I was mortified by the thought of publicity. Fear of the indignity made me cringe. I was conditioned to believe in the concept that image is the paramount thing. This was a personal and private matter between my husband and me. We would work it out. I wanted no-one to know – least of all my mother.

'I'll stay in the room till you get back,' I promised. 'Tell everyone I've gone with you.'

Mustafa was visibly relieved. Dai Ayesha was assigned

to smuggle food into the room She also applied poultices to my face to quell the swelling.

Mustafa journeyed to Islamabad, where Bhutto appointed him as special assistant and chief political adviser, with Cabinet rank, and sent him immediately to the Punjab to ease the tension. At a mammoth public rally in Rawalpindi, wearing his trademark Mao cap and waving an open palm in an imitation of an imam's blessing, Mustafa told a spirited crowd that the opposition should realize that Bhutto and the People's Party were showing restraint. 'We shall retaliate, if pushed any further,' he vowed. 'We can match fire with fire. If they are crying for our blood, we too will go for their throats.' Once more Mustafa blessed them with the same palm that he had used to lacerate my face. The crowd roared in approval. The Lion of the Punjab was back.

Meanwhile, I waited quietly in the bedroom for four days, pretending not to be there. The time I spent in hiding made me even more convinced that exposure of my husband's violence would reduce me to Sherry's position. Too many people were waiting to prove my mistake and mock my humiliation. My marriage would lose credibility and Mother would not think me significant. Mustafa was correct when he said, 'If they think I don't respect you, why should they?' My insecurities and inadequacies paled the event, and I wanted it erased quickly.

More than two weeks passed before we deemed it safe for me to journey out to see doctors. By then, my face was an approximation of the original. I visited an ear specialist, a physiotherapist, and an eye specialist who told me that the burst capillary in my right eye would bother me for the rest of my life. The thin red latticework appears even now, whenever my eyes become tired.

The psychological damage was worse. Now, whenever Mustafa came home, I shuddered in fright. His unpredictable word was law. It was not for me to reason. My love for the man had now turned into fear. I knew that anything that I might say or do could make him angry. Sometimes even a sullen look would send him into a rage. 'Who are you thinking of, a lover, Anees?' he demanded. I was suspect because I had betrayed a husband; my track record sentenced me repeatedly.

I began to say my prayers under my breath constantly: to keep him cool, to soften his heart toward me, to make him love me. I was incapable of thinking of any other issue. Nothing else was significant.

Mustafa told me one day that I was not allowed to read a newspaper; I obeyed without a squeak of protest. From then on, when he found me in a room that contained newspapers, I felt caught, and prayed that he would not think that I had actually attempted to read one of them. My prayers usually went unanswered. If he walked into the room and saw a paper, he was likely to ask, 'Did you read a newspaper?'

I would answer, trembling, 'No.'

Invariably he raged, 'Don't lie to me!' Nothing further was said. His fists did the talking.

There was not a day that Mustafa did not hit me for some reason: the food was late, his clothes were creased. With a shudder, I realized that I had become just like the now-discarded Sherry. Perhaps the greatest tragedy was that, like her, I stopped questioning his violent outbursts. I just tried my best not to provoke him. If I dared to object in some meagre way, the beating was only worse. At last I understood Sherry's dilemma – by the minute I became like her.

He continued to use my first marriage as a stick to beat me with; my divorce and remarriage had proved to him that I was capable of adultery. This produced complete sexual confusion in me. I was afraid that my slightest response to his advances would reinforce his image of me as a common slut. This was a feudal hang-up: his class believed that a woman was an instrument of a man's carnal pleasure. If the woman ever indicated that she felt pleasure, she was a potential adulteress, not to be trusted. Mustafa did not even realize that he had crushed my sensuality. His attitudes were contradictory: he expected response, yet disallowed it. I was on automatic pilot, responding as much as was important for him, but never feeling anything myself. If he was satisfied, there was a chance that he would be in better humour. It was at these times that I realized that prostitution must be a most difficult profession.

I could only develop in the direction that he chose. To think independently was a crime that he had the right to punish. Many of his beliefs ran counter to everything that I considered right, but there was no way that I could dare to engage him in a rational debate. His values were steeped in a medieval milieu, a mix of prejudices, superstitions and old wives' tales. High on the list was the role of the wife. According to feudal tradition, a wife was honour-bound to live her life according to her husband's whims. A woman was like a man's land – 'The Koran says so,' he said. This was a revealing simile. A feudal lord loves his land only in functional terms. He encloses it and protects it. If it is barren, he neglects it. Land is power, prestige and property. I interpreted the Koran differently. To me, land had to be tended and cultivated; only then could it produce in abundance. Otherwise, it would be barren. But, of course, I was expected to accept Mustafa's interpretation without question.

Yet he was not completely backward. He was a feudal lord who had been exposed to the modern world, and his philosophies were eclectic. He kept me suppressed and cloistered, but then again he treated me as a companion. He discussed politics with me and expected me to take an active interest in his work. I was like a wall on which he could bounce off ideas, but I was expected to bounce them true, rather than attempt to deflect them in any way. He also allowed me to drink wine, but only in his presence and when he chose. In fact, he insisted upon it. 'It will make you relax,' he would say. 'You are too tense in bed.' But no matter how much I drank, I never allowed myself to forget in whose presence I was. I discovered that the human mind was strong enough to control the effects of alcohol in times of danger.

I became incapable of thinking logically; indeed I was afraid to think, for irrationally I was certain that he could penetrate my mind. He fed this fear frequently, by saying, 'I know what you're thinking, Tehmina, believe me. You daren't think of anything that I have forbidden you to think about.' My brain was washed, bleached and hung out to dry. I was afraid to sleep, lest I dream images that would annoy him.

Mother's words, based upon her interpretation of the Koran, rang in my memory: 'If I tell any of my children to jump from the roof, they must obey without hesitation or question.'

Only the schizophrenic quality of his behaviour – and my own ambivalent reactions to him – allowed me to survive. When he was in a sunny frame of mind he was loving and considerate. He fed me with his own hands. He dreamt with me. He promised to be a good husband. I grasped desperately at these signs of his approval. My goal was to keep him in this mood.

He was obsessed with my knee-length brown hair. He would not allow me to sit with my back to a fire, lest the hair suffer damage. In his tenderest moments he returned to this passion, oiling and combing my tresses. He made me promise that I would never cut my hair, or even trim the split ends.

I knew that I could not leave him. I had entered into a controversial marriage, and I had to strive to keep it intact. I recognized that there was always an effort and a price to pay for success; I must not fail at any cost. A lasting and happy marriage was my only value. Under its respectable shroud, alongside my powerful husband, my mother would not be able to shun me, and the fear of that happening became equal to – or even greater than – my fear of him. The two fears kept me shaken and traumatized. I did not have the confidence to walk away. I reasoned that Mustafa would hunt me down, and find me, no matter how far I ran.

Then he would murder me. I was convinced of it.

By the time I was eight months' pregnant, Mustafa's rich, force-fed diet had caused me to balloon from my normal eight stone to almost eleven stone. I looked and felt like a bloated cow.

We moved to the State Bank House in Islamabad, so that Mustafa could be at Bhutto's side during what had become a deepening political crisis. We lived amid intrigue, and were forced to maintain strict security procedures. We were guarded by a live-in gunman named Matin.

One of the men whom Mustafa frequently encountered at Cabinet meetings was General Zia-ul-Haq, the Army Chief of Staff. He was noted for his silence and apparent obsequiousness, and he seemed to hold Bhutto in awe. On the evening of 4 July 1977, my grandmother and I were waiting for Mustafa at a restaurant, where he was to meet us after a Cabinet meeting. When he finally arrived he was both very late and very disturbed. I asked what troubled him. Anxiously he reported, 'General Zia suddenly seems to have opinions of his own. The man was disagreeing with some of the plans we were putting forward. His attitude change means that he is being manipulated by bigger powers. I warned Mr Bhutto. Something's brewing.'

That night, at 3 a.m., Matin rushed into our bedroom. Instantly alert, Mustafa reached for his rifle. Matin indicated with his hand that Mustafa should follow him. I was only vaguely aware of this, and drifted back to sleep.

Ten minutes later I was reawakened by a loud banging on the front door. Tired and sleepy, I stumbled out of the bedroom and encountered Matin, who told me in an urgent tone to go back inside. I retreated, but left the door slightly ajar and peeped through the crack. Within moments I was startled to see two uniformed men walk past stiffly. Five soldiers followed, with their Sten guns at the ready. One took up a position in the corridor and noticed that the bedroom door was ajar and that a light was on. He turned quickly and kicked the door into my protruding belly. I winced in pain. The infant in my womb kicked back. I banged the door shut and sat on the bed, trying to figure out what was happening.

Had the army come to arrest Mustafa? Had Mustafa annoyed Bhutto again, or was this a coup, initiated by the proverbial midnight knock on the door? Was this drama being played out in houses across the length and breadth of the country?

The clock on the bedside table ticked loudly. Half an hour passed.

Finally Mustafa returned to the bedroom. He was calm, and I could almost see his mind working out permutations, analysing, trying to plan. He told me that the army had moved against Bhutto; martial law was declared. He ordered me to pack his suitcase and added, 'Don't forget my vitamins – and my cigars.'

'Is it going to be dangerous?' I asked.

'I don't know. It might be a bloody coup. They've come to get me. You'd better go to Ghulam Arbi and Saima's house today.' Arbi was his brother. 'Don't worry,' Mustafa said. I packed his things. He kissed me on the forehead and left.

I stared out of the window. In the darkness I could make out a jeep filled with army officers. Mustafa got in, and the jeep sped off.

At Arbi and Saima's house I listened carefully as General Zia gave a televised speech. He had assumed power, but he promised to hold elections within ninety days. He said that the politicians were being held in protective custody, but would be freed soon.

For fifteen days I knew nothing of Mustafa's whereabouts. Then he was able to send me a note. He was well. He was in Abbottabad, north of the capital.

Three weeks before my baby was due, Mustafa and other political prisoners were moved a short distance to detention facilities in one of the state guesthouses in Murree – the mountain resort where I had studied – and I was allowed to visit him there. I remembered how different my father's imprisonment had been. There was no shame in political incarceration and yet I was conditioned by Mother's behaviour in her situation to be naturally in a state of mourning – a good wife whose life had come to a standstill because her husband was in trouble. My conditioning suited Mustafa. I shopped carefully and brought along a great deal of food, concerned for the welfare of my poor, suffering husband.

To my shock, I found Mustafa and the others living in conditions that would be the envy of the common man. The prisoners decided the menu and the food was served by uniformed waiters. The politicians who, only weeks before, had shuffled the fate of our nation, now sat around all day shuffling cards. Only the sound of marching boots outside their quarters shattered the illusion of tranquillity.

I shifted temporarily to Murree, spending the days with Mustafa and the nights at his friend Taj-ul-Mulk's home.

Even in incarceration, within the Prime Minister's house in Murree Bhutto held court. Each day his imprisoned advisers were driven in a van to see him. Over dinner they discussed the current situation. Bhutto was furious with Zia and, even now, arrogant. He charged that the generals had violated the Constitution; Article 6 outlawed military intervention and martial law. He openly abused the generals and accused them of treason. He swore that he would make them accountable. Mustafa and others gently warned him against such reckless statements, but Bhutto persisted.

Bhutto clung to legalisms, ignoring the fact that the generals had the guns. At times, he mellowed and spoke of the future, of how the next five years were imperative for him to consolidate and implement the reforms that he had begun and that would grant him an exalted place in history. He felt short-changed by the generals, a Man of Destiny locked out of his own future. He believed that the VIP treatment that he and the other People's Party captives were receiving was a tacit acknowledgement that Zia still needed them. These conversations were most certainly taped and, as the generals listened to them, their determination to rid themselves of Bhutto must have grown.

I could sense that the time of my delivery was at hand. I visited a doctor in Murree and was astonished when she told me that the Civil and Military Hospital in the city did not have the facilities to deliver my child. I had no choice but to return to Arbi's house in Islamabad and wait for the labour pains to begin.

Three days later a huge, black limousine with military licence plates arrived. We were all shocked to see Mustafa emerge, smiling. Zia had allowed him special permission to visit his pregnant wife. He spent the night with me and left early the following morning in the dictator's car.

This aroused that suspicion in the minds of Bhutto and Mustafa's fellow inmates that Mustafa had struck a deal behind their backs. The generals fanned the suspicion by holding Mustafa in Rawalpindi for the next few days. Mustafa had requested the meeting with me in all innocence, but he was now suspect and became somewhat isolated from his allies.

Two days later Zia released Bhutto and all the political leaders. Bhutto flew back to Islamabad in a helicopter, and Mustafa was returned to us.

And a few days after this, on 29 July, I gave birth to our daughter Naseeba. She slept in our bed with us. Mustafa instructed Dai Ayesha to fashion a semi-circular enclosure of clay to hold the baby's head as she slept. This was a medieval custom that he said would make the shape of her head flat and beautiful. I shuddered as I saw the contraption take shape. Finally the trap was ready and Naseeba's tiny head was placed inside it. She was very uncomfortable in this strange, restrictive device. Her head directly faced the ceiling. She could not move it at all, and wailed all night long. She grew purple with agitation. I feared that she would choke and desperately wanted to put her on her tummy, but this was not allowed. Her bawling disturbed Mustafa, and he ordered me to quieten her, but he would not allow me to remove her from the 'head-trap'.

I was very frightened. Servants had told me stories about his behaviour toward Sherry's daughter, Amna. If the poor baby howled as he tried to sleep, Mustafa picked her up and shoved her under the bed!

On a number of occasions, Mustafa stifled Naseeba's yells with his hand, or with a cloth. He reacted so fiercely that I feared he would suffocate her. My beautiful baby girl, instead of being a source of joy, became a cause of new, frightful tension. Now I had two of us to protect.

But at least the arrival of the baby tempered my mother's mood. She flew in from London to stay with us for a time and, especially in the context of her previous disapproval, I sought to hide the brutality of my marriage from her. I knew that Mother would approve of my life only if we were happy.

Mother was invited to a ladies' dinner, and she wanted me and two-week-old Naseeba to accompany her. Mustafa reluctantly granted his permission, to avoid drawing my mother's attention to his true nature, but he was irritable and said that it was the last time he would permit such a thing. He set a firm curfew of

10.30 p.m. and ordered me to handle the situation on my own, next time, without involving him.

Here was a form of mental torture. He pitted me against my strong-willed mother, but disarmed me by removing the weapon of truth. It was left to me to create the proper lie that would enable me to meet Mustafa's arbitrary curfew. I spent much of the evening nervously glancing at the clock. As is common in Pakistan, it was 10.30 before dinner was even served! We had only begun to eat when I was called to the telephone. Mustafa growled, 'If you are not home in the next five minutes, I'll fix you.'

I returned to the dinner table, terrified. I repeatedly hinted to Mother that I had to leave, but she was involved in conversation and waved aside my protests.

We finally arrived home at around midnight. Mother went into her bedroom, still unaware of my tense condition. Clutching Naseeba protectively to my bosom, praying to God for His help and mercy, I rushed into the bedroom. I wanted to get to him quickly, and yet I did not. Mustafa stood in the dark, waiting for us. He snatched the baby from my arms, flung her onto the bed, and slapped me so hard that I fell. I suppressed my cries, so that nothing would carry to Mother's adjacent room. I allowed myself a muted whimper, 'Mother will hear.'

'Come upstairs,' he ordered menacingly.

By now, Naseeba was howling. I picked her up and ran quickly out of the door and up the stairs to another room – a torture chamber – as Mustafa followed. I knew what would happen but my primary concern was that my mother not know my reality. He locked the door behind him. Again he plucked Naseeba from my arms and cast her aside. To the accompaniment of the continuous yells of a bewildered baby, he tore my sari to shreds and beat me savagely, avoiding my face.

Next morning I faced my mother as if nothing had happened. I was learning to hide my feelings – and my bruises – from the world.

*　　*　　*

Bhutto decided to take his case to the people. He arrived
in Lahore, driven from the airport by Mustafa, and was
greeted by a vibrant crowd. In his waning days as Prime
Minister, the people had grown tired of his promises of
bread, clothing and shelter, but now he was the underdog and they wished to forget his mistakes. Bhutto was
elated.

The motorcade moved at a snail's pace toward the
house where Bhutto would stay. Once he was inside,
the crowd, trying to get closer, surged out of control.
The pressure of people broke down the gates of
the house. Excited spectators shattered the windows,
climbed the walls, crowded onto the lawns, nested
in the tree-tops and clung precariously to utility poles.
Everyone wanted a glimpse of the man. Everyone
wanted to hear the stifled voice rise again.

Bhutto stepped out onto the balcony, remarking that
he felt 'as tall as the Himalayas', and delivered a rousing
speech: 'General Zia has committed treason. He has
tampered with the Constitution. The people of Pakistan
will not spare the traitor. The army does not have the
right to usurp power by ousting the people's representatives and deposing an elected Prime Minister.'

The listeners responded with wild cheers. In their
enthusiasm, they did not realize that they were signing
Bhutto's death warrant.

The scene shifted to Islamabad. In a calmer moment,
Mustafa warned Bhutto that he must change his hard-
line stance, or the generals would eliminate him. Bhutto
was aloof and cold in the face of this advice. He felt
that his confrontational policies would unnerve the
generals, and believed that the people would stand up
to save their leader. He forgot that tanks and guns were
more palpable than the mood of the people.

Mustafa informed Bhutto that the generals wished to
have a meeting with him, and Bhutto agreed that
Mustafa should attend, since this would give him an

opportunity to assess the military's thinking. During Mustafa's discussion with Zia and two of his compatriots, the three military leaders heaped praise and proclaimed that they needed people like him. But they were hostile toward Bhutto, and declared that he could survive only if he tempered his arrogance. The generals said that they were not opposed to the idea of Bhutto going into exile, if he would guarantee that he was retiring from politics for ever. This, Mustafa thought, was like asking a human being to live without oxygen.

When he reported back to Bhutto, Mustafa tried to convince his leader to flee the country, and asked permission to do so himself, to 'live to fight another day'. Bhutto granted the latter request and paved the way. He invited the ambassador of the United Arab Emirates and introduced him to Mustafa. He then wrote a note to Shaikh Zayed bin Nayan, the ruler of Abu Dhabi, presenting Mustafa as 'my brother' and asking him to provide all necessary assistance.

As for himself, Bhutto proclaimed that he understood the gravity of the situation, but he had no choice other than to stay and fight.

Soon after this meeting, in September, Bhutto was re-arrested, on a charge of attempted murder, and a witch-hunt rounded up his key supporters. Mustafa was called into secret sessions with several generals. One night he informed me that we had to leave for England immediately, before dawn, without Naseeba. He said it would be too inconvenient, and dangerous, to bring her along.

Shattered at the prospect of leaving behind another baby, even for a day, I was panic-stricken at giving instructions for her routine – but it had to be. My pining meant nothing to anyone at this serious, difficult time, least of all to Mustafa. I suffered alone, just as I had suffered for Tanya.

I did not know what sort of understanding Mustafa had achieved with the generals. I smelled betrayal, but

I did not dare voice my suspicions. Mustafa sensed this and lectured that, in politics, compromises are necessary.

We boarded a 6.30 a.m. flight from Islamabad. As the aircraft waited for clearance at the end of the runway, I saw beads of perspiration form on Mustafa's brow. The veins in his temples pounded. There was fear on his face. We both knew that the generals were capricious.

Finally the aircraft moved slowly into its take-off roll. The pilots pushed the engines up to full throttle and the craft picked up speed. It rose into the air, and Mustafa's face showed relief; he had sidestepped the gallows.

We had no definite plans. All we knew was that we would first stop in Mecca, to perform the pilgrimage of *umra*, then head on to London. We had only 50,000 rupees (just over £1,100) with us – which would exchange to a pittance of British Sterling.

Immediately, I was lonely. I had lost both my babies. I glanced out of the window, and saw our country fall away beneath us.

Part Two

LAW OF THE JUNGLE

6

In Mecca, Mustafa placed his hand on the *kaaba*, the house of Allah, and swore that he would never look at another woman in his entire life. For a Muslim, there is no greater testament.

As we flew on to London, Mustafa was recognized by a Pakistani immigrant who was anglicized enough to call himself Harry. The two men passed the six-hour flight in philosophical conversation and, by the time we landed, Harry had converted to our political cause and was our friend. There were no problems passing through immigration: Mustafa's political affiliations with Bhutto and his position caused no problem at all. We were granted political asylum. Harry offered us hospitality, and Mustafa accepted.

Harry lived in a small, uncomfortable council flat in Earls Court. Mustafa adapted easily to the crowded conditions. He was in exile, and exile meant sacrifice and discomfort. But I lay awake most of the first night, embarrassed that we had run away, leaving Bhutto in what was certainly his death cell. I did not know how Mustafa had arranged passage out of the country, but something told me that he had bartered his honour for his life. I resolved that if I was ever confronted with a similar situation, I would stand and fight on my own soil. Finally I fell asleep and dreamed of revolution and marching. I held my head high as I stood on the gallows, and I did not flinch as the noose tightened around my neck.

I pined for Tanya and Naseeba. There was no other equivalent pain. Tanya and Naseeba merged into one deep agony. Every time I saw an infant on the street or in a pram in the park, my maternal ache was stirred, as though they might replace it, but I sensed that Mustafa viewed this as weakness.

He did not tell me the details of the bargain he had struck with the generals, but by picking up shreds of information and overhearing telephone conversations, it was not difficult to discern. He had won his life by promising to return to Pakistan the following month, November, bringing documents from London that would incriminate Bhutto. What documents they were supposed to be I never discovered, and it was most probably a hoax, though I did not know so at the time. I could not understand the Brutus-like betrayal. When his leader was fighting for his life against an unscrupulous regime, Mustafa conspired with the executioners. I expressed my qualms to him, but he replied in a philosophical tone, 'Time will tell'.

He spent the first few weeks in London contacting other exiles, making his presence felt. He was in his element, making and breaking alliances, plotting, scheming, persuading the sceptical. In exile, a political activist quickly develops an inflated opinion of his importance, and Mustafa came to believe that he was *the* man who could unite the expatriates in a victorious struggle to overthrow Zia and his cronies. Mustafa saw his great chance to remould the People's Party under his influence.

Nevertheless, he knew that it would be difficult to unite Bhutto's fanatical admirers behind him. He was contaminated by his own past. Mustafa had helped to found the party, but then he had abandoned it. True, he had rejoined, but his vacillation made him suspect in the eyes of the hard-liners. They remembered how he had tried to humble Bhutto. They thought that he was too ambitious. Many also doubted his integrity, because of the manner in which he had left Pakistan. The party-in-exile was paranoid; infiltrators and informants were everywhere.

As the deadline for the delivery of the documents approached, I sensed Mustafa's restlessness. If he did not comply as promised, he would raise the unforgiving ire of the generals and could not return to Pakistan. Mustafa decided to prove his loyalty to Bhutto and the party by reneging on his agreement with the generals, and I heartily approved. I declared that it was better to live on the run and in poverty than to return home to play Judas. I was very comfortable with this decision.

He called one of the generals in Pakistan. In a nervous conversation, he managed to extend the deadline, buying an additional two months to test the strength of his support among the exile community.

My family was living in London and I talked to my mother on the telephone frequently. But my father adamantly refused to accept the scandalous Mustafa into his family.

Mother and Father currently had their own problems in the form of my sister, Minoo, who had just turned eighteen. In England this fact emancipated her. One day Minoo called and said, 'I have to see you urgently.' We arranged a rendezvous at a restaurant. Minoo told Mustafa and me that she wanted desperately to study photography at a boarding school on the Isle of Wight. The problem was that it was a coeducational institution, and my parents could not conceive of such an environment for their daughter. But the more they refused, the more adamant Minoo became. She disclosed to us that she planned to run away. We tried to dissuade her, but she would not accept our counsel. Mustafa advised me, 'Don't get involved.'

The following day Mother called me, supremely upset. 'Minoo has run away!' she wailed.

Mustafa took the phone from my hand and spoke directly to Mother. 'No matter what happens, I'll get Minoo back,' he promised.

With that one vow, Mustafa built a special relationship

with my mother. His voice carried the power and authority that Father could never summon. Without really knowing my family, Mustafa had assumed the mantle of the big brother. Mother was immediately relieved. Before Minoo had taken her desperate action, Mother had planned for the family to journey to its continental retreat in Marbella, Spain. Mustafa told her to go, and pledged to bring Minoo to her there.

Minoo called us, as we knew she would, and Mustafa employed his powers of persuasion to convince her that she could get what she wanted without severing her family ties. His key argument was financial. Without money, how was Minoo going to live, let alone go to school on the Isle of Wight? 'Come to Spain with us,' he said. 'We'll sort it all out there.'

The three of us flew into Malaga, rented a car, drove to Marbella and checked into the Holiday Inn. Soon after our arrival, Minoo phoned Mother and attempted to begin the process of reconciliation. Mother snapped, 'You can't ever leave again.'

Minoo responded by screaming her frustrations into the phone, but Mustafa yanked it from her hand and said sternly, 'You cannot *dare* to be rude to your mother in my presence.' He lowered his voice and spoke into the mouthpiece: 'We'll call later. I have to talk to her.'

He hung up and turned to my sister. From the expression on Minoo's face, I could see that she realized that she was trapped. The small motel room suddenly seemed claustrophobic. Minoo bolted for the door, but Mustafa grabbed her and threw her on to the bed. He held one strong hand against her throat, choking her. I attempted to pull him off but was pushed aside by his free hand. Minoo struggled briefly, then realized the hopelessness of her predicament and became subdued.

Mustafa released his grip. He sat on the edge of the bed and allowed Minoo to catch her breath. Then he lectured calmly, in a gentle, caring tone. 'If you're going to react like this, they'll never let you go,' he advised. 'You have to play another game. Don't shout at them.'

Too stunned to speak, Minoo sat on the bed, suddenly docile and acquiescent. Her eyes told me that she realized that she was surrounded by enemies. She had to wait to fight another day.

While Minoo was in the bathroom, Mustafa phoned my mother and told her that Minoo's only problem was that she was spoiled. She needed control and discipline.

Mother cried about the difficulties of bringing up young girls in the permissive environment of England. 'We are a conservative family,' she said. 'We don't know what to do.'

By now, Mother had convinced my father that it was time to accept us back into the family fold. In her brief dealings with Mustafa, she had found him to be an honourable man, and it was a time of adversity for him. She felt it inappropriate to continue the boycott. She invited us all to a reconciliation dinner and sent a car to drive us to their villa overlooking the sea.

Father met me amidst tears and affectionate hugs; he was cordial to Mustafa. Obviously, Mustafa's strong hand with Minoo had gained him favour. I was glad that our isolation was over. I respected my father's principles and was quietly proud that he had stood by them in spite of the anguish of our separation. It had caused us both much pain, however, for I knew that I was his favourite. And I knew that he was ready to accept our marriage, convinced that whatever other faults Mustafa might have, he was a family loyalist.

Minoo was on her best behaviour, feigning cheer-fulness. Our younger sisters were also there. Fifteen-year-old Zarmina, an aspiring clothes' designer, had outfitted herself like a senorita, in a frilly Spanish dress set off by a rose in her hair. Adila, the youngest, was thirteen. She wore black jeans and a T-shirt and seemed very curious about us. I sensed that she admired my rebellion in standing up to our dictatorial mother and running off to marry this famous man with a notorious past.

As soon as he could speak to me alone, Father outlined his manifesto: 'I'm making up with you today despite the fact that I'm hurt and upset by your decision. This is your second marriage and I don't want you, for any reason at all, to leave him. You can only leave his home in a coffin. This is the point on which I take you back into the family.'

Over dinner, Minoo chattered non-stop. Zarmina was very affectionate and caring. But I felt something strange between Adila and Mustafa; there was a sense of pre-sentiment in the air, as if two minds – who had never encountered one another – had established a silent bond. I tried to shake off the apprehension caused by the familiar glittery glaze in Mustafa's eyes.

We remained in Marbella for two weeks and during that time my father made the arrangements to cement my happiness by sending for Naseeba. Dai Ayesha travelled from Pakistan with my baby and I felt nearly complete once more. Naseeba's three young aunts were captivated by the tiny bundle and my father was a proud progenitor. Mother and Mustafa got along well and I found, to my surprise, that she and I enjoyed one another, too. The only void was the absence of Tanya, a topic that I dared not discuss with Mustafa. I filled the emptiness by becoming obsessed with five-month-old Naseeba. I fussed with her constantly and found myself lying awake at night, meticulously planning her breakfast.

My parents maintained both a home and an apartment in London. Happy with the reconciliation, they offered to let us live in the apartment, and we accepted the invitation immediately. Marble Arch was much more comfortable and stylish than our first lodgings with Harry in Earls Court. We returned to London with Zarmina and Adila. Minoo was to be accompanied by my parents.

Mustafa and I assumed a new life as fashionable exiles. We invited some old friends from Pakistan for dinner. I wanted to borrow Mother's silver, so Zarmina and Adila brought it over, and stayed to help us prepare. As I arranged the apartment, Mustafa cooked, Zarmina fussed over the baby and Adila attacked the liquor. By the time Zarmina and I noticed, our baby sister was floating in an alcoholic haze. She sashayed about the living-room in an unsteady attempt to be provocative. Zarmina and I tried to pull her into the bedroom, but she pushed us away. I worried that the guests would arrive and see her in this condition – and I worried even more that my parents would hear about this. I found Mustafa in the kitchen and said, 'You have to do something. Give her hell and get her to leave.'

Mustafa moved toward Adila, unsure of himself He grasped her by the shoulders and she struggled. But she struggled closer, rather than away. For a brief instant they stopped, almost sharing an embrace. Then Adila relaxed and suddenly agreed to go home. Zarmina and I knew that if our parents learned of this incident, they would brand me as a bad influence and keep us apart, so we conspired to keep the secret.

Meanwhile, the Minoo situation deteriorated. My parents, unable to emulate Mustafa's heavy-handed style, attempted to purchase her compliance. They bought her an expensive car, filled with luxurious accessories.

'This is the wrong way to deal with her,' Mustafa said to me. 'They're giving in to her under pressure. She's the winner.' He suggested that they ship Minoo back to Pakistan and take away her passport.

Indeed, Minoo once more ran away from home. No-one knew of her whereabouts until a week later. Mother called and informed us tearfully that Minoo was *working* in a *record store* on *Tottenham Court Road*! Mother considered this to be a rather sleazy area of London, and I suppose that it was – although the depths of its degradation could not approach Mother's dark fantasies.

In the midst of this latest crisis, we moved into my parents' home at Beech Hill, in order to be close to the family. The house was set in two acres overlooking a golf course. It was richly decorated with old Moroccan sofas, heavily carved pieces of furniture from Damascus and chairs from King Farouk's palace collection. My mother's display of Persian carpets and paintings made this huge house a perfect setting for her to glide through like a queen. The family had a cook, two maids, a chauffeur, an accountant and a butler to attend to every need.

Mustafa resented the opulence, yet he relished it. My family's style seemed to come naturally; they unknowingly mocked his country origins just by being themselves. Mustafa chose to behave with inverted snobbery. He wore boorishness and earthiness like a T-shirt slogan.

Father played the perfect host, offering Davidoff cigars at the appropriate moment, but he remained formal. Mother, on the other hand, was captured rather quickly by Mustafa's personality. She was very interested in politics and listened with rapt attention as he regaled her with vignettes. He analysed Pakistan's fluid political situation with great insight. Gradually, even Father warmed somewhat. Mustafa was, after all, a member of *their* generation, a contemporary.

At first I found irony in this situation: I had escaped from the domination of my mother by climbing into the lap of a tyrant, and it was somewhat amusing to see the two dictators magnifying one another's egos. But slowly I began to feel isolated. Mustafa became a part of the family from which I had tried to stand apart.

Mustafa watched the dynamics within my family with a keen and manipulative eye. He correctly identified the Achilles' heel. Father – and especially Mother – would do anything, sacrifice anything, to save face. For example, the potential scandal regarding Minoo was too much for my parents; they capitulated, rented a flat for her on the Isle of Wight, furnished it and allowed her to enrol in photographers' school. Mother made Minoo promise to come home nearly every weekend and on every holiday, but it was clear that Minoo had won.

As January approached, Mustafa was afflicted with the common ailment of the exile – chronic optimism. He told me that General Zia's days were numbered. 'He won't last more than six months,' Mustafa predicted. 'You'll see.'

He acted upon this optimism, informing the generals in Pakistan that he would not honour his agreement to return with documents incriminating Bhutto. For his troubles, he was sentenced *in absentia* to fourteen years of rigorous imprisonment, and all his assets were confiscated. Personal injury was added to political insult when Mustafa's mother was denied a passport. We had hoped to bring her to London to join us, but the authorities in Pakistan obviously believed that they could use her as bait to lure Mustafa back. He was very attached to his mother, and this action crushed him. He sat quietly in his chair, with tears in his eyes, as he contemplated this latest twist.

Mustafa's malaise was only temporary. Soon he began a long-distance campaign to save Bhutto, even as, at home, the trial of the former prime minister began.

Our fights were now centred around my family. Mustafa picked up on tiny snippets of dinner-table conversation and used them against me. In vulnerable moments, I had made the mistake of telling him of the difficult childhood relationship I had had with my mother, and he turned this information against me. He was on her side now, and cast me in the role of an ungrateful, untrustworthy child. He methodically widened the gulf between mother and daughter, isolating me even more completely on the island of his tyrannical rule.

At other times he suddenly posed as my ally. He would say, 'I think I will discuss with your mother your misgivings about your relationship. All these things you have told me must come out. She must be made aware of the pain that has been caused to you.' He knew that I would panic. I lacked the strength to take on both Mustafa and my mother. I pleaded with him not to follow through with his plan, and I submitted even more willingly to his cruel whims in order to buy his silence.

Each morning Mustafa woke early and did his yoga. Then he sat in my parents' bedroom, drinking coffee and discussing the latest news from Pakistan. Mother and Father were – or at least pretended to be – unaware that this charming person had, the night before, battered their daughter.

I camouflaged my bruises and buried my humiliation. I started taking Valium to calm my nerves. My father wondered why, and objected, but my mother agreed that I needed the tranquillizer to relieve my tension. I suspected that she knew the cause, but she believed ruthlessly in keeping one's private life locked away. The most she would do was speak in general terms. She advised me: 'If a husband behaves in a strange or unreasonable manner, you should treat him like a sick human being, like someone who needs medical care and treatment. Deal with him like a psychiatrist.' I took this counsel to heart, and it helped. My body suffered, but my mind was spared.

I wanted desperately to shed the uncomfortable and unattractive pounds that I had retained after Naseeba's birth. Mustafa would not allow talk of a diet or other weight-loss strategies, so I secretly obtained a supply of diet pills. I lost most of the extra weight, but I still felt matronly. Often I looked with envy at the women in England, moving about, laughing, participating in life.

Although we had travelled extensively and were now living in this free society, in my mind I might as well have been sequestered behind the veil in Mustafa's village of Kot Addu.

Mustafa felt increasingly isolated too. I was quite amazed to realize that I understood his predicament and wanted to help him deal with it. My tired mind at times was able to analyse and rationalize. I could empathize with his frustration. He missed having a bevy of disciples. He missed being chief. He disliked being in a foreign country. He missed the panoply of power.

I reached out to him and tried to build his morale. I learned to forgive him his temper and abusive nature. I subsconsciously submitted to the role of whipping boy and allowed the man who had once run a province with an iron hand to rule me instead. His hand never once trembled.

Fortunately, Naseeba was safely out of the way, almost always in the care of my sisters, who became the proverbial fussy aunts. This, at least, meant that I had one less person to protect from this abnormal man living in abnormal circumstances.

I was always acting, petrified that the truth of my marriage would be exposed. I tried my utmost to avoid any clash with Mustafa. He realized my paranoia and exploited it fully. He forbade me to talk to anyone about my secret torment, with threats of severe consequences, but this was unnecessary since I felt as if I could trust no-one. It was a schizophrenic existence. The humiliation of not being able to keep my husband happy and of falling short of my mother's definition of the ideal wife was becoming more frightening than the beatings. The physical abuse was not his crime – it simply affirmed my own inadequacy.

Mustafa never allowed me to go out alone. Mother frequently asked me to accompany her to lunch, or to a doctor's appointment, or merely to go shopping – and I always had to come up with a plausible excuse. I was forbidden even to *ask* Mustafa's permission. I was to handle it on my own. Mother saw my refusals as selfishness. I longed to tell her the real reasons, but I forced myself into a tortured silence.

Despite all the problems I had with my mother, I felt an overpowering urge to become her child again. She symbolized strength. I saw her as the only force that could countervail Mustafa's evil. Whenever he hurt me I cried out for her, and prayed that she would come and save me. I longed to describe to her in detail what was happening to me, but I was sure she would react by taking his side, that she would find some way to trivialize my torment and reject me.

By a process of elimination, I attempted to learn how to mould my personality so that Mustafa and I could live in harmony. I tried to emulate whatever attitudes I knew that he had appreciated in his previous wives, but nothing seemed to alter his savage behaviour. At times I even found myself perversely thankful for the beatings, because they would be followed by his grovelling remorse. To see this man, larger than life, reduced to such a degrading position brought a twisted measure of glee.

When he surrendered to a tender moment he praised my fortitude: 'Do you know how much you mean to me? I am incomplete without you. This has been a very frustrating period in my life. It will pass. You'll see – I'll change and make it up to you. I've been so close to a nervous breakdown. It has only been your love and devotion that has kept me sane.' His eyes would well with tears as he continued: 'You came into my life at a most difficult period. Everything around me has crumbled, but you've stood by me. I wish you had come into my life earlier so that I could keep you wrapped up in silks. I've put you through hell. I'm really sorry. Can you ever forgive me?' He cried at my feet. He confessed that he had tried to destroy me and was amazed at my tolerance and resilience. 'I never thought you could cope with my temper,' he admitted. 'I always thought you were too delicate and fragile. You proved me wrong. You're a strong woman. You're the only woman who has the tolerance to cope with me intelligently. I will never, ever let you down. Promise me that you'll never think of abandoning me.' I promised, washed ashore on his tears, proud of his high esteem for me, hoping that he would tell Mother.

Sitting on my prayer mat, I regularly asked for deliverance. I did not ask God to resolve my crisis in any specific way; I merely asked Him to help sort out my life, and to change Mustafa for the better and to lessen the punishment for my mistakes.

Adila stood five feet, four inches tall and had the figure of a siren. She craved attention. My other sisters kept their distance from Mustafa and, when they were together, were very correct in their behaviour. But Adila was younger and wilder; she seemed to sense that she and her brother-in-law were soul mates. Mustafa indulged her spoiled whims and laughed at her childish pranks.

Initially, it was quite touching to see Mustafa remove his dictatorial mask and play big brother. We ascribed Adila's coquettishness to juvenile cockiness.

My parents left for a fifteen-day trip to the Middle East, and Adila went with them. Mustafa remained irritable and restless during this period, and turned the smallest issue into a terrible fight. With the house to ourselves, he knew that he could thrash me with impunity. Once, he grew very upset as I talked to my brother Asim on the phone. 'Why did you speak to him for so long?' he growled. 'Is he your brother or your lover?'

I glanced up at him, amazed, and responded, 'He's my brother, Mustafa, really.'

'Are you answering me back?' He used this so-called impudence as an excuse to pummel me with his fists.

On another occasion he kicked me down a staircase. When I landed at the bottom in a mangled heap, he ran down the stairs and resumed his savage kicks and blows. I cried out, 'This is my father's house and I do not think that you should dare to lift your hand on me here!'

This brought a stunned silence. For the first time I had said what I felt, and I had scored a key point: I was not his chattel, but had other ties that were stronger than the ones that bound me to him. This realization brought only a moment's respite. A feudal lord understands the strength of blood ties, but he also understands the power of physical violence. Mustafa beat me with increased venom, until my screams weakened to tired whimpers and I was nearly unconscious.

Later, in order to avoid yet another beating, I apologized for what I had said. I knew that my comment had shaken Mustafa, and he now had to plan some way to crush the tiny flicker of my remaining spirit.

There was a brief hiatus when my parents and Adila returned. Then Mother and Father travelled to Luxemburg for two days, and left Adila at home with us. She nagged me to allow her to skip a day of school. When I grew weary of her pestering I agreed, and she made plans for a shopping and luncheon expedition. But on the evening prior to the outing she said that she had changed her mind and wanted to go to school after all.

In the morning our driver Erik, perhaps confused by the change of plans, did not show up to take her to school. Mustafa was going into the city anyway, so I asked him to drop her off at school. As they drove away, I waved and turned my attention to Naseeba. I thought nothing more of this until the middle of the afternoon, when Adila called to report, 'I bunked school today. I've gone to a friend's place.' She chattered on about only missing a half day of classes and said that she would go to school for the rest of the afternoon. 'Can you send Erik to pick me up later?' she asked.

It was all very confusing, but I let the incident pass. I

looked forward to my parents' return, so that they could resume their duties with her. Dealing with my youngest sister was a twenty-four-hour-a-day job.

Adila changed her manner of dressing. Suddenly, all western outfits were discarded and replaced with traditional eastern clothes, borrowed from our mother's extensive wardrobe. She draped herself with a veil and even covered her head for effect. She decided to grow her hair long like mine, and in fact began to resemble me. She ferreted out the sensitive topics in our lives, and wandered brazenly into them. In an innocent tone she would mention how much I had longed to marry Anees and how much he loved me. Every night I suffered Mustafa's wrath.

My other sisters noted Adila's deliberate insensitivity and scolded her about it but she carried on regardless. Minoo complained to Mother that Adila was trying to cause problems between Mustafa and me, but Mother dismissed the allegations. Adila was her favourite daughter; she was the only person who could do no wrong. Mother blamed the rest of us for fostering sibling rivalry.

I deeply resented Adila's mischief-mongering. Her sole aim in life was apparently to make Mustafa angry with me. I became increasingly irritated by his indulgence of her, and told him so. I felt that he gave her too much attention, and that she took advantage of it. Mustafa revelled in the family intrigue. He and Adila shared private jokes and often turned their sarcasm on to me. Mustafa said, 'See, Adila, how Tehmina is behaving. Why is she jealous of you?'

In the midst of this tension, and because of his prohibition against precautions, I learned that I was pregnant once again.

Mustafa and I both knew that we had to get away from my family. We did not discuss the matter, but I was very relieved when he arranged for us to move to the Hampstead home of Jam Sadiq Ali, one of Mustafa's political colleagues. He was an important feudal lord from Sind who had been one of Bhutto's ministers, and now was in exile like us. We had our own bedroom in this large house and our host family treated me with affection.

Mustafa exhibited a restless attitude. Although I preferred not to, he frequently insisted that we visit my parents. One Sunday, during such a visit, Mustafa was doing his yoga exercises on the patio. I walked in, followed by Dai Ayesha and Naseeba, and saw Adila seated next to him, leering at his body, drinking in the sight of his muscles flexing and relaxing. I snapped impulsively at Mustafa, 'If you had to exercise, you should have done it at home. Why are you doing it here?'

He turned casually toward Dai Ayesha, who stood behind me, and said jokingly, 'Get hold of her long hair and throw her out.' Adila giggled.

I could have died of shame, but I found it impossible to react in any sensible manner. Mustafa had turned me into a vegetable. I glanced towards Naseeba, took her from Dai Ayesha's arms, clung to her and, sobbing, ran out of the room. My baby was the only person in this lonely world who could give me solace.

There was no way out. Mustafa had got me in a corner and I did not dare defy him. The consequences of the slightest rebellion were too critical. At that moment, something inside me snapped.

I handed Naseeba back to Dai Ayesha. Like a sleep-walker, I trudged into my father's bathroom. For a moment, I stared at the medicine cabinet, then I opened it. I examined several bottles. There were tablets from a clinic in Spain, some capsules for high cholesterol, nine or ten Valium. I took them all and slipped them inside my clothing. My decision was final.

That evening, we left Naseeba and Dai with my parents. I waited until we returned to Jam Sadiq's house. Mustafa was involved in a political meeting downstairs, so I went to our bedroom, sat alone and pondered. I thought of Tanya back in Karachi with Anees. I thought of my beautiful baby Naseeba. I thought of the unborn child in my womb, four months along. The images made me hesitate, but only for a moment. The void in my life was too frightening to endure. I felt burdened to the point of extinction by these lives that had come from my own. I opened the bottles and gulped all the contents down.

I stood in front of the mirror wondering why I was born in the first place. I remembered Mother's words, every time she had been upset with me: 'Why did you not die when you had meningitis?' Strange, I thought, that was when Mother was pregnant with Adila. My youngest sister came to life at the moment that I struggled with death. Perhaps I had cheated death. Perhaps I was meant to die then. Now Adila was living and I was dying, once again. I had suggested the name Adila, which means 'justice'.

I saw fire engulf me in the mirror. Would death be worse than life? Suicide is a ticket to hell. I moved quickly away, feeling the numbness in my head. No, I decided, nothing could be worse than life. I staggered into the bedroom and sat alone, staring at the palm of my hand, examining the fate line. The line began to sway and shift. I reeled, and slipped to the floor. I watched a wave billow over me, spraying me with peace.

They told me that I had been upstairs alone for about half an hour when Mustafa walked in unexpectedly and found me sprawled across the floor. He called out for Jam Sadiq and the two men tried to revive me by splashing cold water on my face. They called a doctor, who summoned an ambulance. Before long I was in the intensive-care ward at Royal Free Hospital in Hampstead. My stomach was pumped, but the toxins had already entered my bloodstream. Mustafa asked the doctor, 'Will she live?'

'Is she a fighter?' the doctor asked.

'Yes.'

'That's our only hope then.'

From the hospital, Mustafa called my elder sister Rubina who was visiting from Pakistan. 'Tehmina tried to kill herself,' he told her. 'God only knows why. She's mad. You had better come and, er, better not tell your parents. They'll panic.'

The night passed slowly. I *was* a fighter, but at the moment I was not interested. What are the dreams that come in this twilight world between life and death? I do not remember them in detail, but they were not sweet.

Slowly I began to improve. I saw misty visions of Rubina and Mustafa, hovering over me.

Two days passed before doctors agreed to discharge me, along with the news that my pregnancy had been unaffected. The baby seemed more resilient than I wished; I wanted an abortion. I still wanted to die. Mustafa took me to my parents' home to recuperate. I was still groggy and completely disoriented. Mother played the ostrich to perfection, pretending not to know that my wretched life had driven me to suicide. My father avoided the subject.

As I slowly surfaced I saw, looming in front of me, Mustafa's smouldering wrath. My crime, to him, was not against my body, but against his honour. 'You embarrassed me,' he snapped harshly. 'D'you realize that you were examined by male doctors. Male doctors! You have humiliated me. I shall not forgive you. You will pay for this stupid act. You just wait and see.' I was petrified, and miserable to have survived.

Mother's house was filled with other guests, so she set up a sofa bed in the study. There I returned to a coma-like sleep, with Mustafa at my side. Sometime during the middle of the night, I felt the presence of someone else. My still-sedated mind noticed that Mustafa rose from the bed and left the room, but I was too sleepy to pay attention.

Much later, I woke once more. Instinctively my hand reached out to feel for Mustafa, but he was not there. I recalled the earlier, dim scene, and wondered where he had gone. I pulled myself from bed and staggered toward the kitchen. Whoever was in there heard me coming, and a shadow fled upstairs. Then Mustafa, half-dressed, came toward me and asked, 'Why have you come out?' There was a distinct note of sheepishness in his voice.

'I was looking for you,' I explained.

'Go back to sleep. You shouldn't be walking around in this state.' I did as he suggested, too tired to ask any further questions.

In the morning, when I was more lucid, I asked Mustafa, 'What happened last night? Someone came into the room. Who was it?'

'Oh, it was Adila,' he answered.

'Adila?'

'Yes. She's involved with an Iranian boy and is having problems. She wanted some advice. She came to discuss it with me.'

'Yes?' I asked, my confused tone searching for more information.

'You were sleeping. I didn't want to disturb you so I took her to the breakfast room.'

'You should have spoken to her here. It's not right for you to talk to her alone in the middle of the night. Suppose my father had come down.'

Mustafa dismissed my comments, and stuck to his story that Adila needed to confide in him – like an elder brother. He declared that his advice would keep her from getting hurt. He was now playing the role of saviour of the family honour.

My only strategy was to get through each day and each endless night. I was mortally afraid of the depths to which I would now have to sink. My greatest fear was that Mustafa would seek to punish me for my suicide attempt by somehow taking Naseeba away from me. I devised strategies to keep her away from him and his temper.

139

Meanwhile, in March 1978, Bhutto was sentenced to death. Mustafa intensified his political efforts, joining forces with two of the former Prime Minister's sons, Mir Murtaza Bhutto and Shah Nawaz Bhutto. Mir had been studying at Oxford, but Mustafa convinced him to scrap his education in order to campaign for his father's release. We moved from Jam Sadiq's house to a shabby, claustrophobic flat in Hampstead, and Mustafa crowded it by inviting the Bhutto boys to live with us. Conditions were so cramped that I left Naseeba and Dai Ayesha with my family. At times I was even thankful that Tanya was not with me.

Immediately Mustafa began to educate the young men in the art of politics and sought to raise them as symbols of resistance to the junta. Mir was a novice, but he learned fast. Younger brother Shah Nawaz exhibited the idealistic, faraway gaze of the revolutionary. They established a sort of headquarters of disgruntled Pakistanis in our flat, and plotted Zia's overthrow. The flat was always full of their friends, who kept odd hours and sprawled out wherever they could find room.

The two young men related to my background and sensed my predicament. I grew fond of them. Shah Nawaz made a point of chatting to me as I moved from room to room, picking up cups and plates, emptying ashtrays and gathering the laundry to send off to my mother's house. I wondered how they viewed me; I was not a part of their intense debates about the future of our country, or of their fanciful schemes to bring about change.

Mustafa introduced Mir to the exiled Husna Sheikh, the woman Bhutto loved. This was somewhat embarrassing for the boy, but he pushed aside his personal considerations because Husna had valuable contacts who might save Bhutto's life.

I desperately needed to talk to another woman, to gain reassurance that I was not going mad. I found Husna to be the first person in whom I could confide. 'Just leave,' she advised me, when I told her about Mustafa's constant beatings. 'There's no reason why you should take this.' Husna planted the seed, but it lay dormant.

Mustafa and Mir set off on a mission to persuade various world leaders to pressure the generals to spare Bhutto's life. Mustafa was also certain that these powerful friends would extend financial support to the exile movement. They received campaign funds from Libya's Colonel Gaddafi and from Shaikh Zayed bin Sultan Al Nahyan, Sultan of Abu Dhabi. Asad of Syria promised to keep pressure on the Zia regime.

Our drawing-room was converted into a firing range. Mir set up a target at one end of the room and practised his marksmanship with an air gun. I was not terribly impressed; he seemed to be just a spirited youngster playing at terror. My concern was for the slugs that peppered the carpet. For his part, Shah Nawaz looked more like a suave terrorist, but his soft eyes gave him away. He did not seem to be able to force a steely-cold look into them.

One day Mustafa informed us, in a conspiratorial tone, that Yasser Arafat, the leader of the Palestine Liberation Organization, had a plan to liberate Bhutto: Palestinian commandos would attack the Rawalpindi gaol, create a diversion and snatch Bhutto from his cell. An aircraft from a friendly country would be waiting at the airport to whisk Bhutto to safety. Mustafa told Mir and Shah Nawaz that their father would soon be with us to carry on the fight in exile.

Mustafa was livid when he came into our room. Apparently, a call disclosing details of the plan had been put through to Benazir – even though it was known that the telephones were being bugged by various intelligence agencies. Suddenly the Rawalpindi gaol became a fortress, guarded by militant right-wing troops.

In the privacy of our bedroom Mustafa snapped, 'How could anybody do such a dumb thing? They have ruined everything by their childishness.'

*　　*　　*

Although I continued silently to ache for the absent
Tanya, a part of me was glad that she was safe in Karachi
with Anees. Increasingly, I had to protect Naseeba from
her father. He loved her only up to a point. He cuddled
her and played with her, but the moment she became
distracted or failed to respond to him, he grew agitated.
He could not countenance her tears, so I trained her not
to cry. As with Mustafa, I tried to anticipate all her
needs, so that she would not complain. Like a sprinter
consigned to a marathon, I was exhausted by the end of
each day.

One morning as Mustafa shaved, Naseeba was in the
bathroom with him. She splashed about in a bubble bath
for a while, until the water was no longer a novelty and
the bubbles ceased to fascinate her. The moment I heard
her whimper, I rushed in and said, 'I'd better take her
out. She's tired.'

'No,' Mustafa said calmly. 'Leave her there.'

'But she's tired.'

'You *can't* take her out. I have ordered her to stay
there.'

'Ordered? But, Mustafa, she's only a year and a half.'

'So what? She'd better learn to obey from this age.'

I stood there, flustered, helpless and desperate to avert
a crisis. Naseeba's wails increased, and Mustafa's anger
rose in proportion. I tried to divert my daughter's
attention by splashing her with water, but she only cried
harder. He told me coolly, 'Leave her and go.' I was as
frantic as he was calm. For a few moments there was a
stand-off. Mustafa continued to shave, Naseeba kept
crying and I stood at the door, frozen with fear.

Suddenly Mustafa turned towards Naseeba with
menace in his eyes. She screamed, looking at him
with her big, frightened eyes. He grabbed her and
pushed her head under the water. I ran to them
and begged him to let go, but he shoved me aside and
held her under, with an expression on his face that said

he was determined to teach us a lesson. My mind flashed through horrific alternatives. My baby was drowning! But if I struggled with him, I would only increase his anger. I pleaded with him, but he would not relent. An eternity passed before me. Then, when Naseeba's struggles finally diminished, he released his grip.

I pulled my baby out of the water. She coughed and spluttered. Her eyes bulged with fear. I shot a sharp glance at Mustafa, but the look in his eyes was so evil that I could only clutch Naseeba and run out.

Naseeba was afraid of water from that moment on. Bath-time was an ordeal, a punishment. Water and screaming went together, and I made sure that I bathed her when her father was absent.

I was afraid to let Mustafa take her out on his own. An innocent walk in the park might turn into an excursion to hell.

I dreamed of release, but reality stood in front of me like a stone wall. Divorce was just not possible. British and Pakistani law might be on my side, but in the feudal world, a man retains control of his daughter, and I knew that Mustafa would use her as a hostage to assure my loyalty. I was willing to forsake everything – except Naseeba. I began to hope secretly that Mustafa would die, but I buried these thoughts quickly and deeply, terrified that he would somehow discover them.

A prisoner ultimately settles into a monotonous routine. Anger recedes; senses dull. The spirit is crushed.

It was increasingly apparent that money was pouring in from various sources to support the cause. (Later on Kabul and Syria would also help them.) The Bhutto boys, who a short time earlier were more or less normal young men enjoying the casual benefits of western society, were now transformed into well-financed revolutionaries. Mustafa benefited, too. A courier arrived from Agha Hasan Abidi of the Bank of Credit and Commerce International, delivering a briefcase containing £50,000. Mustafa asked me to deposit the cash in my mother's safe.

The new-found status as politicians inspired Mir's confidence, and he very quickly challenged the power and authority of his teacher. He was, after all, a Bhutto, and the surname worked magic. It became unnecessary to share anything with Mustafa. Husna fed this. She warned Mir that his father had never completely trusted Mustafa, and advised him to strike out on his own. Both brothers moved out of our flat and into a suite.

The young Bhuttos' revolution went jet-set. Tailored suits replaced blue jeans. The self-conscious demeanour of the young student gave way to swagger. Women and other accessories of the fast lane were now available to them. While their adventurous lifestyle of subterfuge, intrigue and high risk had proved irresistibly romantic to other young men of their age, now they were increasingly seen in the company of mink-clad ladies. One of Mir's longstanding companions was the glamorous – and much older – wife of a Mediterranean politician. To me, the Bhutto boys seemed like mixtures of Che Guevara and characters that had stepped out of a Harold Robbins novel.

Although the relationship was growing strained, Mustafa continued to work with the boys. They decided that the People's Party needed to demonstrate to the world that it stood by its imprisoned leader, and called for a rally in front of the Pakistan Embassy in Lowndes Square. In Pakistan, this would have been an open invitation to slaughter; but in the UK it could be civilized protest. The question was: Would the expatriate masses turn out?

They came in spontaneous waves, from all over Europe, carrying home-made banners and placards. The legend *Save Bhutto* was emblazoned on their T-shirts. They gathered solemnly at Speakers' Corner and marched off to save their leader from the hangman's noose. The serpentine procession snaked its way from

144

Park Lane and assembled in front of the Embassy. Mustafa, Mir and others gave fiery speeches.

We could only hope that the international news coverage would pressure Zia into sparing Bhutto's life.

We moved to a little cottage in Arkley Lane in Barnet, very close to my parents' home. Compared with the flat it was an improvement yet it irked me to be the mistress of a home that was decorated so distastefully. I tried to improve it, but the cheap reproduction French furniture stuck out hideously, no matter what I did to hide it. Nylon carpets made it all worse. I felt terribly disoriented in this new environment.

As I waited out my pregnancy, the political intrigue deepened. Bhutto's nephew, Tariq Islam, visited his uncle in prison and related the event to us in England. He said that his uncle weighed only six and a half stone. His hands and feet were swollen. His chronic gum ailment had been exacerbated by neglect. Stomach cramps left him in a permanent state of agony.

Even so, Tariq said, his uncle was mentally alert and eager to discuss politics. He wanted to know about developments both in Pakistan and abroad. He was pleased to hear that his sons had become active in politics and were campaigning to save his life. He asked about Mustafa, too, wanting to know if his protégé was a good orator. When Tariq said yes, Bhutto declared with a wry smile, 'Not better than me.'

As the conversation continued, Bhutto grew more confused and depressed. He could not understand why the people had not stormed the prison gates to free him. Where was the spontaneous uprising that would sweep away the dictator?

Tariq requested that Bhutto give him a message to carry to the People's Party leaders that would revitalize the party. 'Do they want me to spoon-feed them?' Bhutto replied. 'Don't they know what they have to do?'

*   *   *

145

All the Bhutto brothers' international campaign came to naught. Zia made sure that Bhutto died many times before he was finally hanged. During his time in prison, he was constantly humiliated and insulted. The proud former prime minister was forced to use a noxious, open toilet in the presence of a guard. A brigadier was placed in the opposite cell expressly to provoke him to a frenzy. The brigadier knew the pressure points; he used the most foul language to debase Bhutto's mother, mocking and taunting until the former prime minister would lose his composure.

On 3 April 1979 Benazir was taken to see her father and informed that it would be the last visit. She was dismayed to find herself separated from him by iron bars and a large table, but when she pleaded with the guards to allow her to embrace him, he admonished, 'Don't ever beg them for anything.' She had brought him his favourite perfume, Shalimar, and some books. He accepted the perfume but refused the books with a wry smile, explaining, 'I don't think I'll have time to finish these.' She handed him a razor and he said, 'Good. I'll shave this beard off. I do not want to die like a bloody mullah.'

Here, accounts merge fact and fiction. What actually happened may never be known. It is said that the brigadier, Bhutto's tormentor, walked into the cell at about one o'clock in the morning following Benazir's visit. He handed Bhutto sheets of paper and a pen, and demanded his confession. Bhutto started to write. His mind must have been clogged with memories – the triumphs, the adulation of adoring crowds. Where had it all fled? Here he was, terrifyingly alone, with a blank sheet of paper in front of him. He knew that the proper words of compromise might save him. But, on a sudden impulse, he tore up the paper and flung away his life.

The brigadier rose and kicked Bhutto in the stomach. Some say that Bhutto was beaten unconscious, but that he regained his senses as he was carried off to the gallows

– that he staggered, fell, stood up and walked the final steps with dignity and defiance. Others say that he was already dead when the body was hanged.

Whatever the truth, the outcome was the same. The People's Party, and Pakistan, had a martyr.

7

I was in the last stages of pregnancy. Father was away on business in Japan and Minoo was at home on holiday from school when Mustafa and I went to visit.

Adila was dressed as if she were ready to go to a dinner party. She wore a crêpe de Chine shirt and trousers, draped with a stylish chiffon veil. Her face was fully made up. She paid special attention to Mustafa, leaning forward, drinking in his every word.

Mother interrupted the conversation at one point and instructed, 'Adila, make some coffee.'

My younger sister pouted. 'I'm not feeling well,' she complained. 'Zarmina should make it.'

With a sigh, Zarmina went off to the kitchen. Adila resumed her worshipful pose. She expressed great interest in Mustafa's assessment of the current political situation in Pakistan and leaned forward expectantly, awaiting more. She did not appear ill.

Suddenly, in a tone that allowed no argument, Minoo snapped, 'Adila, get up and leave the room!'

Adila was shocked, but complied.

I was curious to know why Minoo objected so sharply to Adila's presence in the room and, after we had returned to our own home, I called her and asked. Minoo was very agitated. She told me that she had seen Mustafa pick up Adila from school and drive off with her. She did not know where they went, but they were gone for three hours.

I felt my body freeze.

Minoo explained, 'When you and Mustafa entered today, I kept looking at Adila. I wanted to see her reaction. She had dressed up only after she was told you were coming. Her whole being responded to him. The way she was sitting, the glances they exchanged, were tell-tale. I could not tolerate it. I had to tell her to leave the room. There is a limit to such blatant flirtation. I am surprised no-one else in this family noticed.'

I was certain that Mustafa had.

'I had it out with her after you left,' Minoo reported. 'I gave her hell. Mummy and Zarmina were there, too. This sort of behaviour is just not acceptable. Who does she think she is?'

After I hung up the phone, I stood paralysed for a few moments. Then I went to Mustafa and confronted him. He stared straight into my eyes and denied the whole story. 'It's pure nonsense,' he contended. 'I never picked her up from anywhere.'

I was not convinced, but I had no way of discovering the truth.

Mustafa was quick to implement the proper defence. He suggested that Minoo still resented him, due to their first encounter. Once again he undercut my moorings: isolate the enemy and then crush him. I did not know who or what to believe. Was Minoo doing this because she harboured ill will for Mustafa? Was she upset because of Mustafa's obvious preference for the baby of the family? Were all my sisters attempting to win his affections, to become the favoured sister-in-law?

The following morning I received a frantic phone call from Mother. Adila had run away from home and no-one knew where she was. 'It's all Minoo's fault,' Mother snapped. 'Adila was accused of all sorts of terrible things. She is obviously very hurt. Minoo implied that something was going on between Mustafa and Adila.'

Mother was characteristically more terrified by the prospect of a developing scandal than by the reality of the matter. She was determined to keep this entire episode under wraps, so she now turned to the villain

149

for help. Mustafa was supposed to travel to Liverpool that day for a political meeting, but he agreed to cancel his trip to help us locate Adila. He left to search London, as I headed for Mother's house.

Throughout the morning Minoo phoned Adila's friends, trying to track our runaway sister. Mother feared the worst, but she tried desperately to conceal her hysteria behind a calm exterior. She paced about, gulping coffee.

Mustafa called during the afternoon to report no success. Mother broke down on the phone and begged him not to give up the search. Mustafa offered reassurance; he was coming over to discuss a plan. When he arrived, he disclosed that his plan was to tap Mother's phone, as well as ours. (As this sort of thing goes on in Pakistan all the time, we accepted what he said.) He was positive that Adila would attempt to contact someone in the family and, when she did so, 'We'll be able to trace her,' he explained. 'I've spoken to the appropriate authorities. They've agreed to help us find her.'

Mustafa and I left for our own home, along with Dai Ayesha and Naseeba. On the way Mustafa stopped to buy two bottles of wine. 'How could you think of wine at this time?' I asked. 'Everything is in such a mess. When will you find time to sip this wine?' He mumbled a confused reply – something about us having run out of stock. He dropped me off at the house with instructions to sit by the phone, then went off to continue the search.

It was 10 p.m. when Adila called, sounding very hurt. She vowed, 'I'm never going back to that house. They all hate me. They have accused me of having designs on Mustafa. Mustafa is like my brother. Even you don't trust me. I'm not going home, ever. I'll call later.' The telephone clicked dead. I immediately called my mother and reported the conversation.

When Adila called back about an hour later, I insisted that I had to see her, and reminded her that Father would be furious if and when he found out about her latest episode. She relented and said, 'Come and see me at the Hilton Hotel, in the lobby.'

Before I had a chance to leave, Mustafa called and I reported this latest development. 'Why don't you come there and handle her,' I suggested. 'We have to get her to return.' He agreed to meet me at the Hilton.

With Dai Ayesha and Naseeba in tow, I rushed over in a taxi. Dressed in a caftan that doubled as a maternity gown, I walked into the hotel only a few moments before Mustafa appeared. As Adila made a grand entrance into the lobby, I noticed that Najeeb, who had spent a lot of time with us at the Hampstead flat and was a close friend of Mir Bhutto, also happened to be there. He remained in the shadows.

We sat at a table, in the lobby and spoke in hushed tones. I tried to reason with Adila, but when I saw that she remained obstinate I tired of her shenanigans and told Mustafa to pick her up and drag her to the car. 'If she were your daughter, you would have killed her by now. You wouldn't sit around a table negotiating her return. Don't you remember Minoo?' I asked. 'Just put her into the car. She doesn't have a choice.'

Adila was adamant that she would not go home. 'I'm in love with an Iranian boy,' she announced with a pout. 'I'm going to stay with him. You can't stop me.'

I stared daggers at her, waiting for Mustafa to assume the role of a protective and domineering brother-in-law, as he had done with Minoo. But I was astonished to hear him suggest, 'Listen, I think that we should send her to him with Dai Ayesha as a chaperone.'

It was an incredible proposition, and completely out of character with Mustafa's feudal standards. I was disgusted. 'How can you even suggest such a thing?' I asked. 'Adila has to go home. There's no other way.'

Adila's manner grew more aggressive. We raised our voices, and I heightened the emotion by pulling at Adila, trying to get her out of her chair to move her towards the door. She struggled against me, and ripped my caftan at the neck.

At first Mustafa was a passive spectator to our wrestling match. But then, in an apparent attempt to avoid a scene in this five-star hotel, he hammered out a compromise. If Adila would not come with us, and if I would not leave her on her own, we would all have to stay here together for the night until we could sort out our disagreements. Najeeb suddenly emerged from the sidelines and stood next to Mustafa at the front desk as he booked a room. I found this strange, but could not decipher why. I shook my head as if to shake off the confusion, located a phone and informed our mother of the plan. Adila stood by my side, making sure that I did not disclose where we were.

That night, Adila and I shared a bed with Naseeba. Mustafa and Dai Ayesha slept on the floor.

Very early in the morning, mother and Minoo barged in. Mustafa jumped up in surprise and offered a quick excuse to leave on his delayed trip to Liverpool. I thought he looked very sheepish as he walked out of the door, but I turned my attention to the tense family crisis. Mother angrily explained that she and Minoo had played sleuth all night, calling the security officers at every hotel in London, complaining of an under-age runaway. They had finally discovered that this particular room had been booked *the previous morning* by Najeeb, in the fictitious name of Samina Khan!

Pieces of the puzzle suddenly came together. Images flashed through my mind. Had Mustafa and Adila spent the day here together? Was he with her when she called me? Were they laughing at us? I shot an involuntary glance at the bed where I had slept all night. Had they been there? On those same sheets? I felt sick.

Still, my vegetable brain refused to acknowledge what was now so clear. Adila told us that she had met up with the Bhutto brothers, who were friends of the Iranian boy. She claimed that she had spent the entire day with them. Minoo had doubts, but both Mother and I used Adila's explanation as sand in which to bury our heads. Each of us maintained our personal charade. Adila insisted on coming home with me. When Mother refused to let her, she snapped, 'Why can't I stay with Tehmina? If I can spend nights with Rubina, I can spend nights with Tehmina. I'm not going home. I want to stay with Tehmina. You will not let us get close to her. You hate her for some reason.'

Mother gave up arguing, due to mental exhaustion, but her permission was temporary. She ordered Adila to leave my house and come home the very moment that Mustafa returned from Liverpool.

I desperately wanted to talk to Adila that day, but as soon as we walked into my house she gobbled several sleeping pills and went to sleep. She woke only when Mustafa arrived. I reminded her that she was under Mother's order to leave now, but she was freshly defiant.

Mustafa old me that Adila wanted to speak to him privately. 'I think I have to sort her out,' he said. 'I have to put some sense in her head. So if you could leave us alone for a while, we could talk.'

'I don't see why she can't talk in front of me,' I responded. 'She's my sister. What's she afraid of?'

'She doesn't trust any of you. You'll tell your mother about her problems. She needs to talk to someone she can trust.'

I gave in, as he knew that I would. I did not want to believe that I was being betrayed. I was confused. For too long now, Mustafa had pulled all my strings, like a puppet master, and now those strings were hopelessly, perhaps permanently, entangled.

That evening, Mustafa had to contend once more with my mother and Minoo. They arrived unexpectedly and marched into the house. Mother, appearing broken but severe and resolute, was armed with the Koran. She commanded, 'Adila, get into the car!' Adila began to object, but Mother silenced her with a sharp slap in the face. Then she turned to Mustafa and said, 'I am carrying the Holy Book in my hand. In its name, get out of our lives! You're a cunning and evil man. You're destructive. I warn you not to play with our family's honour. I want you to send my daughter to me immediately. I won't let her remain in your house.'

'What do you know?' Mustafa retorted. He took Mother by the arm and guided her into the living-room. He tried adopting a more reasonable tone. 'I have saved this family's honour,' he claimed. 'But I had rather not talk about it.'

Minoo interrupted and rudely accused Mustafa of corrupting the morals of a minor. 'Don't make up stories to cover up the truth,' she warned.

My response was that of a conditioned zombie, who could neither discern the whole truth of the matter nor deal with it. I was a dutiful wife, only conscious that it was my role to defend Mustafa. I ordered Minoo out of my house, because she was insulting my husband.

Mother dragged Adila to her car and they drove off.

I needed to hear the truth from Mustafa and I reasoned with him to clear my doubts. I told him that if I was to defend him to my family, I needed to know the facts.

Mustafa read from a new script. 'Minoo was right,' he said. 'I did pick Adila up from school that day. I didn't want to tell anyone what I was doing with her, so I denied the story. Adila was pregnant. It was that Iranian boy. I had taken her to a clinic for an abortion. I was protecting your family's honour. For this I am being painted as a dishonourable man. It's a strange world when you're condemned for your kindness.'

I wanted desperately to believe my husband, and so I did. Armed with this fresh evidence of his innocence, I went to see my mother. She demanded proof – the receipt for the abortion. Mustafa did not have it. Mother wanted to know where the abortion was performed. Mustafa would not tell. At this point Mother decided that she would have no more to do with Mustafa and me. This was not a workable relationship.

I discussed my mental anguish with my obstetrician. She was a Welsh woman who was very sympathetic to my plight. Her face reacted with revulsion when I told her how Mustafa beat me. 'He's very violent,' I said. 'I'm miserable with him.' I asked for tranquillizers, and she wrote a prescription for Valium, assuring me that it would not endanger my child.

My father had prepaid the childbirth costs prior to our current estrangement, so on 27 December 1979, when I went into labour, Mustafa drove me to a small, exclusive clinic in the Hampstead area. His expression carried a sense of mild rebuke. He considered these facilities to be excessive for mere childbirth. My obstetrician greeted me warmly, but was cool to Mustafa. I missed my family intensely, once again cut off from them when I needed them most.

Apart from the physical pangs of childbirth, I was racked with guilt. I was tortured by the prospect that my baby might not be normal, owing to my suicide attempt. Throughout my labour I prayed to God to forgive my selfishness and spare my baby from punishment.

My heart pounded with fear as I strained for the first look at my new daughter Nisha. Instantly my anxiety evaporated and was replaced by unconditional love. I removed the locket from my neck – inscribed with the name of Allah – and placed it around hers to protect her from the evil eye.

Two hours after my daughter's birth, Mustafa came into my private room and sat by my bed. I could see that he was tense and angry. He was in the mood that I most feared, yet I could not restrain myself from pouring out my own frustrations. I wondered: even if my suspicions concerning him and Adila are not true, how could a man of Mustafa's intellect allow this mess to take over our lives? One of the reasons I had married him was to elevate myself in my mother's eyes, but all I had found was additional humiliation and pain. Now, I realized, I had been allowed a safe moment to vent my rage. He would not dare strike me here in such a public place, at such a time.

I complained: 'Mustafa, you've messed up everything. Here I am in a hospital, all alone. You have created havoc by your connivance and intrigue. You're like an old, petty village woman who thrives on carrying tales and keeping families apart.' He listened to this tirade with mounting fury. I saw the rage growing, but I could not stop. 'You have cut me off from my family,' I accused. 'I have four sisters. I have a brother. Parents. Where are they? Why aren't they with me today? Think about it. Who's responsible? Think.'

Mustafa rose from his chair and slapped me hard, two hours after I had delivered his child. With methodical movements, he lashed his hand across my face, back and forth. Then he resorted to his favourite tactic, twisting my forearm until I thought the limb would crack in two. I bit fiercely into my lip to avoid crying out.

He left me, bruised and battered in my hospital bed, and went to the airport to meet his thirteen-year-old son Bilal, who was flying in from Pakistan to live with us.

My obstetrician found me alone in my room, weeping. Why should I be so devastated at such a joyous moment? She knew, and she listened quietly as I sobbed out the details. Then she advised softly, 'Nobody can help you unless you help yourself.'

I knew that she was right. Why did I not cry out as he beat me? Why did I not attract the doctors and nurses and demand that someone call the police? What could they do? What could the police do? They would admonish Mustafa, but sooner or later I would be alone with him, in a worse predicament than before. My silence was not to protect Mustafa; it was to protect myself.

My father did not call to see me or the baby, but he sent me a locket with a prayer inscribed on it. I was touched by the gesture – which told me that he had access to me through his prayers. I needed them.

My obstetrician helped me in the only way she could, by finding purported medical reasons to keep me in the clinic for a few extra days. When finally it was time to leave, Mustafa arrived with a present for me, a very expensive white Cashmere coat. Quite obviously, this was supposed to be compensation.

With the execution of Bhutto in April 1979, a portion of the exiled community rallied around his sons and distanced themselves from Mustafa. Adventurism was in the air. The would-be terrorists had outgrown their air guns and, by 1981, were shopping for the real thing. The revolutionary group known as Al-Zulfikar, aka the Pakistan Liberation Army, was born. The Bhutto brothers and their supporters compiled hit lists, planning to assassinate the key figures of the Zia regime, leaving a power vacuum that they could fill. They moved to Afghanistan and set up a secret training camp in Kabul.

The Americans were supporting Zia against the Soviet invasion of Afghanistan. The constitution had been violated by the man they supported. The young Bhutto boys' father had been murdered by hanging, their mother and sister were confined. They had no option but to take up armed struggle with the help of those few countries which were prepared to guide them and provide shelter.

Mustafa was not privy to the plot, but he learned a few of the details, and he argued the futility of attempting to dislodge the generals forcibly. He understood the impatience of the Bhutto boys, but he could not condone their plans. Pakistanis are repelled by acts of sabotage and assassination. Mustafa knew that Al-Zulfikar would attract not only hard-core activists, but infiltrators from the world's intelligence services. He worried that Al-Zulfikar would give Zia the pretext for a witch-hunt to eliminate any trace of People's Party support. Terror was certain to be met with terror, and the innocent would suffer torture, imprisonment and the gallows. In sum, he was convinced that this outlaw arm would tarnish the image of the entire party and would only slow down the peaceful struggle for the restoration of democracy.

Mustafa favoured a more prosaic style of politics. He travelled across the country and the continent, addressing large public meetings, stirring sagging spirits, rebuilding the party, always with me in tow. He became the tireless cheerleader, arguing for sensible change. Old friends and colleagues dropped in constantly, and the subject was always politics. I enjoyed their conversations, and slowly realized that, whatever the horror of my private life, I could find reason for existence in working for the liberation and betterment of my homeland.

On 18 February 1980, my twenty-seventh birthday, my father telephoned to extend the family's forgiving hand. Three months of estrangement had passed. No-one in my family had seen Nisha. Father asked what I wanted for my birthday and I answered, 'To see you.'

He replied in a choked voice, 'Come tonight.'

Mustafa happily agreed.

That evening, as we climbed the stairs to the upper section of the house, we encountered Adila, coming down. Mustafa had no choice but to ignore her and follow me up; to me, it signalled my ascent and her descent.

Stuttering a little at first, family life began again and gradually became more coherent. But it seemed that each step closer to my family took me further from my husband.

Mustafa's obsessions took perverse forms. Whenever he saw me laughing or joking with my parents, his mood darkened, and I knew that the next moment we were alone he would find a pretext for an argument that would lead to violence. A spiral of allegations began as soon as we returned home at night and continued until daylight seeped through the curtains. He picked up my own words and hurled them back at me until I lost the thread of logic. He underscored intermittent points with his fists or his shoes. Inevitably, I apologized for whatever supposed outrages I had committed. 'Are you really sorry?' he would goad.

'Yes.'

'Are you sincerely sorry?'

'Yes, yes.'

'Your tone is wrong. You don't sound as if you're sorry.'

This was as it had been during my childhood years, when I obeyed Mother, but did not *look* obedient. I replied, 'Mustafa, I'm exhausted. Please believe me. I'm sorry.'

'But you don't really feel that you did something wrong.'

'But I do. I do.'

'Two hours ago you were explaining your position. You were defending yourself.'

'I thought—'

'—Thought? Thought? You thought you could justify your actions. Do you still think?'

'No. You have proved that I was wrong to think.'

Our relationship had become one long argument. These nocturnal verbal skirmishes were almost the only way in which Mustafa communicated with me. He had a repertoire of abuses so vile that they would make a whore blush. He could shred me to ribbons with his tongue.

I bore the sole responsibility of camouflaging our relationship from others. Mustafa was extraordinarily clever. He had the facility to point all blame at me, and if others were to learn of my humiliation, it would be turned around to reflect badly only on me. In Mustafa's male-dominated society, he would always emerge smelling like roses.

Despite the bitterness that pervaded our lives, we continued to act the gracious host and hostess as we entertained friends and political contacts. Media men, powerful politicians and old acquaintances from abroad constantly arrived on our doorstep. In preparation for our dinners, Mustafa played the role of the Great Chef as Dai Ayesha and I served as his menials. Mustafa conjured gastronomic fantasies; Dai chopped and peeled; I cleaned up the mess. Mustafa had a fit if we altered his instructions in the tiniest detail, or if we were too slow – or if I had failed to anticipate any item that he might require. The proximity of huge, sharp-honed knives added a chilling dimension to these cooking sessions. Dai Ayesha was as fearful as I. She was a servant; thus, Mustafa did not have to justify his thrashings of her at all. No errors were allowed. The simplest omission brought his hand to her face or his foot to her buttocks. To Mustafa her name was simply: 'You bloody bitch!' There was no possibility of her altering her lot She spoke no English and had no money. If she dared to run away, Mustafa's family would vent his wrath upon her aged mother and other relatives in Kot Addu. She was in bondage.

Mustafa watched me constantly, and my every action became staged and stilted. He enjoyed seeing me squirm. I was even supposed to please him when he was not around. He journeyed to America to conduct some vague financial and political business and, quite oblivious of the time difference, called me very early every morning. If my voice sounded groggy, he was upset. It was my duty to be awake, alert and awaiting his call. I was supposed to miss him.

It was during one of these trips that Mustafa granted me permission to go shopping with Zarmina and Adila at Brent Cross. I bought some magazines, but warned my sisters not to tell Mustafa about them; he thought that they were a waste of time and money. We giggled like schoolgirls, sharing a 'wicked' secret. When Mustafa called the following morning, he cross-examined me about the shopping trip. He wanted to know in detail what I had bought, and I told him about everything except the magazines. 'What else did you buy?' he asked. His voice carried a tone of oneupmanship.

'Nothing,' I lied.

'I asked you what else you bought. Answer me truthfully. What else, huh?'

'Nothing.'

'I know you bought something else. I *know* you did.' The sinister tone scared me. 'I will always find out,' he warned. 'You disobeyed me. You bought some magazines, didn't you? Come on, tell me. Didn't you?'

I broke under the pressure of his cross-examination, and as he abused me over the long-distance line, I thought: Adila!

Mustafa was exercising downstairs when the phone rang. He answered, just as I happened to pick up the extension. Adila was on the line. I heard my sister ask my husband, 'Do you love me? Tell me. Do you love me?'

I heard my husband respond to my sister, 'More than you will ever know.'

I came downstairs numb, feeling dirty and used. But I could not bring myself to confront Mustafa. What was the best strategy? I was unable to react to this latest horror. Then the phone rang again, and I overheard Mustafa promising to arrange a passport for someone.

Within moments there was a third call. Dai Ayesha picked up the phone and announced that the caller was Choudhry Hanif, one of Mustafa's 'comrades'. As Mustafa took the phone, I sneaked back upstairs. Steeling myself, I quietly picked up the extension and heard Mustafa say to Adila, 'I'll get you a passport. Don't worry. I'll get it done, but it'll take some time.'

'Hurry up and do it,' Adila insisted. 'I can't stand

161

being without you any more. I want to get out of here, now. I want to live a new life with you – only you.'

I felt as if I would vomit. I was still unable to do anything at the moment, but my mind began to fashion a counterattack.

That afternoon, we visited my parents. I was burning with silent anger and pain, but if Mustafa sensed this he did not show it.

I found a moment to draw my mother and Adila into my parents' bedroom, and I took the offensive. I complained to Mother, 'Mustafa told me about Adila – how she's chasing and harassing him. He's fed up. Adila's trying to wreck my marriage. My husband is warding off her advances. This must stop now. It is her fault. She is my sister. He has asked you to control your daughter. This girl has surpassed all limits of decency.'

Adila exploded and called my bluff. 'He could never say all this,' she declared. 'Tell him to come here and say it to my face. I will say nothing in my defence without his presence. He is involved in this. Let him confront me.'

Mother lectured Adila on morality and told her to stop her childish games. She warned that if our father learned of this, he would kill her.

I added, 'Adila, I have enough problems without you compounding them. Leave us alone. We are in a difficult and uncertain phase of our lives. We are uprooted, living in exile. Why are you bent on making our lives into a hell? I cannot cope.'

'I have done nothing,' Adila responded. 'Why don't you call Mustafa in? We will soon find out what is happening. You are lying, not him.'

Her confidence forced me to back off in disarray. I was trapped in a maze of strange motives, trying to cover my humiliation by defending the major party to the crime. He was on her side of the fence and I was screaming in isolation from my side, trying to eye-wash his role in this affair, to protect myself from the degradation of his not wanting me. My ego could not accept Mustafa and my sister together. I wanted Adila to feel that he had dumped her. And I wanted Mother to feel that the man whom I had chosen to protect me from the complex legacy of my childhood was, indeed, honourable. But the smirk on Adila's face tore me apart.

When we returned home, I waited until Dai Ayesha took my babies to their room, and Mustafa's son Bilal had gone to his own room. Mustafa and I stood in the midst of the large living-room. The few pieces of furniture – a sofa, an armchair and a television set – sat about the edges, leaving an immense void at the core of the room. Here, I suppose, I felt relatively safe. It seemed like space to manoeuvre. My anger over the primary issue receded; instead, the one I had created at Mother's house became paramount. How should I tell him? My heart thumped with fear. I knew that I had to choose my words carefully, to stress the point – the truth – that I had attempted to defend *him*, and thus myself. I began by explaining that I had overheard his telephone conversations with Adila. Then I told him how I had confronted Adila in front of my mother in such a way that the blame would fall upon Adila, so that my parents would not lose respect for him.

The wheels turned in his head and instantly I realized my mistake. I had put Adila on the spot. Cornered, she might find a reason to tell the truth! If Mustafa thought that I had saved him, he would have been ecstatic. Instead, he was trapped. It was all topsy-turvy. Suddenly I became the guilty party.

It happened in an instant. Mustafa's eye fell upon his double-barrelled shotgun, which stood against the wall next to the TV set. In one swift movement he reached out with his right hand, grabbed the barrel and swung it at me. The wooden butt of the gun slammed into my side. I fell, but instinctively scrambled to my feet. I screamed, 'You have destroyed my life!'

He silenced me with another blow. I crumpled to the floor and drew my feet up against my belly for protection. He struck me repeatedly with the heavy gun stock, aiming for my back, my side, my legs, but he was in sufficient control to attempt to avoid striking me on the head. His face was a blur, an object that I must fear and obey without question. I tried to stifle my screams, lest Dai Ayesha and the children hear, but I could not. I knew that, by now, they must be huddled nearby, frightened to death.

I began shouting for Bilal's help. Mustafa only stopped when he saw evidence of obvious damage. Some of his blows were errant. My mouth showed blood. 'Ring up your mother this instant!' he raged. 'Tell her you are mad. Tell her you made up everything. Pick up the phone!'

'I – I can't do that,' I sobbed. 'She will never believe me. I can't change my story. She will suspect—'

The force of his blow interrupted me. 'Stand up, you bitch!' he commanded. There was a new, ominous, more methodical timbre to his voice. 'Stand up.'

I was barely able to rise, but I did as he ordered.

'Take off your clothes,' he shouted. 'Every stitch. Take . . . them . . . off.'

I trembled, clutching at the cloth of my baggy shirt, and when he saw that I could not respond he grabbed one arm and twisted it behind my back until I shrieked in pain and screamed that I would obey.

He backed off and sat in an armchair. He watched as I slowly began to remove my shirt.

Again I was aware of the emptiness of the room, but this time it looked unsafe. There was no place to hide, nothing to which I could cling. I slipped out of my trousers. Clad only in a bra and panties, I stared at him, pleading, begging, crying for him to allow me to stop. But there was no reprieve. I felt blood drying on my swollen lips and nose. With trembling fingers, I pulled off my underclothes.

He sat in the chair with his arms extended on either side, like a king on his throne. His eyes ran up and down my naked body, invading. His expression was grim, his lips tightly pursed. His eyes narrowed, searching, glinting, gloating.

Never before had I felt so totally humiliated, so utterly controlled. I could see on his face the awareness of the importance of this moment. This episode would cripple my spirit – perhaps beyond salvation. From this moment forward, it would be nearly impossible for me to function as an individual. There was not one iota of self-esteem left. The shame had burned it down to ashes. I was exposed as nothing.

'Please, Mustafa,' I cried, 'for the sake of the Prophet, let me wear my clothes.'

'Pick up the phone. Make the call first. Then we'll see.'

'How can I call without my clothes? Please, let me put them on first.'

He hurled profanity at me. He dragged my family through the gutter. Emptiness engulfed my senses. I could not reach out to anything. I could barely stand. My knees knocked against each other. My hands and arms were not sufficient to cover my nakedness. I wanted to grasp something. I tried to kneel on the floor, but as I bent my knees, he screamed. I rose immediately.

I stood there for many moments, begging and pleading, invoking the names of Allah and the Prophet.

'I'll call,' I whispered. 'Let me wear this, please.' Finally, he reached to the floor, grasped my crumpled, blood-stained shirt and threw it to me.

He nodded, lips still pursed, watching intently as I slipped into the shirt.

Burning with shame, I called my mother. But my mind and tongue would not co-ordinate. I babbled. Instead of saying that what I had told her were lies, I fluffed my rehearsed lines and said that it was all true – at the moment, I did not know the difference.

165

Mustafa grabbed the phone from my hand, slammed it into its cradle and beat me with renewed vigour. I cried out for forgiveness and begged for another chance.

Once more I called. I was trembling and crying when I told my mother what Mustafa wanted me to say. Then he took the phone, with a look of triumph on his face. 'Tehmina isn't well at all,' he said with feigned compassion. 'She's going mad.' He referred to the meningitis that had struck me down as a child; he knew that my mother still attributed my rebellious nature to that episode. 'She's imagining things,' he contended. 'She fantasizes. She hates Adila for some reason. Perhaps you will know better, as her mother, what her complex about poor Adila is. I promise you, Adila has never committed the crimes Tehmina says she has. I'm dumbfounded by her allegations and suspicions. She has confessed the truth now. She makes up vicious stories about everyone, to torture them, but mainly to torture herself. She then goes into a cocoon and sobs and cries inconsolably. I have had to bear all this with great patience. What she did today is an example of what I have to go through each day. She wants to be a tragedy queen.'

That night, Mustafa begged me to forgive him for inflicting such humiliation upon me, but attempted to shift the blame on to me. He insisted that my ears had imagined the telephone conversations between him and Adila. 'These things happen to people in love, you know,' he said. 'They love with such intensity that they can hear things that worry them – they auto-suggest and go mad. You are, in any case, not mentally strong because of the meningitis. It is not really your fault, and I should have controlled my temper.' He bestowed a benign smile upon me, opened his arms and warmly commanded, 'Come to me.' Like a zombie, I came. He hugged me and cradled me in his arms. I clutched back at him and cried uncontrollably. I knew that he was lying, yet I did not know what to do about it. My mind was dead.

For a long time after this night, no matter how many layers of clothes I wore, no matter with whom I was, I felt naked.

A week passed before Mother called us and, in a furious tone, proclaimed that Mustafa should be sent to an asylum.

I was surprised by the outburst. What had happened now? I wondered. Then Adila came on the line and I realized that Mustafa's apprehensions were justified. Adila had finally confessed to Mother and now, in measured words, she admitted to me, 'I've been sleeping with him for three years. I'm telling you this not as a sister but as a friend. Mustafa hates you, Tehmina. Everyone hates you. Mother hates you, too. There must be something wrong with you. I'd leave him before he leaves you. Have some respect for yourself.' Adila was graphic in the details, disclosing that Mustafa's son and Dai Ayesha were both in on the long-term deception. 'Bilal arranges the meetings,' she said. 'He is our go-between. He books the room in West Lodge Park Hotel. Dai Ayesha has known all along. Ask her. He had sex with me at the apartment that day when he dropped me at school, remember? There was no Iranian boy; it was always Mustafa. I was with him that day at the Hilton – all day. When he called you, I was there.'

What this fifteen-year-old sister of mine was telling me was that Mustafa had been having an affair with her since she was thirteen years old!

Full of anger, I questioned Bilal and Dai Ayesha.

'You'll have to ask my father,' Bilal replied softly. Dai nodded.

Their reluctance to speak was an eloquent confirmation. I felt my anger rise, but I stifled it. These two were like me, totally subjugated to Mustafa's will. Like me,

167

they had no options. I counselled myself to redirect my anger.

Mustafa came home soon and found me in the bedroom. My body shook with both fury and fear. My voice quavered. But from some deep reservoir I found the courage to confront him.

He denied *everything*, attempting to be glib, but I could tell that he was as shaken as I. I put him to the test, asking him to call Adila in Spain and expose her cruel game of deception. He refused, but luck was not with him this day. The telephone rang and who should be on the other end of the line but Adila herself! Mustafa spoke to her, aware that I was listening on the extension. 'I love my wife and children,' he proclaimed. 'I love you too, but like a sister. You mustn't behave like this. You're hurting a lot of people with your behaviour.'

After the call, he stood in front of me, placed his hand on the Koran and swore that the 'affair' had occurred only in Adila's obsessive mind. He contended, 'She has some severe, deep-rooted problem with you, Tehmina. She wants our marriage to break at any cost. You know her. She's mentally unwell, very unwell. How can you believe all this? Can you not see that she has related and adjusted all the incidents to the times that she knows you were suspicious? Don't let them get you. Your mother eats out of her hand. Don't become gullible like her. We must fight her attack on our home together.'

I did not believe a word of what he said, yet I was prepared to live with the lie because I was relieved to hear him say something against Adila, and I was also unprepared to face the prospect of life on my own. Escape was not an option. He would take the children. He would take the money. He might even take my life.

I realized that our marriage was sustained not by the relationship, but by complicated external forces: my ego, fear of failure in the eyes of my family and society, fear of losing my children, fear of losing my status as a married woman. But the most important ingredient was Adila. If my marriage broke she won and I lost.

I rang up Mother in Spain to where she had rushed off with Zarmina and Adila, spiriting her youngest daughter away from the scene of the crime. With boldness born of resolute despair, I told her that my husband was not to blame if my sister was a slut. With that statement, Mother and I once more severed our ties.

In Spain, my mother instructed Zarmina to pamper the errant child, serving her breakfast in bed and otherwise catering to all her whims – as if Zarmina were her personal maid. Mother bought the fifteen-year-old's entire trousseau in Marbella, to pacify and divert her mind, and justified it with the explanation that Adila 'has suffered heartache and betrayal at a very young age. She was impressionable and he exploited that.'

Zarmina brooded over the injustice of it all and cried silently for her own and my predicaments.

8

We flew to Sharjah in the United Arab Emirates. Only when we were aloft did Mustafa reveal that we would also be visiting India for a meeting with Prime Minister Indira Gandhi's son Rajiv. According to Pakistani law, it was an act of treason – punishable by death – to ally with India, but Mustafa did not believe for one moment that his actions were unpatriotic; he saw the Indians as a means to an end. Working with India against Pakistan was not treason; he justified it as 'Bhuttoism'.

In Sharjah, the night before we were to fly on to Delhi, we spent the evening with a People's Party politician who knew nothing of our secret mission. Mustafa blundered, breaking security when he mentioned that we were going to Delhi the next day. The politician expressed a desire to go, but said that he did not have a visa. Mustafa surprised me by boasting that he could 'fix it'.

When we arrived at the Delhi airport, intelligence officers whisked us through, but they stopped our friend. A well-known woman journalist from India was also on the flight, and the incident raised her eyebrows. She wanted to know how *we* could get in without visas. What kind of Pakistani politician was Mustafa? How could the Indian government allow this?

The unwanted attention was poorly received by our host. Learning of the airport incident, Rajiv Gandhi refused to compromise himself by meeting Mustafa. In a firm but polite message, he explained the danger of drawing attention to our clandestine visit.

Nevertheless, the treasonous contacts continued in

England. Unbeknown to me, Mustafa managed to arrange a meeting with Prime Minister Indira Gandhi herself!

And it was during this time that I became pregnant with my fourth child.

Mustafa was again travelling to India. I was in the second trimester of my pregnancy when I learned from a friend that my seventeen-year-old sister Zarmina would marry Riaz Quraishi, the son of Nawab Sadiq Hussain Quraishi. I was sad to receive such important news through a third party. Mustafa's intrusion into our lives had caused havoc, and Mother had dictated that my name should not be mentioned in her home.

I knew that Mustafa would be emotionally and politically opposed. Riaz's father had been Governor of the Punjab during the time when Mustafa served as Chief Minister, and had been appointed by Bhutto to succeed Mustafa after the two fell out. Sadiq Quraishi had withdrawn from politics following Zia's take-over and now concentrated upon the business world; he owned the Pepsi-Cola franchise in Pakistan. His was an ultra-conservative family that sought to indulge its women.

For Zarmina, whose world was fashion, this arranged marriage was a perfect match, despite the fact that she had met Riaz only once – for tea with the family – before the proposal was accepted. Subsequently they spoke briefly via long-distance telephone. Riaz had visited London during the engagement period, but the couple was not allowed to spend any time together without a chaperone. I was very happy for her and knew that she felt her prayers had been answered. Zarmina had been a happy child despite the preferential treatment that our fair-skinned sisters had received from our mother. In age she was sandwiched between the beautiful and spirited Minoo and the manipulative Adila, and was openly known as the 'Cinderella' of our household. Her current status as Adila's handmaid was torture for her. This marriage would free her.

The groom and his relatives travelled from Lahore to London for the elaborate event. Zarmina and I had been very close. I wanted desperately to be there, to sing, to dance and share Zarmina's happiness, but of course I was not invited.

During the week preceding the wedding, I visualized Zarmina in her bridal clothes and tried to picture all the exciting events that I knew she was experiencing. My reverie was interrupted by the ringing of the telephone. When I picked up the receiver, no-one spoke. I listened closely and heard wedding songs in the background and the unmistakable beat of the *dholki*, a silver spoon used as a drumstick to accentuate the rhythm of the music. There was laughter in the background 'Who is it? Who's there?' I asked, but my questions were answered with a cruel silence. Then the phone went dead.

This became a diabolical game. Someone was playing with my mind, exploiting my isolation. As the wedding week continued the calls accelerated. I recoiled every time the phone rang but I could not keep myself from answering. Who hated me enough to do this? Adila?

I sent a friend to the wedding as my secret envoy. I wanted my sister to know that, despite my enforced absence, I loved her and would always pray for her happiness, so I smuggled in a note telling her this. When she returned from the wedding, my friend told me that Zarmina wept over my note. My spy displayed Polaroid photos of Zarmina in her stunning dress of silver silk. The tissue-like fabric was embroidered with silver and turquoise. Diamond jewellery sparkled in the light of the camera flash. The pictures made me sob inconsolably. My little sister was the Princess and I was the stay-at-home Cinderella.

When Mustafa returned from his trip I told him about the cruel and mysterious phone calls that I had received during the week, but he sloughed them off, accusing me of taking mental field trips into dark fantasy. He attempted to distract me with new clothes he had purchased for me, and with news. He had met Indira Gandhi. He dismissed this act of treason as easily as he discounted the crank phone calls. To him, India was the traditional enemy of Zia's Pakistan, not of the new nation that he was fashioning. During the hour-long secret discussion at the Prime Minister's residence in New Delhi, she was articulate and approachable. They spoke of Bhutto's execution and the prospects for restoring democracy in Pakistan. The Prime Minister of India and the exiled Lion of the Punjab tried to analyse the reasons for the continued hostility between their two nations, and both concluded that the Pakistani army had a vested interest in maintaining border tensions; it made them necessary.

Mustafa was smug. He had pulled off a daring political coup. He saw this as the first step in bringing a dramatic change to the people of Pakistan.

A large segment of our population shared Mustafa's belief that the Pakistani army has been the root cause of our problems. Proponents of this theory argue that the military, jealously guarding their power and budget, are always suspicious of democracy. Indeed, historically the military have played a visible, interventionist role in Pakistan's politics. Mustafa theorized that Bhutto's great mistake was that he attempted to coexist with the military. And, in fact, it was the army who toppled him, and General Zia who ordered his execution.

The People's Party was split on this issue. Right-wingers recognized the army, with all its faults, as necessary protection from the perennial Indian threat. But Mustafa and many others caught the anti-army virus and nurtured it. It was a confusing malady, complete with a fever that caused Mustafa to believe that the Pakistani army had to be crushed. Only then would the politicians have a free hand at restructuring the lop-sided system. But how could this be done? Mustafa's supporters did not have an armed force of their own, of course, so they decided to look to India for salvation.

Mustafa indoctrinated me into blind acceptance. He conditioned me to respond to any mention of the Pakistani army with hate and revulsion. He lectured: The army gobbles up Pakistan's scarce resources, diverting them from industry. It keeps the people poor. It prevents the nourishment of democracy. He wanted nothing less than to foment another India–Pakistan war. He was convinced that once the Indian army had defeated the Pakistanis in battle they would roll back across their borders and allow civilians to get on with the business of running our country. He did not believe that India wanted hegemony over Pakistan. That country, too, needed to divert its precious resources to industry, without the necessity of spending enormous sums to defend itself against our menacing armed forces.

Indira Gandhi warned Mustafa: 'We will have to crush and humiliate your army. Only then can our two countries live in harmony. Only then can you hope to restore the rule of civil law.'

As Mustafa related all of this to me, his gaze took on a statesmanlike quality. 'What I am about to do will be misunderstood,' he acknowledged. 'The people of Pakistan are illiterate. They are rigid and do not have foresight – but that is the difference between the leader and the led. For them, the Indians are the Number One enemy. They don't realize that the army, which syphons off our country's money, and deprives them of a better future, is the real enemy. Mine is a long-term plan, for our future, for our children. The élite will not understand. They will oppose the plan as too radical. They know that we will not just stop at the army. They, too, will have to give up their ill-gotten wealth. Reforms will be extensive. The destruction of the army is just the first step!' His voice grew hushed. He added, 'This is a dangerous secret.'

Mustafa waited only a short time after his return from India before he dropped a more personal bombshell in my lap. We were plagued with strange phone calls, from some unidentified person who would talk only to Mustafa. I found the whole thing juvenile. 'You're an old man now,' I chided (he was actually forty-four). 'Grow up.'

It was then that he 'confessed' to me that the Indian film goddess, Zeenat Aman, was madly in love with him and wanted to marry him. They had met during his trip to New Delhi. Mustafa reported with barely concealed pride that she was pursuing him, harassing him. He said that the spate of calls was from her, and protested that he was growing tired of them. But his phone conversations – if, indeed, they were from the mysterious Zeenat Aman – did not convey the message that he was trying to brush her off. I walked into the room during one call and heard Mustafa growl, 'If that man looks at you again, I'll shoot both of you.' He realized that I had overheard this and he quickly hung up. His expression was sheepish.

'So that's a brush-off, is it?' I asked sarcastically. 'You sounded more like a jealous lover.'

He had an explanation for everything. 'I knew you were there; I heard you,' he claimed. 'I was teasing you. There was no-one on the phone.' Then he opened his arms wide and grinned a Cheshire-cat smile. 'Come here,' he commanded gently.

It was only a couple of hours later when he once more complained that Zeenat Aman was making his life miserable. 'She won't take no for an answer,' he said. 'She wants to marry me. What shall I do?'

What a question to ask a wife! My sarcasm returned, and I lectured: 'Mustafa, you must be honour-bound to your word, either to her or to me. If you cannot think of me – and our two children and your child resting in my womb – as important, then I think you should leave us. If you feel that your commitment to Zeenat Aman is more sacrosanct than the one you made to me, go to her. But please be loyal to somebody. I'd like to see some sense of loyalty in you, for somebody, anybody – even another woman.'

'I could never leave you or the children,' he vowed. 'I love them. I love you. I'd die without you.'

The constant making and breaking had taken its toll on me. The cracks in our marriage could not be papered over with words.

Mustafa said that he had arranged to meet Zeenat Aman this very night, outside a pub. It was to be their last meeting; he would make a clean break with her. He wanted me to come along, as a witness to his good intentions, and he asked his friend and 'comrade' Sajid to accompany us.

I felt as if I were losing my senses as Sajid and I sat inside the pub while my husband went outside to meet his girlfriend. Unbeknown to me, whoever he was meeting had arrived in a chauffeured car. I ordered a Bloody Mary and set about converting it into a curry; I dosed it with tabasco and Worcester sauce and gulped at it. Sajid remarked on my tolerance, and I told him that I was not sure why I was still with Mustafa. My only defence was the weak and very tired explanation, 'Since I married Mustafa I have been clinically dead.'

Mustafa came back into the pub and announced that he and Zeenat had argued, and she had left. He appeared quite shaken. He told us no more.

That night, at home in bed, he clung to me like a child frightened of the bogeyman. He was tired and agitated. He spoke very emotionally: 'I'll always love you. I've been a terrible husband. I couldn't have had a more tolerant wife. I don't know how or why you have stuck it out with me. I've given you nothing. All the reasons you married me for have remained unfulfilled. I have made you suffer in exile. I forced you to endure my fears and my problems. I have put all my burdens on you, and you have carried them with dignity. Whatever frustrations I've had, I've taken them out on you. I don't know how I could have survived without you. I know you will leave me. Take the house in Islamabad. Go there with our children and please try to forgive me.'

His disturbed tone softened me. I did not know what, but some thing – or someone – was putting pressure on him. I lowered my gaze and felt the tears well in my eyes. I fashioned a response, and lifted my face to address him.

He was asleep! Clearly he had made peace with whatever demons were chasing him. The man delivered his passionate speech and then drifted off, as if he had resolved the problem. My anger returned with full force, and I was ready to lash out with my tongue, to rouse him from his stupor, when the telephone did the job for me.

Mustafa bolted upright, grabbed the phone and spoke to the caller in Punjabi dialect. He repeatedly assured whoever was on the other end of the line that he would sort out the problem in the morning.

'Who was it?' I asked.

'It was Zeenat Aman's mother,' he said. 'She told me that I should marry her daughter tomorrow, otherwise they will publish the news of our romance. If they do so, it would be my political death.'

I snapped, 'In that case, I suppose you must marry her.'

'I suppose I'll have to,' he whispered.

We lay there for several moments, not speaking. Soon, the sound of his breathing told me that he had gone back to sleep. I was stupefied – and suspicious. I slipped out of bed and headed for the downstairs telephone. I called a friend who followed the Bombay film scene. 'Is Zeenat Aman in London?' I asked.

'No, she's in Bombay,' my friend replied. 'I think she's doing a film there – several films, in fact.'

'Tell me, does her mother speak Punjabi?'

'No. Why do you want to know?'

'I'll tell you one day.'

I returned to bed, confused. This whole story about Zeenat Aman was so much tripe! But if Mustafa had not met Zeenat Aman outside the pub, whom did he meet? I prayed desperately to God and, if He did not answer, He at least allowed me to drift off to sleep.

I dreamed that Zeenat Aman walked into our house and vanished. Then images of Adila and my grandmother appeared. They stepped inside my home and, suddenly, we were enveloped in flames. I smelled smoke and burning flesh. I woke in a cold sweat. Could it possibly be Adila again? I wondered. Was she back to haunt me? After all I had given up, all I had been through, could Mustafa dare to involve himself with my sister again?

Early the following morning, my grandmother arrived at our house. She had journeyed from Pakistan for Zarmina's wedding, but I was startled to see her here. My mother had announced that anyone who had contact with us must sever all ties with her, and my mother was too domineering for anyone in the family to challenge her, my grandmother included. Suddenly I realized that it was *she* who had called the previous evening – she spoke Punjabi. When Mustafa saw her, he left the room quickly. His manner was that of a guilty person.

My grandmother, breathless and very agitated, sat on my bed. In tears, she told me that Adila had informed my mother that she wanted to marry Mustafa and had given him an ultimatum to divorce me. Mustafa had vowed to marry Adila, but had stalled for time, using my pregnancy as an excuse. He based the delay upon the Koran, which, he said, forbade a man to divorce a pregnant wife and also prohibited marriage to two sisters at the same time. The real reason, I was sure, was that the scandal would ruin his political image. To confirm Adila's story my grandmother had called Mustafa.

My grandmother could not bear to see me deal alone

with this continual suffering, but she was also angry with me for bringing such a sick man into the family. My mother had sent her to me this morning with a message: Mustafa has ruined you, but your sister is young; you must not allow her to fall under his evil spell. To spare Adila, you must sacrifice the remaining years of your life by not allowing him a divorce. If you leave Mustafa, your parents have said that you should *never* think of returning to them.

Her words emptied me. I could see the future, and it was blank. I would have to be the martyr, the shield for the family who had abandoned me – for the sister who had betrayed me. There seemed no choice.

Leaving my grandmother alone upstairs, I went to talk to Mustafa, surprised at my own sense of calm. He fell at my feet and begged me to toss a scrap of forgiveness into his bowl. 'I'll treat you like a queen,' he vowed. 'I won't beat you any more. I'll be your slave. I'll do your bidding – whatever pleases you. Please don't leave me.'

It was traumatic as always to see such a brutish monster reduced to a pitiful, grovelling mess. I *knew* that this would be a short-lived transformation, yet I grasped at it.

Together, we went back to my grandmother. He sat with his head bowed while she told us that my mother had run out of patience, and she delivered an ultimatum: 'There is a sword hanging over the neck of this family. It is time to drop it. Let the bloody deed be done. We will throw Adila out of the house. You can take her in if you want to.' I knew that would never happen and that she was speaking for effect, to force this man to withdraw.

Mustafa's reaction belied everything he had said to me a few moments ago. 'Fine,' he declared. 'If that's your decision, fine. I'll go and bring Adila into my house.' But he promised my grandmother, 'As long as Tehmina is in my house, I'll not touch Adila.'

The message was devastatingly clear. I knew that with

the birth of my baby I would be discarded. His only restraint, by his interpretation of the Koran, was to keep his hands off Adila while I was still pregnant. The years of abuse, sacrifice, lies and manipulation bubbled in my head like some sort of poisonous stew. I became hysterical, the shrieks emanating from a place I could not even identify. My screams brought Sajid running upstairs and our neighbours to our front door. I was completely out of control, in a state of total madness. Sajid gave me two tranquillizer tablets, but they had no effect. In the midst of my agony, my grandmother left, saying that she had to be with my mother. She disclosed that my mother had just had a cataract operation, and conjectured that she had ruined her eyes by crying endlessly over this mess. My father, she warned, was in hospital, being treated for chest pains. We were all victims, devastated by this one man.

I fell silent for some time after Grandmother left. I could feel myself falling into the snake pit. I was deluged by images of my life of humiliation and helplessness. My nerves were threadbare from years of marriage to this man. I collapsed on to the bed and allowed myself to scream relentlessly. Even in the midst of my hysterical despair, I wondered why it had taken me so long to reach this point.

In an incoherent state, I listened as Mustafa called Adila. 'Tehmina has had a nervous breakdown,' he told her. 'Your mother is taking all this badly. Your father will probably die. We should stop all this for their sakes.' My screams grew more hysterical; I knew that he was merely stalling for time. It was not over.

That night, we were supposed to attend an important dinner. Mustafa insisted that I go, but even he could see that it was impossible. He went alone.

I lay in bed, trying desperately to get to sleep before Mustafa returned. The effect of the drug had worn off. I felt, as always, trapped in the darkness. It had been dark in the bedroom that night in Pakistan – so long ago

– when he first beat me severely. Night was the time when I had to face him alone. Night was when he had no other distractions and could concentrate his fury upon me. Darkness was accompanied by evil. I thought of how I had met him and why I had married him. Every other reason faded as my mother magnified. I thought she would treat me better because I was married to an important man with a strong personality, someone who could hold his own. His treatment of me and his preference for Adila had reduced me to a worm, one that was slithering in the muck and filth of dishonour and degradation. Never again could he serve the purpose of winning Mother's approval for me. My anger rose, even as hopelessness invaded my entire being.

I heard the car pull up outside the house and I was disgusted that he was home. I heard the front door open and close downstairs, and I shook with anger. As his footfalls on the stairs grew louder, my breathing nearly stopped.

He entered the room. I feigned sleep. He undressed, climbed into bed and had the audacity to touch me – paw me – suggestively.

I pushed him away roughly with both hands, the first time that I had ever dared to deny him.

His fury was instant. He hit me on my face, cutting my lips, raising black-and-blue blotches on my cheeks. He clutched at me and pulled me from the bed. He threw me to the floor, kicking out at me even as I fell. My forehead crashed against the corner of the bedside table and I screamed in horror as blood gushed into my eye.

Seeing this, Mustafa instantly sobered. The gash on my brow was large and deep. He glanced about the darkened room, found a towel and tossed it to me. I pressed it against my forehead, but blood continued to flow. I was sure that I would faint.

'We'd better go to the hospital,' he said. 'You need stitches.'

During the hurried drive, my mind was spinning. Why had he chosen this moment to beat me? Throughout the anguish and turmoil of the day, he had kept his cool. He had bottled the rage. Why did it explode now? I realized that, on this occasion, he had actually lashed out in self-defence. Today, thanks to my grandmother, the truth had emerged into the cold, clinical light. Prior to this we had all known about his affair with Adila, but chose to utilize our various strategies to maintain the façade. But now the worst had happened. Adila, Mother, Grandmother, Mustafa, and I had all openly acknowledged the truth. As with my mother, truth, to Mustafa, was the unpardonable sin. His weaknesses were now well defined. He was vulnerable as never before. He could not control my family, but he *had* to control me. He had to crush the seedlings of rebellion, especially so because the reasons for it were genuine and adequate.

At the hospital, I told the doctor that I had fallen down the stairs. On the drive home, Mustafa played chameleon once more. He apologized, using the same threadbare words. Even as he pledged his undying love and compared me favourably to Adila, I thought: Who is he to choose? Why have I given this man the privilege of choosing between me and my sister? Why are we queuing for him to make his decision?

In a measured tone laced with menace I dictated, 'Mustafa, call Adila. Tell her in no uncertain terms that you love me and the children. Tell her to get out of our lives. She has messed up our lives. She must be told by *you* to get out. Now!'

He refused.

'In that case,' I replied, 'drop me off at my father's house.'

He agreed, but he made it clear that I would have to leave the children with him. He drove without speaking, unable to keep the smirk off his face. He knew, better than I, the priorities of my family. My own priorities were so simple – I just needed an excuse to forgive and forget, but it could only happen if Adila became convinced that she had lost him to me.

I walked into my family's home and encountered a maid, Adila's long-time ally, who had helped arrange their clandestine meetings. No-one else was at home. They had all gone to the clinic to visit my father. I looked around sadly and realized: this is not my home; this is the home of the other woman. I stood alone in the large house, broken and desolate, my head throbbing, my heart aching for my children. *I can't come back here!* I thought. *And I have nowhere else to go!*

I phoned Mustafa and asked him to pick me up. He smugly agreed. Then I left my parents' house and stood outside, crying loudly and uncontrollably, awaiting his arrival at the gate. Other than the time Mustafa forced me to stand beaten and naked in the living-room, this was the most humiliating moment of my life. I wished that I had never come here. Now my husband knew that *I* knew there was no place for me to go, no place of refuge. When the car arrived, I opened the door and slid meekly back into the inferno.

The *Economist* printed Mustafa's four-page article discussing Pakistan's relations with India, wherein he expounded his thesis that military rule prevented progress and that he would re-enter Pakistan on Indian tanks, if necessary. This was a surprise to those who knew Mustafa as the Lion of the anti-Indian Punjab, and created a great deal of controversy.

Ever since Zia had taken power, desperate People's Party leaders had maintained contacts with Indian political leaders and their intelligence arms. Zia had totally allied himself with the United States in their policy on Afghanistan. Afghanistan was a Muslim country on Pakistan's volatile western borders and its invasion by the Soviet Union was unacceptable. To stall Moscow's advance further south, Pakistan had become a front-line state. This helped Zia in his efforts to attract all-out political support of right-wing forces in Pakistan and to a great extent neutralize those who were working against martial law and for the restoration of democratic order. The United States and the West gave him their total support, and he was able to continue his regime.

Being an ally of the Soviet Union, India was obviously against the United States–Pakistani axis. Besides, Afghan governments, before during and after the Soviet invasion, had essentially been pro-India, whereas the Mujahadeen fighting against Kabul and its patron were pro-Pakistan, and were operating from a country they considered their second home. Zia's stance on Afghanistan and his covert assistance to Sikh separatists had earned him the wrath of the Indians; the Bhutto brothers and their followers were far more palatable. Heavy security measures were adopted lest word leak out and the People's Party leaders lose the bulk of their support. However, the Punjab stood in their way. The Punjabis would oppose any alliance with India. The Indians needed a strong leader in the Punjab to plead their cause.

They chose Mustafa. He was put into contact with a man named Joshi, a high-ranking intelligence officer assigned to the Indian High Commission in London. They communicated via code-names: Mustafa was 'Dilip' and Joshi was 'Asif Ali'. They met at various locations, mostly in Wimpy bars dotted around London. Over burgers and fries they discussed the futures of their two countries.

I spent the next two months in a deep silence, which withdrew me from my surroundings. I felt tired when I tried to make even a small conversation; a single sentence exhausted me. I lived only because of heavy sedation. Mustafa did not even notice.

I had been seven months' pregnant when the Adila issue erupted – just as Sherry had been when she walked into the prefabricated cabin to find me, her husband's other wife. I had felt embarrassed and awkward at the disturbance I had caused her. Now I felt her pain. The concepts of crime and punishment drove me to spending the nights crying over the Holy Koran for forgiveness – but only after I had completed my duties as a sexual object. When Mustafa slept I bathed and performed my ablutions, then drew away from him to the only One who still received me: Allah.

It was 5.30 a.m. on 23 January 1981 when I felt the beginning of labour pains. Mustafa drove me to the National Health hospital, complaining that all this fuss about childbirth was a western concept. He lectured, as he had before, about how the women in his village delivered in the fields, and then went back to work immediately. My father had paid my previous maternity expenses, but now he was out of my life and the responsibility fell upon a reluctant Mustafa.

At the hospital I asked him to leave. 'This could take a long time,' I demurred. I was frightened, but I wanted to bear this child without Mustafa's shadow falling over us.

As I sat alone in the waiting room, the pains grew suddenly worse and I screamed in panic. The doctor was not there and the nurses, unaware of my emotional state, scolded, 'Stop this nonsense, or we'll send you home.' The pains of labour melted into the accumulated agony of my absurd life, and I broke down completely. A collage of angry faces blurred in front of me as the hostile nurses chastised me for my hysteria. They would not believe that the baby was coming so quickly, although I continued to scream as the pain ripped through me. Finally, they rushed me into the delivery room. They had not even contacted the doctor in time and had to deliver the baby themselves.

My hysteria had grown so wild that the physical agony of childbirth unleashed all the other pains of my life. It was clear to me, even during the height of labour, that I might never have another chance to vent my feelings without drawing attention to the dormant crisis of my heart and mind. Nobody comprehended my nervous collapse. Instead, I felt anger and irritation from the people around me, as if they would have suffocated me into silence if they could.

As I pushed this new life out of my body, I abandoned Mustafa, my family and all my friends. I turned to God, the Holy Prophet, his daughter Fatima and especially her husband, the Prophet's cousin, Hazrat Ali. I begged them to come and stand by me, to protect me. A calm descended over me, as if they were at my side, as if they were my family. It was a miracle.

I named my first son Ali.

When the doctor finally arrived, she asked if I wanted her to inform my husband, but I did not feel it necessary. Mustafa did not know until two hours later, when he called after completing his yoga. He was thrilled that I had, finally, produced a son and heir.

An heir to what? I wondered.

My brother Asim was the only person in our family who maintained contact with us. Despite my mother's orders, he had established a forced civility with Mustafa, often bringing him gifts of Dom Perignon champagne, and bearing expensive presents for my daughters. Now he came to visit and was shocked to see me lying in an open ward at a National Health hospital. I covered up for Mustafa and said that he could not afford anything better, but he, in turn, said to Mustafa: 'I'm disgusted. If you can afford to go on expensive shoots and buy expensive wine, why couldn't you get your wife a room?' Mustafa shrugged off Asim's disapproval as inconsequential.

There were benefits to my stay at the hospital. In the presence of other, everyday people, I came alive again; I learned about their ordinary, everyday problems, which they all shared with one another. I, on the other hand, shared nothing about my life, amazed at the trivial troubles they took so seriously.

*　　　*　　　*

As much as I could, I avoided Mustafa. To me, he was now Adila's husband. I endured him, but when he slept I arose, bathed and went downstairs to the prayer mat. I read the Koran and cried, soaking the sacred words with my tears. I cried out to God, desperate for His help. Night after night I sat there, hoping that God would notice. I tried to escape into religion, but even there my life would slip in with me and I would become completely distraught in front of Allah – the only One who would hear me.

I grew increasingly detached from Mustafa, and drew my strength from my children. My new son Ali gave me a sense of spiritual peace. The pain of childbirth had brought me closer to God.

I began to analyse my life. What had happened to me? Why was I so afraid of everything? Why did I not react like a normal human being to insult and humiliation? I understood that my husband had crushed my spirit. He had complicated my already strained relationships with my family. He had isolated me from my friends. He had led me into a maze, and I did not know how to find my way out of it. He took away all my supports and anchored me securely to his own island. All I could do was wander through the labyrinth, too tired to talk or think.

His extremes made it difficult to focus on his true personality. Both of his selves – the angry one and the contrite one – were very convincing. I was afraid of the former and felt pity for the latter. One moment he punished me like a disobedient child; the next, I was a mother-figure who was supposed to forgive his transgressions. I could not react swiftly enough to his mercurial changes.

I had diagnosed his illness – he was a confused and insecure product of his background – and I had to find a cure. My reformer's zeal – and my ego – would not let me accept defeat by running away from the problem, no matter how daunting and intractable it appeared. I became his psychiatrist.

Mustafa's behaviour towards the children gave me a glimmer of hope. His initial bouts of insanity toward Naseeba had not recurred. He was still volatile and unpredictable but he was often a considerate and loving parent. I clutched at this straw.

I knew that my own personality had to change. I had become submissive and weak – just like his previous wives. I had, somehow, to learn to deal with him on a different level. God answered my desperate plea. The dust of inertia was blown away.

We were in the kitchen; I was at the stove, warming food for the children. Mustafa wanted us to go somewhere with him, but I did not want to take Ali out into the cold. Mustafa insisted and I resisted. He pulled me by the hair, swung me around and employed his favourite threat: 'I'll break every bone in your body.'

I grabbed the pot from the stove and threw it at him. He screamed in pain from the burning brew. For a moment he was paralysed. Then, as he raised his hand to strike back, I pushed him in the chest and yelled, 'The next time you raise your hand to me I will pick up a knife and kill you!' There was power and conviction in my voice, although my heart was beating madly. I had declared war.

Mustafa backed off.

I gave him some ointment for his burns. As he applied it he muttered dark threats, but he appeared subdued. Was it that easy?

I pushed my advantage. 'Mustafa, I've taken enough,' I said. 'There's no reason for me to take any more. This is a voluntary relationship, a relationship of choice. I'm not your sister or your mother. I'm your wife. I'm not bound to you by ties of blood. We have a contract to live together. I can tear that up whenever I feel like it. Get that into your head. Learn to respect me and appreciate my living with you. I find no necessity at all to live in this concentration camp. You correct your ways and make our lives worth living – or I'm leaving.' The last words were said with mounting fear of dire consequences, but I camouflaged that condition with an expertise that had become part of my nature.

He listened intently, and then fought to regain lost ground. He threatened, 'If you ever mention leaving again, I will not spare you. This is not an atmosphere that I can afford in my home. I have growing daughters. Do you understand? I shall fling acid on your face. I'll maim you and take my children away from you. I can deprive you of your beauty like—' he snapped his fingers in an arrogant fashion '—this.'

He left the house, and I went about my work, praying under my breath for safety from a monster's wrath. That night he sensed that I had once more weakened under the threat of darkness. He was correct, but only partially so. He began with a barrage of verbal abuse. My mother and sisters – even my grandmother – were dragged through the gutter. It was always an attack on the women. The men always degraded what they considered the most sacred areas of their honour.

When he was finished, I said quietly: 'You sound terrible using such language. It doesn't suit your status. It shows up your family background.'

He rose to strike me, but I reacted with disdain. 'Don't be foolish, Mustafa. Grow up. You don't need to hit me. Talk to me like an adult. Sit down,' I ordered.

For a moment, he actually sat on the edge of the bed and glared at me with a puzzled expression. But then his fury was unleashed and he lunged toward me.

I kicked him in the belly with both feet, sending him reeling from the bed. He attacked once more and I scratched and shoved him as hard as I could. I clawed at his face and pulled his hair. No woman had dared do this to Mustafa Khar, and I could tell that his mind was devising new blueprints of terror.

He spun me around and pinned me from behind. His

right forearm crushed against my windpipe. His flesh was an inviting target, and I sank my teeth in deeply. He yelped in pain and slugged me with his fist. His superior strength prevailed and he pummelled me with intensified fury until I was nearly senseless, perhaps only a few blows from death. Then, breathing heavily and still cursing, he slunk back.

He watched me stagger to bed. I refused to cry. I stared at him with sheer contempt, and I could tell that he was confused and even frightened by my resistance.

I tortured him with indifference. I did not sulk. I demanded no apology. He tried to offer one, but I brushed it aside with the admonition, 'Forget it, Mustafa. Sorry is a very inadequate word. Events have overtaken it.' In the past, my tears, my arguments, my pleadings had been like applause to his great acts of misplaced masculinity. Now my composure upset him; my silence weakened him.

9

On 2 March 1981, hijackers took control of a PIA aircraft in Karachi and ordered it to fly to Kabul, capital of Afghanistan. They demanded the release of forty of Zia's political prisoners and, to prove their intentions, shot an army captain and dumped him on the tarmac. Mir Bhutto did not have anything to do with the plot, but seized the opportunity to claim that his Al-Zulfikar organization was behind the terrorist act.

The hijacking was an ISI plan created by Zia to malign and isolate Mir and Shah. The international support that they were able to muster for their father had disturbed the General, who understood Western aversion to terroism. Mir was called by the Kabul authorities because the hijackers demanded to see him. His role was to try to save the passengers, but this was used against him. Mir went on the international terrorist lists and was unwelcome at home. It was a cruel conspiracy against two young students.

Mustafa and I were in the car when we heard the news over the radio. I expressed my delight that, at last, someone was taking action. 'It's a mistake,' Mustafa pronounced. 'There will be a witch-hunt now.'

He was right. Zia caved in to the pressure and released the political prisoners. But once the hijacked passengers were freed, Zia sent them to Mecca at government expense to perform *umra*. He made sure that television crews were on hand to interview them concerning their ordeal, to paint Al-Zulfikar and, by extension, the People's Party as a collection of thugs. All over Pakistan, anyone even remotely connected with the tricolour flag of the People's Party was in danger. Thousands were arrested, flogged and tortured. Some very fine youngsters were sent to the gallows. Bhutto's widow and daughter Benazir were placed under house arrest.

The lease expired on our Arkley Lane house and we rented a small, single-storey cottage in Mill Hill. Mustafa liked it because of the large garden at the back. For my part, I was tired of living like a gypsy. I suspected that Mustafa would continue to move us from place to place as long as we remained in exile. He was extremely restless. As he waited for plans to develop, Mustafa needed some outlet other than Adila for his excess energy and decided upon an old hobby – dogs. His craze took us all over the country, and he spent as much as £300 on a single dog.

He was obsessed by his new pursuit. If a dog developed a crooked tail, he doubted its pedigree and got rid of it. If a dog failed to respond to training, Mustafa lost patience. These were expensive show dogs, but Mustafa had no idea how to care for them.

He bought a Great Dane pup and installed it in an outdoor kennel. It was winter, so I turned the heater on at night but Mustafa, seeking to save money, turned it off, causing the poor animal to shiver. When the soft bones of the Great Dane pup affected the 'shape' of his legs, Mustafa gave the animal away to an humane society. Then he bought a full-grown Rhodesian Ridgeback, and soon after that a champion bull terrier arrived. He became bored with the Ridgeback and gave her away also. The bull terrier was the next to go. Then came a succession of six Irish Wolfhounds. Mustafa could see himself as the envy of Pakistan's hunting set. Mumtaz Bhutto, Bhutto's cousin, had about sixty hunting dogs, and Mustafa considered taking his dogs home in order to upstage Mumtaz.

This hobby was his, but the rest of us were stuck with it. In particular, Dai Ayesha was terribly upset whenever

In Marbella. I still had long hair and was in love with my
second husband, Mustafa Khar.

Mustafa Khar at the start of his political career.

Mustafa and Zulfikar Ali Bhutto looking in different directions – a reflection of how their political careers would end.

Mustafa Khar, the Lion of Punjab, being greeted by his followers.

London, 1985: In exile with our four children, Naseeba, Nisha, Ali and Hamza. I am holding the newborn Hamza while Ali sits on his father's knee.

Ali, Naseeba and Nisha at the time when Mustafa was trying to prevent me from divorcing him. This photograph appeared in all the English and Pakistani daily newspapers.

My grandmother, who has taken care of me all my life,
even when my parents rejected me.

Hamza, at the time of Mustafa's imprisonment.

The family returning to Pakistan after nine years in exile. Mustafa is carrying Hamza. As soon as he arrived, Mustafa was arrested by General Zia's secret police and imprisoned for three years.

Mustafa in captivity.

With Mustafa and the children leaving Lahore at the start of his electoral campaign once he'd been released from prison.

LEFT: Mustafa with Ali at a Pakistani People's Party rally after our divorce.

CENTRE: With Mustafa at a political meeting.

BOTTOM: Mustafa with Benazir Bhutto in 1989. Their paths would cross again in 1994 when Mustafa became a minister in her government.

1994: I decided to write this book and break the tradition of silence.

Mustafa commandeered her to help walk the dogs. She pouted as Mustafa pulled on his Wellingtons and she tucked the cuffs of her baggy trousers into gumboots. This was a woman who was revolted at the thought of touching an unclean animal and in Pakistan, even as a lowly servant, would never stoop to such work. Mustafa took charge of two Wolfhounds and strode off, looking like an Englishman in India who, having forgotten his solar hat, had remained outside too long in the August sun. Dai followed behind, with as many as three dogs tugging and dragging her. She made sure that her curses were too soft to reach Mustafa's ears.

I chose not to get in the way of his latest obsession; it was expensive and very inconvenient, but it diverted his attention from me.

Much time passed in uncertainty. We rode a financial roller-coaster. Mustafa was a slick salesman who managed to persuade various people to finance his fight for democracy, but his expenses were high and he cared little about accounting for them. Agha Hassan Abida of the Bank of Credit and Commerce International made a regular monthly payment of £2,000 through his trusted private secretary, Mr Osmani, but never disclosed the primary source of these personal funds.

We also received considerable financial support from a Pakistani named Seth Abid. We knew that he was very close to one of Zia's Cabinet ministers and that his brother-in-law had turned state's evidence against Bhutto. But these negatives were outweighed by Seth Abid's reputation as the man who had slipped nuclear secrets into Pakistan. He was also well known for dealing in gold. In a country like Pakistan men such as Seth Abid flourish. They are not viewed as criminals; for them, it is a form of trade where the risks are high and the profits are higher. Despite his reputation, he moved in lofty social circles; his wealth bought him acceptability and secured him from accountability.

Seth Abid offered us the use of his enormous, six-bedroom house (all bedrooms with en suite bathrooms) in Brondesbury Park, so we moved once more. The house was richly furnished, like a shaikh's fantasy gone wild. The space was a luxury that allowed Mustafa and me to coexist without getting into each other's way. Here we threw lavish parties for the glitterati and literati of Pakistan.

Mustafa lost interest in the dogs and soon all of them were gone. He turned his attention to canaries and finches. At first he housed them in beautiful brass cages, but as the number of birds increased he stopped buying cages after the fifth. He converted the dining room into an aviary, where his several hundred birds could fly about in relative freedom. Their droppings were everywhere – on the carpet, the floor, the dining table – and it was my lot to clean up after them. It became almost a daily ritual to catch the zooming birds, put them back into their cages and then scour the dining room prior to the evening's party. The next day they were flying again.

Eventually Mustafa grew bored with the birds too, and he decided simply to open the doors and set them free. I told him that they were too defenceless and domesticated to survive in the wild, but he insisted that they would be fine. He released them from bondage and our patio was sprinkled with confused little yellow-and-orange birds which had no idea where to go or what to do. I watched in horror as aggressive jays swooped down and devoured them. It was a massacre.

Mustafa's initial contacts with junior officers of the Pakistani army were tentative. The first meeting took place at the home of a mutual friend in London. The participants were young men who were disgruntled with Zia and who believed that the military had no business interfering in the politics of the country. They viewed Mustafa as the sort of courageous politician who would usher in the necessary reforms, and the fact that he was the Lion of the Punjab and had been a colleague of Bhutto was a bonus, since any effective movement toward the restoration of civilian rule would need the co-operation of the Punjabis. The 'boys', as we came to call them, believed as Mustafa did that Zia and his corrupt cohorts had to be physically eliminated, that repeated periods of martial law in Pakistan were used to serve a few generals who made the army their constituency to increase their power.

Mustafa was quite pleased with the results of the initial meeting, and more surreptitious contacts followed. He had found a chink in the armour of the military; the smell of mutiny was in the air. A plot was hatched. The 'boys' would plant a bomb, timed to go off when Zia convened a meeting with the top brass. Simultaneously, groups of rebel officers would take over the television and radio stations. With Zia's death, all the exiles would return, and the will of the people would prevent yet another general from seizing power. Although she knew nothing of the developing drama, the conspirators planned to install Bhutto's daughter Benazir, the leader of the People's Party, as Prime Minister, and Mustafa would be number two man in the new government. All those involved in Zia's 1977 coup would be tried for treason. The slogan was whispered quietly: 'Generals will hang from every pole.'

It was Mustafa's task to arrange for the purchase of arms and ammunition, as well as their delivery. Over yet another rubbery burger, the Indian agent Joshi consented to handle the purchasing details; delivery was trickier.

On 14 August 1983, the struggle to overthrow Zia began in earnest. In Pakistan, a coalition of opposition parties known as the Movement for the Restoration of Democracy (MRD) defied the ban on political meetings. When many of the demonstrators were arrested, spontaneous uprisings occurred, particularly in Bhutto's home province of Sind. Sindis are stereotyped as docile and timid and the army was caught by surprise. For days Pakistan's lifeline, the National Highway, was clogged by wave after wave of volatile demonstrators. The death toll mounted. Gaols were overflowing.

India's Prime Minister Indira Gandhi issued a statement praising the courage of the Sindis and extending her moral support. As far as the Punjabis were concerned, this was a great blunder. They withdrew from the struggle and the Sind was isolated.

Mustafa was aware that the MRD movement could not survive without the wholehearted participation of his home province, and he decided that action was necessary to revitalize Punjabi support. He chose seven exiles who had been tried in absentia by military courts, and sent them to Pakistan from London on 5 September. But in his somewhat garbled official announcement he declared that, as a gesture of defiance, *nine* valiant People's Party workers were on their way home to court arrest as a contribution to the MRD movement. The fact that the actual number was seven, rather than nine, took on aspects of black comedy.

The seven spent most of their flight spouting slogans in favour of democracy and its figurehead, Mustafa Khar – much to the annoyance of other, disinterested passengers. When the aircraft landed in Karachi, it was ordered to taxi to a position a great distance from the terminal, where it was surrounded by commandos and armoured cars. The seven returning exiles disembarked into the hands of the police, who immediately wanted to know where the other two were. Choudhry Hanif (a Member of Parliament and a follower from the early days when Mustafa took on Bhutto) and Sajid tried to convince the authorities that only seven men had arrived. But the head of the police party was under instructions to bring back nine people from the plane. He arrested the apolitical brother of one of the group, as well as an innocent boy who was returning from a visit to his aunt in London and was, in fact, a Zia supporter. All nine were trucked off to the Ohjri prison camp. (The two innocent boys spent twenty-two months in gaol, a longer term than any of the others.)

Choudhry Hanif later described for us his cell at the Ohjri prison camp as 'worse than any conception of hell we may have in our mind . . .'

Each of the seven felt betrayed by Mustafa and cursed him for his callousness. Each had a common prayer; they pleaded for death.

If he was to finance a complete revolution, Mustafa needed much more money than was available through his early contacts, and his attention centred upon Ali Mehmood, an expatriate Pakistani who had made a fortune on construction contracts in Abu Dhabi and Kuwaiti oil. They discussed a political deal whereby Ali Mehmood might become Finance Minister in the new government in return for bankrolling the rebellion.

This relationship precipitated another move as we joined Ali and his vivacious wife Billo at 'Ayott Place', their mansion in Welwyn Garden City. The intrigue deepened.

Benazir Bhutto arrived in London, having finally been freed from imprisonment by Zia. An adoring crowd of exiled Pakistanis met her at the airport, with Mustafa at the forefront. She was now the focal point of the struggle to restore democracy in Pakistan, but her task was enormous. She was young and inexperienced; her father had been hanged; she had spent three years under arrest. Everyone expected great things from her, but no-one was willing to give her time to learn her political craft.

The joy of reunion was short-lived. Mustafa had reservations about Benazir's youth. He still remembered her as a child whom he had called 'Pinkie'; she had called him 'uncle'. For her part, Benazir felt more comfortable with a younger generation of politicians and distanced herself from her father's contemporaries. Her young 'kitchen cabinet' told her not to trust people like Mustafa, who were ambitious and had pretensions of leading the party. They reminded her that Mustafa had left the country under suspicious circumstances.

On a personal level, Benazir was wonderful. She tried to extend a hand of friendship to me, but Mustafa would not allow me to respond. 'I don't know how long my own relationship with her will last,' he explained. 'You are the sort of person who will become her friend. You will complicate matters between us. Your petty friendships and my politics cannot mix.'

One day I happened to be alone in Ali and Billo's fabulous Kensington apartment where they had their work base when a young man of about twenty-five came to call; he was looking for Mustafa. I told him that Mustafa would not be back for some time but he insisted on waiting. I disliked him instantly. He was insolent and coarse, and behaved – unlike anyone else dared – as though he was here as a favour to Mustafa. When Mustafa returned home, he talked privately to the young man for about an hour. Then he came into my room and asked me for £200. I handed him the money, but I was surprised – it was not Mustafa's nature to hand over such sums idly to distressed or friendless party workers – and I questioned him. 'The poor kid has come all the way from my home district to see me,' Mustafa explained. 'I want to help him.'

Ten days later I received a frantic phone call from the same young man; he said that British authorities had arrested him at the airport for attempting to smuggle heroin into the country 'in his socks'. I jotted down this disturbing message and gave it to Mustafa as soon as he came home. He was furious at me for speaking to the man and worried that I might have said something stupid to implicate him. 'You should have just said that you did not know who he was,' Mustafa shouted. 'You talk too much.'

'I thought that you would have wanted to help,' I said, confused. Only two weeks earlier Mustafa had shown compassion for the boy. 'How was I to guess that you wouldn't want to know him any longer – especially when he's in trouble? Maybe you *can* help?'

Mustafa grew pensive, then picked up the phone. He spoke to a police officer and asked what the problem was. They allowed him to talk to the boy and he asked him angrily, 'Why did you do this silly thing? Look at the mess you've made.' He slammed the phone down and began to pace the room.

Illegal heroin is plentiful in Pakistan. Fields of poppies grow in abundance in the northern region; smuggling occurs in even the highest circles. I found myself wondering how much heroin £300 would buy in Pakistan. I felt very uncomfortable with the whole business.

When the case went to court, it made headlines. Mustafa was called to testify. He swore under oath that he knew that the boy was from Muzaffargarh, but maintained that this was the extent of his knowledge concerning the case. The young man testified that he and some of his friends in Pakistan had been falsely implicated in an act of sabotage – an attempt to derail a train. He said that Pakistani authorities promised to release his friends if he would carry heroin to London and plant it inside Mustafa Khar's house. 'I was carrying the heroin under duress,' he claimed. 'The martial law regime wanted me to plant it in Mr Khar's house to implicate him in a smuggling rap.' To me, the story sounded contrived and rehearsed; in fact, it was just the sort of fantasy that Mustafa might conjure up to wriggle out of a tight spot. But it made good copy, and it was widely reported both in Britain and Pakistan. Mustafa's reputation rose – he was now deemed important enough to be the target of an international scam. It proved his nuisance value as a critic of Zia's regime.

The young man was sentenced to five years in prison.

From his cell he plagued us with letters, begging Mustafa to contact his family in Pakistan, to send them money, to intercede for his release. Mustafa threw the letters into the dustbin without even reading them.

Meanwhile, planning for the coup escalated. Joshi arranged for the necessary arms to be stored in an Indian village near the Pakistani border. Mustafa now sought someone who could smuggle them across. Indian border guards would not present a problem, thanks to Joshi, but the rebels needed a trustworthy person who was familiar enough with the terrain so that he could slip past the Pakistani checkpoints.

A rupee note was torn in half. The Indian contact was given one half; in order to take delivery of the arms, the smuggler had to produce the matching half. To me, it all seemed like a scene from a cheap thriller.

Mustafa settled upon Seth Abid for this critical role and instructed me to telephone him. I did not think of disobeying, of course, but I was consciously perturbed. Seth Abid, as I have said, was very close to one of Zia's Cabinet ministers. He had first come into the limelight in the mid Sixties as an important member of an international network of smugglers. In Pakistan he is a big name in the underworld. He is also known to have assisted in the development of Pakistan's 'modest' nuclear programme. I was abetting treason. If Seth Abid's telephone was monitored – and this seemed a very likely possibility – it would be my voice on the tape played at intelligence briefings. Mustafa was hiding behind my skirts!

When Seth Abid picked up the phone, I introduced myself. He responded with a polite salutation. I got straight to the point: 'My husband wants you to come to London. We have important work for you. We need your assistance for something I cannot speak to you about on the telephone.'

The man stammered a response. 'I . . . I don't think I can . . . can . . . talk to him,' he said. 'I don't think I

. . . I should. I'm living in Pakistan. Please think of my family. Please understand.' He paused, then he suggested, 'Listen . . . er . . . call me back . . . on the same number in half an hour.'

I told Mustafa that Seth Abid was too nervous to help and that I was convinced that his phone was tapped. Nevertheless, he ordered me to call back as instructed.

During the second conversation, Seth Abid was very composed and spoke freely. He drew me out, and made me repeat my statements clearly. 'Mustafa wants you to come and see him,' I said.

'Oh, Mustafa wants me to come and see him?'

'It's very urgent.'

'It's urgent? Is it something to do with politics? Does he want to discuss some plans with me? OK, I'll let you know when I can come.' I could almost hear the tape reels whirring.

After the call, I conveyed my new apprehensions to Ali, Billo and Mustafa. 'The man is taping the call,' I said. 'He cannot be trusted. His attitude has changed in half an hour. Why did he become so relaxed? I can smell a rat, even at this distance.'

Mustafa stared at me irritably and put my reaction down to an attack of feminine nerves. 'Stop hallucinating,' he warned. 'Don't interfere in matters you don't understand.' The moment we were alone he abused me for making the Mehmoods nervous. 'If they back out, everything will go to the dogs. My hard work will have been for naught because of your "thinking".' The final word was laced with sarcasm.

Suddenly we came into a great sum of money; I never found out how much it was, nor where it came from. We started looking for a house to buy, and Mustafa was quite willing to defer to my judgement on this point. His only condition was that it be somewhere in the country; he hated London's polluted atmosphere and congestion. We found a beautiful home in Haslemere, West Sussex, on eleven acres, at the very headwaters of the river Whey. The home boasted a bit of history. Apparently Britain's first rhododendrons were planted in these gardens. Dai Ayesha was captivated by the beauty of the location. Upon laying eyes on it, she remarked, 'This is just like Kot Addu!' Mustafa and I laughed, for these lush, rolling hills were nothing like the dry wastelands of his home village. I realized, then, how homesick Dai was.

Mustafa had owned property before, and he always made sure that it was solely in his name. He told me quite blatantly that he did so because he was never sure how long his marriage was going to last. But this time, he insisted that our new house be titled as joint property, explaining to me, 'I want you to know that I will never leave you. You are the only woman I can think of as a wife. I want you to feel completely secure.'

Was the nightmare turning into a dream? I owned a home: at last, a measure of security!

I had a flair for interior design. I had all the windows moved so that, from every room, we had a view of the undulating lawns, the quiet pond and the bubbling stream; the sensation was that of sitting out in the landscaped garden. I decorated the entire house in different textures of pale beige – with the garden as the only colour. I bought old carved pieces to set off the contemporary furniture.

We had to build an ugly chicken coop, and I had this constructed behind the camouflage of a large tree. In the morning, the children walked up the hill to gather free-range eggs.

Canada geese lived on our pond and provided comic relief. Every day about 10 a.m. they made their way up the hill, where they sat in the sun for precisely one hour. In the evening they marched in single file and sat on our front lawn until 6 o'clock – I could set my watch by them – when they waddled up to our front door and honked until we responded with food.

We entertained often, hosting barbecues for as many

as one hundred guests. Thank God, we had another servant now. Farid, related to Dai Ayesha, was our cook and chauffeur. We put up marquees outside and huge coal pits where the food was cooked. Mustafa had a reputation as a great chef and people came in droves to sample his delicacies.

On these occasions Mustafa brought home as many as fifty live roasting chickens and slaughtered them one by one. Reciting the *Kalima* to render the bird kosher, he cut a neck artery and flung the victim away from him. The chicken jumped about in agony and quivered horribly before it died. The children and I pleaded with Mustafa not to let the birds suffer, but he laughed and said that the last mortal tremor of the chicken was an indication of the soul leaving its body. When he was finished, the patio resembled a slaughterhouse. We raced against the clock to clean up the mess while he cut and cooked before the guests arrived. By then, we were all exhausted.

Sometimes he would bring home a goat and slaughter it himself. The children and I suffered its pain as we heard it bleat in fear for what seemed an age before silence confirmed that the deed was done.

Mustafa relaxed slightly in this idyllic setting, but he still lost his temper frequently. He was unable to control his tongue, but he tried to stop short of hitting me. Instead, he increasingly turned his fists upon poor Dai Ayesha. She was his serf; it was her lot to be pummelled. I felt sorry for her, because I knew that she was a surrogate. On one occasion I heard her praying to Jesus, begging Him to loosen the bonds of her servitude or, at the very least, arrange for her return to Pakistan. I asked incredulously, 'Dai, have you become a Christian?'

'No,' she replied, 'but I am willing to try anything.'

Mustafa loved the open countryside, for it reminded him of the wilds of Pakistan. He rose at 5 a.m. daily and began his two-hour regimen of yoga exercises on the veranda. Gradually he would move to a spot in the gardens or at the top of the hill. Even when it was snowing he found a covered area, somewhere outside, to exercise.

We were never allowed to keep the central heating on at night, and the bedroom windows remained open even when the outside temperature was below freezing. I kept myself warm with a hotwater bottle and a goose-down coverlet.

In matters of physical health, I have never known a more self-disciplined person than Mustafa. He bathed in freezing tap water because he believed that it was excellent for blood circulation and for thwarting the ageing process. His diet was devoid of *any* sugar, starch, or unnecessary calories. He consumed much yogurt and skimmed milk. Wild honey manufactured by the 'small' bee was flown from the Frontier Province in Pakistan. Brown husks of wheat were ground in his presence at a mill in Haslemere. There were no biscuits, no carbonated drinks.

Mustafa bought two dogs, an English springer spaniel and a Labrador retriever, whom we called Bruno. He would not allow the dogs inside the house because they were 'unclean', so they took up residence in our garage. I worried about them in the middle of the night, and often walked out to cover them with an old rug. Eventually I had a kennel built for them. I always felt as if they had been sold off to bad foster parents and were unused to the harsh nature of their new lives.

Whenever she was assigned the distasteful task of caring for the dogs, Dai Ayesha lightened her load by carrying on extended conversations with the animals. I overheard her one day imploring, 'Bruno, I'm looking after you. You pray to God that He will get me out of here, get me home to Pakistan. God will listen to you, because you are *bezuban*.' Literally, the word means 'without a tongue'; figuratively, it designates those most helpless forms of life (like animals and children) to whom Allah must surely respond. I was saddened. By this time in her life, Dai had spent nearly eighteen years in Mustafa's service, as nanny to Bilal, Amna and my own three children. She cleaned the house, washed the dishes and cared for the children. She was beaten for the slightest error and abused for the most minor of mistakes. After years of violence, abuse and fear, her once-beautiful skin had lost its glow. Although she remained slim due to overwork, she was fatigued and her eyes filled with tears at the slightest mention or remembrance of her country. Dai's mind had died long before mine and, even as I was trying to recover, I could sense that she was giving up.

We realized that we had misnamed the dog when Bruno gave birth to a single puppy. I called him Blot, because that was what he appeared to be on the land-scape. I tried to keep him in a basket in the entrance hall, but Mustafa turned him out. Blot wandered freely about the estate. Inevitably, he strayed on to the road, was brushed by a car and came home limping. Mustafa wanted to put him to sleep, but the children and I begged permission to take him to a vet for surgery. Mustafa wanted perfection; he was not interested in a damaged dog, so he neglected Blot, until we decided that we must give him away.

Mustafa looked bemused whenever he saw me worry over any animal. He admitted to me that it had never occurred to him to show compassion for pets; to him, a dog was a purely functional creature who was required to respond to his master's commands with complete loyalty. That sounded familiar.

He told me of an incident from his past. He was a young man, on a partridge shoot, when his retriever defied him. Instead of bringing the prey back to the feet of his master, the dog took off with the dead bird hanging limply in his jaws. Shaking with fury, Mustafa sent his henchmen after the dog with the instructions, 'Find him and bring him to the village.' They captured the dog after a long chase. He was panting heavily, and his eyes showed fear of pending terror. As the men dragged the poor beast toward Mustafa, the dog splayed out his legs, desperately trying to resist. Mustafa directed his men to tie the dog's legs together; then, he ordered them to beat the dog with bamboo staffs. The animal's howls tore the silence around Kot Addu. His body writhed in agony. Still, the men bent to their task, breaking countless staffs across the poor dog's back. They stopped only after the dog's eyes clouded over, and he fainted. At that point, Mustafa said, he felt instantly sorry for the beast. He ordered his men to take the dog away, and walked off, overcome by guilt.

The story shocked me. I could not believe that Mustafa's irrational violence could be directed so blindly toward a helpless animal who could offer no defence or excuse – or apology. But to Mustafa the issue was clear: if a dog begins to stir from the dust, rebellion is in the air. He had to crush it immediately.

I suffered repeated nightmares about the dog, and I finally spoke to Mustafa about them. I said, 'You know, I think that all your difficulties are due to what you did to that dog. I dreamed last night that the dog had cursed you. Imagine – you may carry a dog's curse. What could be more terrible?'

Surprisingly, my speculation worried him greatly. He confessed to me, 'When I sit on my prayer mat I think of that dog. I lift up my palms and pray to God to grant me respite. I end up begging for a dog's forgiveness.'

Initially, Mustafa had been willing to give Benazir Bhutto, who was now twenty-nine, a chance to take over leadership of the exile community. He was quite prepared to play the role of senior statesman. But, each time he returned from a Central Committee meeting he seemed more disillusioned. He reminisced about the old days, when Bhutto ran forceful meetings that addressed issues squarely and resulted in firm plans of action. Benazir's meetings, he said, were uninspired, and resulted in only a generalized call for 'strengthened agitation' against Zia.

Finally he decided to take her on. The crucial issue was the party's stance regarding Al-Zulfikar. Mustafa's contention was that the radical, terrorist wing was a liability. He wanted the party to dissociate itself from Mir's group. He warned that the Bhutto boys were indulging in romantic adventurism that merely strengthened Zia's hand.

Benazir's reaction was that of a sister rather than co-chairman of the party. She declared that she would not have her brothers discussed 'in such a derogatory manner'.

Mustafa retaliated: 'You have to discuss this issue. It has a serious bearing on our party. We must announce that we have nothing to do with terrorism.'

Benazir burst into tears and fled from the room.

Others persuaded Mustafa to go after her, to console her. He found her crying alone in a bedroom. She said, 'You people keep pushing me into a corner. I don't know who to trust and who not to trust. I don't know how to deal with all of this.'

'This is politics,' Mustafa explained calmly. 'You must understand. You'll come across a lot of people who won't agree with you. You can't throw a tantrum every time. You must pull yourself up and be stronger.'

Seth Abid arrived in London and received a warm welcome from Mustafa and his fellow plotters. He listened to the details of the planned coup and agreed to play his designated part. He gave his word that, on the specified date, he would deliver the arms to an empty house in Lahore. Upon Mustafa's instructions, I gave him the smuggler's half of the torn rupee note.

As D-Day approached, I was drawn completely into the conspiracy, unaware of how thoroughly I was being implicated. I was in touch with the 'boys' via telephone, and became quite adept at speaking in cryptic tones. At night I tossed and turned from the suspense, but Mustafa slept soundly, dreaming of his great victory.

Much of Mustafa's day was spent in conference, clarifying details, plugging holes. The planners decided that it was imperative to entice at least one senior military official into the plot. There were a number of known sympathizers among the top brass, and the decision was made to try to cultivate them. The choice narrowed to a Bhutto admirer. A careful contact was made and, according to Mustafa, the general was 'in'. The Indians were elated that they had been able to penetrate the Pakistani army at the higher echelons and Mustafa prophesied, 'I think the cake is about to bake.'

The conspiracy was so high-powered and serious that there was an atmosphere of excitement. Ali and Billo, anxious to play some role in their country's politics, found an opportunity to become part of a revolution against martial law. Our adrenalin level remained high throughout the planning period, and the state of excitement intensified in 'Ayott Place' as the final, finishing touches were completed.

I, at least, had some dormant apprehensions, based on my dealings with Mustafa, but Ali and Billo were completely mesmerized. For them, Mustafa was undefeatable. His discipline and shrewdness added to perseverance and practical action swept them off their feet into the maelstrom of his mad, reckless idea.

Then, at last, Seth Abid informed us that the 'parcels' were in place.

The 'boys' were told to drive to the mall in Lahore, opposite the Inter-Continental Hotel, where a man would give them a slip of paper bearing the address of the safe house where Seth Abid had stashed the weapons. At 7.30 p.m. on 2 January 1987 they were to claim the armaments that would restore democracy to Pakistan. Then they were to call us.

On the appointed night, the conspirators gathered in Ali's London apartment to monitor developments via long-distance. By Pakistan Standard Time, it was past 9 p.m. when the perspiration broke out on Mustafa's brow. He began to pace the expensive rugs. The silence of the phone mocked us. I made a fresh pot of coffee as I prayed, fighting against the images that forced themselves into my mind.

By 10.30 – three hours after the scheduled time of the pick-up – Mustafa instructed me to call the home of Major Aftab – one of the 'boys'. His wife answered and reported in a cold and unnatural voice, 'He's not here. Please don't ring us up.'

I fumbled through my book for the numbers of the others. What had happened? I wondered. I prayed: Please God, help them.

I dialled several numbers before I received another answer. This was the wife of Squadron Leader Tahir. She was sobbing. In a voice full of anguish, she whispered across the continents, 'The house is full of army personnel. They're taking my father-in-law and my brother-in-law away. They're taking my brothers, too. They've ransacked the house. I don't know what to do.'

As I lowered the phone, all I saw in front of me were the sullen and solemn faces of would-be heroes. Each of them dropped his eyes, refusing to meet one another's gaze.

I dialled Major Bokhari's home. His wife said, 'I can't speak now. There are too many people around.' The phone clicked dead.

I could feel the terror in the hearts of the 'boys' as well as the innocent family members. I was angered that we had exposed them to such dangers. What had gone wrong? Who was at fault? Something told me that Seth Abid had betrayed us, and I felt that Mustafa was to blame for ignoring my intuition.

Suddenly the phone rang, causing every one of us to jump. I grabbed for it, and heard the voice of Seth Abid on the other end. He was actually crying. 'I've just been watching TV,' he said. 'On the nine o'clock news they've announced that a raid was conducted, on a tip-off. Crates of smuggled gold have been found. What should I do now? They'll implicate me.'

'Gold?' I asked incredulously. 'What gold? Where are the arms?'

'They don't want to disclose that an arms cache has been found. They don't want the people of Pakistan to know that there was an attempted coup from within the army. They don't want the public to know that the military was involved in an abortive attempt to smuggle in arms. Do you understand? The gold story is a smokescreen. I don't know how all this happened. What will happen to my family? Should I cross the border to India? Can Mustafa arrange for my asylum?'

I felt sick. I knew that the man was lying.

We learned the details later. The 'boys' had driven in jeeps to the house, where they found two rooms full of crates, containing the promised arms. As they loaded the *matériel* into the jeeps, one of them said, 'It serves the damn generals right. We'll put this country back on its rails.'

They prepared to drive away. Keys turned in the ignitions. The jeeps were jammed into gear but as they hurtled forward, the 'boys' suddenly found themselves surrounded. The ambushers opened fire. The 'boys' returned fire, but all were wounded and captured.

They were sent to top-security prisons, implicated not only for their roles in the attempted coup, but accused of acts of treason by negotiating an arms deal with Pakistan's arch enemy India. Their wives were held incommunicado. Their male relatives were arrested and tortured. The 'boys' themselves were denied an open trial and threatened with a firing squad. Behind the glitter of gold was a story of broken homes and broken men.

Publicly the government held to its story that it had broken a gold-smuggling scheme, but in a move of supreme irony compensation was arranged for Seth

Abid's act of 'patriotism' in tipping them off to the plot. Since the 1960s, a huge quantity of gold that he had smuggled into the country had been held by customs officials. This was now returned to him as a result of a 'legal technicality'.

At the prison camp in Ojhri, the 'boys' underwent constant torture. They were made to strip naked and lie on their stomachs. Then a steel roller was crushed against their thighs until the skin broke open. They were hung upside down and beaten.

The seven Punjabis whom Mustafa had sent off to prison four months earlier also came under the cross-fire, subjected to increased torture and intimidation. Choudhry Hanif was moved to the Inter Service Intelligence prison, into a dingy cell without ventilation. A single naked bulb remained lit twenty-four hours a day. He slept on a lice-infested mattress, with a foul-smelling sheet as a cover. His toilet was a tin cup. He was not allowed to bathe or shave. He endured continuous grilling sessions and was made to listen to my voice on tape. He told me later: 'They say that a day spent here is equal to a year spent at the dreaded Lahore Fort dungeons or the top-security prison in Attock. A year there is equated with twenty years in an ordinary prison.' He also reported: 'Every conversation you had with the "boys", their wives and Seth Abid was recorded. They had access to all the information down to the torn rupee note.'

Mustafa showed little concern for the fate of the 'boys', or the seven former exiles whom he had once lauded as patriots. He discarded them as he had the dogs and the canaries. What gnawed at him was that he had failed. Had he succeeded, he would have been hailed as a champion of democracy in Pakistan, but failure pinned the medal of treason to his chest. He was afraid for his life, but he was even more concerned that he would be ostracized by his allies. He was now a high-risk ex-patriate and extremely worried about the reaction of the Indian government.

He met up with Joshi, and returned flustered and disturbed.

But one could not keep Mustafa Khar down for long. He soon visited India again, for a private audience with Indira Gandhi, and he returned with renewed fire in his eyes. 'She said I was a great patriot,' he beamed. The failed plot had, of course, greatly increased tension between Zia's Pakistan and the Indian government, and Mustafa had worried that India would back off. But he was pleased that Indira Gandhi had reaffirmed her belief in the necessity of destroying Pakistan's army. Mustafa prophesied, 'A war is necessary to crush the people's enemy once and for all.' He said that it would be the miracle that we were praying for.

Very privately, I disagreed. I remembered Indira Gandhi as the woman who had hailed the defeat of the Pakistani army in 1971 as 'the end of a thousand years of slavery', implying that Muslims had enslaved the people of India. At the moment, she was in danger in her own country for ordering an attack on the Golden Temple of the Sikhs, which had resulted in the death of their leader. Sikh separatists had vowed revenge, and there were rumours that some of them were being trained in Pakistani camps. I feared Indira's secularism, and I saw her as an opportunist; she would use hatred of Zia's Pakistan to unite her countrymen.

To me, it all sounded like another example of the Indira Doctrine, which postulated that India was the policeman of South Asia, with some sort of portfolio to interfere in the domestic affairs of its neighbours.

War clouds suddenly appeared over the sub-continent. Everyone spoke about the impending conflagration.

On 31 October 1984, Mustafa was out jogging; I was watching the morning news on television when I heard the report that Indira Gandhi had been gunned down by her own guards. When Mustafa returned to the house and I broke the news, he slumped on to the sofa. He cradled his head in his hands and moaned, 'Oh, God!'

10

Once a month Mustafa coloured his hair, glossing over his natural grey with black dye. One evening he was in the bathroom performing this ritual as we prepared for the arrival of dinner guests. I argued with him about this unnecessary vanity. It seemed cheap to me. 'You don't need to do this,' I reasoned. 'Grey hair looks distinguished on a man of your position.'

'I will only stop colouring my hair if you agree not to colour yours,' he retorted smugly. I could not accept this trade-off. Living with Mustafa, I knew that I would be silver-haired by the time I was thirty. 'And besides,' he added, 'it is *sunat*.' This was the term denoting that whatever the Prophet did, you should follow. Mustafa reminded me that the Prophet had dictated that old age should be combated in every way; it helps you to be more energetic. 'The Prophet says you should look as young as possible for as long as possible,' he lectured.

I thought: Here is another example of Mustafa's convenient use of Islam. But his reliance upon Islamic law and custom was highly selective. So I shrugged it off and asked him at least not to dry his head with my white towels. I tossed a coloured towel toward him. He looked at me with disdain, pointedly picked up a white towel and ran it through his hair.

'Mustafa, you're doing this deliberately,' I accused.

'You're looking for a fight,' he warned. 'We're expecting guests. Don't upset me.'

I was too angry to heed the clear warning. I snapped, 'Don't use my white—'

He picked up a jug that happened to be within reach

and flung it at me, hitting me on the shoulder. I ran from the bathroom, slammed the door and locked him inside.

Mustafa banged on the door and screamed, 'I'll kill you!'

I ignored him and went downstairs to answer the doorbell and greet our guests. When they asked where Mustafa was, I muttered a vague excuse; I could hardly tell them that the Lion of the Punjab was locked inside the bathroom!

I allowed twenty minutes to pass before I returned upstairs. Through the bathroom door I said, 'If you can only understand once and for all that I am not here to take your nonsense, I'll let you out.'

'All right, let me out,' he said. His tone was quiet and controlled. I released him, and as he scurried out he growled with simmering fury, 'Let these people leave. I'll teach you a lesson.'

That evening, we presented the image of an exceptionally happy couple. Our guests did not know that as Mustafa carved the roast, he was contemplating murder.

The moment that our friends left, Mustafa headed upstairs and ordered me to follow. I had no intention of going willingly to my punishment, so I slipped into a side room and locked the door behind me.

Ten minutes passed before he came looking for me. 'Tehmina, open the door now,' he ordered. 'Your attitude is becoming unacceptable. I shall fix you.'

'I am not mad,' I replied. 'I know there's a sick, insane animal outside. Do you really expect me to come out and hand myself over?'

Back and forth, through the protective cover of the door, we exchanged views on women's rights. He tried to provoke me, but my answers remained calm and reasonable as I took the opportunity to argue my points. After a time, Mustafa succumbed to the absurdity of the situation and burst out laughing. His temper had evaporated.

A barely perceptible change was taking place: Mustafa was adjusting to me. He began to converse with me almost as if I were an equal. He lectured me on politics, and was pleased to rediscover that I was not only truly fascinated with the subject, but quite willing to accept his opinions.

He gave me an increasing measure of freedom. Often, on his way to a meeting, he dropped me off at Harrods, and allowed me to roam the department store until his return. I took special interest in browsing the book department and brought back material that I felt Mustafa should read. I knew his interests, and I wanted him to absorb as much knowledge as possible during this period of exile – which we both, despite the turmoil, began to regard as a time of meditation and preparation. He read a hundred pages a day, religiously. He learned the delicate, painful task of self-criticism. With a broader horizon, he probed into the causes of Pakistan's prevailing political crisis.

The key to my emotional survival was that I was able to detach my personal life from my political one. Among our friends and allies, Mustafa always knew that I would defend his political causes, but now he realized that I truly believed in them. I learned to argue the issues with the same conviction and vigour as my husband. Our friends noted my transformation from a subdued house-wife to a spirited conversationalist. Even so, I often began my sentences with the phrase 'Mustafa said'; I was his political shadow.

Nevertheless, his compulsions still overpowered him on occasion. Once, as he waited for me in the car, I was delayed because of a telephone call from his travel agent. By the time I arrived at the car, he exploded, furious to be kept waiting by a 'wife'. 'Calm down,' I lectured. 'It's not the end of the world.' He backhanded me across the face, raising an instant black eye. Our errand was called off.

As usual, we had guests due that evening, and Mustafa

instructed me to wear dark glasses in an attempt to hide the bruise. I found this embarrassing. When someone asked why I was wearing glasses, I simply avoided an answer. Mustafa was nervous, knowing that he could no longer predict my behaviour, and his anxiety was well founded. At dinner I coolly removed my dark glasses, exposing my husband's fury. Someone asked what happened and I replied stoically, 'Mustafa hit me.'

Wine glasses were placed quietly on the table. Throats cleared. Bottoms shifted uncomfortably on our dining-room chairs. Mustafa offered defences: I was unreasonable and insolent; I was not co-operative during these difficult times. But his words did not wash.

Later, in our bedroom, my insolence was punished with yet another sharp slap. He called me an exhibitionist, a woman without shame.

I agreed that I was not ashamed and pointed out, 'It's *you* who've been humiliated tonight, not me. You're angry because I caused you shame. Next time, before you do something you'll be ashamed of later, make sure that you can cope with the humiliation. I'm not going to protect you any more. If my face is bruised and battered, I shan't hide it. I want people to see me as I am. I don't want to be a hypocrite.'

He listened to my words in silence. His pursed lips seemed to say, 'Time will tell'.

Mother surprised me with a telephone call. She wanted to see me urgently. I had mixed feelings about her sudden reappearance in my life after several years, but Mustafa agreed that I should go to see her. Later that day, as I waited at the door of my parents' home, I stepped back for a moment to visualize how the house must have looked at Zarmina's marriage. My eyes filled with tears. I did not feel a part of my family any more.

Adila greeted me at the door with an embrace. With her own tears running down her cheeks, she told me that she was the reason that our mother had asked me to visit. Adila said that her long-guilty conscience had produced chronic insomnia. She was now receiving marriage proposals, but she could not accept any one of them until I forgave her. 'God will never forgive me, till you do,' she wailed. 'I know that I can never be happily married because of the pain I caused you. Fate will extract its revenge from me. Please forgive me – I beg you.' When she began to blame Mustafa for her immorality, I cut her short.

'Never speak ill of my husband in front of me,' I commanded. 'If you have something to say about your own behaviour, I shall listen and forgive. Leave him out of it.' With a start, I realized that I was hearing Mother's voice coming from my own mouth; she always defended Father like this. However, in both cases it had more to do with ego than with respect for the man.

By the end of the visit I had truly forgiven Adila. It was a luxury that I could afford, now that I felt more in control of my own marriage.

I was mentally exhausted by the time I returned home. I related my conversation with Adila to Mustafa and saw happiness appear on his face. I told myself with satisfaction: The Adila chapter is closed for ever.

My parents now wanted the children and me to visit as often as possible, but they declared that they did not want Mustafa's shadow to fall upon their doorstep. Mustafa had to drive me to their home and return at an appointed hour, to wait outside in the car. I could expect to find him in a grouchy mood, but we both knew that the family snub was highly deserved.

The tension built slowly. The carefully constructed *détente* between Mustafa and me – fragile at best – degenerated into a cold war. I dreaded the resumption of hostilities and so, for the sake of harmony, began to evade visits to my parents. My priorities were clear. I had to keep my marriage together for the sake of my children and myself. I had invested too much pain and compromise in this relationship to let it go now.

Mustafa and I went to Wellington Hospital, to visit Shireen Jatoi, the daughter of Mustafa's closest friend and political ally. She was in the early stages of labour. Shireen's mother embraced me and told Mustafa, 'I think that for the first time you've found yourself a really good wife. I hope you will appreciate her.'

Grasping my hand, Mustafa declared in a tone of extreme sincerity, 'I could not think of living without her. You can't imagine what she means to me or how good she has been for me.'

Mustafa left me at the hospital. That afternoon Shireen asked for something from my home, so I called to speak to a servant. I tried several times but the line was busy, and I gave up in frustration.

Shireen went into the final stages of labour at about 6 p.m. By then, Mustafa was back with us in Shireen's hospital room, where many of her friends and relatives had gathered. Mother had left on a trip to America and assigned me the task of checking on Adila. My younger sister was due home from boarding school and, within a few days, was to join Mother in Boston. I called my parents' home to assure myself that Adila had arrived safely. She answered the phone herself, and immediately disclosed, 'Tehmina, your husband has been on the phone to me all afternoon.' My heart skipped. I shot a freezing glance across the room at Mustafa, as Adila continued, 'He's been begging to see me. He keeps telling me that I'll never meet another man like him. He insists that nobody can make me forget him, that I should not think of marrying any of my suitors – they would be inadequate.'

Mustafa could not hear these words, but he could see the pain in my face. His own complexion grew deep red. Guilt was inscribed on his features.

Adila maintained that she was no longer interested in Mustafa and I believed her. She had many eligible young men pursuing her. Her voice held a cutting edge when she said, 'I told him that Tehmina always maintains that you love her. He said that you're very foolish. "If I say she has beautiful eyes, she thinks I love her." He pleaded with me to see him. He said that he would drive down and park outside our gate. He just wanted a glimpse of me. He's obsessed with me. He kept telling me that he would die without me. I knew you wouldn't believe me, so I have witnesses. My friend Claudia is here. She heard our conversation on the extension. So did our cook Rehman. Ask them.'

I put the phone down and realized that I had gone into shock. I had reconstructed myself for him to demolish once more.

As if to mock my pain, the waiting room erupted with jubilation at the news that Shireen had given birth to a son.

I burst into tears.

Shireen's mother hugged me and asked what was wrong. I could not allow my misery to dilute this family's moment of joy, so I did my best to suppress hysteria. I mumbled tearful excuses and made an exit.

Mustafa followed me out, like a whipped puppy. We drove home in total silence.

At home, in our bedroom, he donned his most innocent tone and asked, 'What happened? Please tell me. What's wrong? Tehmina, I beg you.' He began to babble, and as his words rushed out, he unwittingly confirmed my sister's report. 'Is it Adila?' he asked. 'My God! that mad girl. Has she said something? Don't believe her – she just makes these things up to upset and torture you. She hates you. She's trying to ruin our marriage. She's not in love with me; she wants to punish you. She wants our marriage to break to fulfil her own perverse desires, to win. Please don't believe her. She did say something, didn't she? What did she say? Tell me.'

I remained silent, and told Mustafa I wanted to be alone. He left the room but insisted that I leave a door open. I wanted oblivion. I turned out the lights and crouched in a corner of the room. I wanted to crawl into my mother's womb. Contorting my body into the foetal position, I wept.

By morning I was calm, and this made Mustafa more nervous. I told him, simply and with finality, that I was leaving.

'Where will you go, Tehmina?' he taunted. 'To your father's? Your father won't throw a bone to you.'

My mind raced. I suddenly realized that I had to do this with great caution. I *was* going to leave. I *had* to. But if Mustafa truly believed that I had decided to divorce him, he would lock me up or take my children away – or both. Outwardly I relented, lulling his fears with silence.

He apologized for what he had said about my father. He tried to embrace me, but my revulsion showed through.

'Tehmina, you are a complete woman,' he said. 'You are exceptional. You have endurance that would outstrip the patience of women from my village. You have tolerated so much. You have coped with so much dignity. You have suffered in silence. You have protected my reputation. You have been a wonderful mother. I have broken this home so often, and you have always reconstructed it. How can you even imagine that I would give you up for that little slut?'

With feigned sincerity I told him that I was forgiving him for the last time. 'Don't disturb my life again,' I warned. 'I managed to cope the last time. You took me on a conducted tour of hell. This time I do not have the energy or the will to walk down the corridors of your deceit.'

Mustafa believed my words. He swore on the Koran that he would never betray me again. He left for business in London, fully reassured.

The moment he was gone, I called for a cab and began to pack my bags. Dai Ayesha dissolved into hysterics, truly fearing for her life. I called my brother Asim and informed him of my intention to leave Mustafa. He was very understanding and booked a hotel suite for me.

When the cab arrived, I walked out of the house with my three children and my bags. I did not look back.

Asim had a table prepared in my hotel suite, laid out with caviar and champagne to celebrate my release. 'You've made a good decision,' he proclaimed. 'I want this to be the first day of the rest of your life. You must now be happy. Forget that man!' He turned to my children and announced, 'From today, I am your father.' He gave me £2,000 in cash. 'I'm arranging for you to go to Spain,' he said. 'You need a holiday.'

After we celebrated, Asim left us alone. The children and I fell into a peaceful sleep.

When I awoke, I realized that in my haste to leave I had forgotten our passports. Quickly I called the house and spoke with Dai Ayesha about the passports. Then I asked where Mustafa was. She said that he was doing his yoga. It upset me to realize that he was not even bothered enough to break his routine.

Mustafa came on the line, and I informed him that I had left for good.

He replied calmly, 'Good. I hope you make a good life for yourself.'

I was confused by his reaction. Had it been that simple to leave him?

The children and I spent a week in London. For the first time in seven years, I visited a hairdresser. I shopped for the children and for myself. I was ecstatic to be among normal people.

I called a lawyer and asked him to draw up divorce papers. In the course of this task, he found it necessary to phone Mustafa to discuss the case. He reported back to me that Mustafa had stonewalled, arguing that we could work out our differences without him. I warned

221

the lawyer that I dared not see Mustafa; he would do his best to persuade me to return, and I did not yet feel strong enough to rebut him. I was afraid of my programmed reaction to his practised routine of guilt and reformation. I told the lawyer to inform Mustafa that he could only make contact with me through counsel.

Asim arranged for me and the children to fly to my parents' villa in Marbella, Spain, and I recruited a friend's nanny to accompany me. Asim gave me more cash, some of his own and some forwarded from Father.

In Marbella, I tried to let my past sink away into the deep-blue Spanish sea. I visited a health resort daily, lazed about and forced memories out of mind. I bought clothes and shoes – too many – for me and the children. The days passed over me like a balmy wind.

I heard that Mustafa was shattered. In keeping with the image of a jilted lover, he grew a beard. He cut a sorry figure, traipsing back and forth among the homes of our many friends, weeping and wailing, trying to convince them to persuade me to return. He drank heavily. He spoke to strangers on the street about the wife whom he loved, who had deserted him. He met Asim and fell at his feet, begging my brother to mediate. He called my mother – for the first time since the Adila episode had burst into the open – and pleaded for forgiveness.

He won crucial sympathy votes. Friends phoned to convince me that he had changed. My family members urged that I give the marriage another try, for the sake of the children. Even my mother switched sides. I was amazed to hear her injudiciously weigh the pros and cons; I knew why: she was unused to Mustafa in the role of the pitiful child. I knew how convincing the false act was, but no-one else did. Everyone saw a strong man dissolve into tears at the mention of my name. They saw him humble and repentant. They saw him grovel, and believed that he had actually changed.

The exuberance of my liberation began to dissipate.

I did not want to live the rest of my life as a two-time divorcée, and I wanted my children to be raised in a stable home, if that was possible. Darker fears beset me, too. At the moment, Mustafa was trying to win me back with petulance and remorse, but I worried what turn his personality might take if these tactics failed. Long ago I had buried my physical fears, but when I stared at the innocent faces of my sleeping children, I sometimes shuddered.

Asim brought a practical solution to the impasse. He had my lawyer draw up an agreement that gave me the right to a divorce – and to custody of the children – should I ever again decide to leave. 'Mr Khar,' the lawyer advised Mustafa, 'I think you should read before you sign on the dotted line.'

'I don't need to read it,' Mustafa responded. 'If this paper brings Tehmina back to me, it's worth signing. I don't need to know the price.' He scrawled his signature quickly.

The children and I returned to Britain. When Mustafa picked me up at my parents' home, Mother proclaimed officiously, 'I want him to realize that you're leaving from your parents' house. He must never forget this. You have a home to come back to.'

Mustafa treated me like a queen. He did not speak to me in a normal tone; he bleated like a lamb. We spent the night at Haslemere and then embarked upon a second honeymoon in Palm Beach, Florida.

In the past, Mustafa was always an irritable shopping companion, but in Palm Beach he followed me around like a baby chick. When he tired, he squatted at the store entrance, with packages strewn about him. He joked with sympathetic customers who took him to be a model husband. 'What a dear,' they said. Mustafa smiled back at them.

We ate dinners on a candle-lit terrace; the sound of the rolling surf attempted to erode my apprehensions. But I was wary, still deeply hurt. I had difficulty responding to Mustafa. I shuddered when he touched me, and I did not allow him to progress beyond holding my hand. When he gave the slightest indication of a romantic overture, I panicked. With a start, I realized that whatever traces of love had remained in my heart were now irrevocably gone. I began to understand that the core of marriage is not necessarily fidelity; it is trust and respect. Mustafa had long ago destroyed my trust in him and, now, I no longer respected him. In fact, I pitied him.

Our one remaining link beyond the children was politics. We talked about returning to Pakistan. I wanted to fight for the things we both believed in, to change what was wrong and fashion a new society. I fantasized about our house in Lahore and, in my mind, planned how I would redecorate it. This was metaphorical; the house was my country and its interior design my politics.

We flew to Boston to visit my sister Minoo and her husband. Much had happened during my years of family exile. At the coed school on the Isle of Wight the worst had happened, as far as my parents were concerned. Minoo had fallen in love with Philip Holt, the best photography student in the school. The fact that he was a Catholic of French and English descent was a stumbling block. Our parents were furious but, realizing that they had no choice, demanded that he adopt Islam and change his name to Ali Habib. They were married in a mosque. Now they had moved to Boston to continue their photography studies. Minoo was happily surprised to see that I was calm and that Mustafa's temper had vanished.

When we finally returned to London, my grandmother came from Pakistan to visit us. She could not believe how well adjusted we had become. The peace in our beautiful country house filled her with gratitude to Allah. She proclaimed that her prayers had been answered.

No, I was not in love. Yes, I felt secure and even content.

Mustafa was desperate to seal our new bond by producing another child, but I was convinced that my pregnancies were cursed. I shuddered at the memory of how I had caused pain to a pregnant woman – Mustafa's former wife Sherry. I believed in crime and punishment. Was it mere coincidence that my pregnancies coincided with the worst times of our marriage? Or did God visit me with the most severe trials whenever the seed nestled in my womb?

Mustafa pleaded, arguing that a child born to us now – in this phase of our relationship – had to be special. He craved a chance to make up for past traumas. His persistence paid off, and soon I was pregnant once more.

The very moment that I told Mustafa that my tests were positive, I sensed a change. The charade was over. Where could I go with a child in my womb and three in my arms? He had me where he wanted me – at his mercy once again. Western women refer to this state of dependency as 'barefoot and pregnant'.

What explanation could I offer for my stupidity? All the friends who had been privy to his condition during our separation and had defended my decision, insisting that he had lost me by his own nature, were dropped. Even Ali and Billo were completely cut from our lives.

The irrational fights resumed. Mustafa demanded that I hand over the agreement that he had signed, guaranteeing me the right to divorce and custody of the children – on demand. I refused to relinquish this passport to freedom. Asim had the papers, and I could not ask him for them.

Mustafa gloated at my fears of pregnancy and began to reinforce them. 'Your pregnancies are cursed,' he proclaimed. 'You were right all along. This is another example of the potency of that curse. You have to suffer for your sins.'

Meanwhile, the saga of Adila's love life took many strange turns. During their visit to America, she and

Mother were invited to dinner at the home of a Washington heiress whose family knew our father through a series of business relationships. Mother was so impressed with the opulent home and its collections of fine art and antiques that she nearly forgot that the family was Jewish and was, in fact, generous in its financial support of Israel. That evening, the heiress's young son fell madly in love with Adila. Mother and Adila fell in love with the family fortune.

The love-struck boy followed Mother and Adila back to Boston. Minoo was astounded that Mother allowed him to visit. The boy pressed his case, proposed marriage and agreed to the extraordinary key point: he would adopt Islam.

Before long, Mother and Adila were en route to Pakistan, on a solemn mission to persuade Father to bless Adila's marriage to a Jew. Mother was confident. She had always been able to twist Father to her will.

But Father had been on his own in Karachi for some time, tending to business. Away from Mother's watchful eye, he had reacquainted himself with his old army drinking buddies, who now occupied positions of power in Zia's government. He was in a more confident and aggressive mood these days.

Mother, as diplomatically as possible, proposed Adila's marriage into a foreign family. In an instant years of pent-up frustration exploded. My father, who had *always* yielded to his strong-willed wife, declared vigorously that if the marriage took place he would divorce Mother.

Trying to soften him, Mother explained that the boy had agreed to accept Islam.

Father screamed, 'There is only one solution. He should take the name Yasser Arafat. Then I will agree. The whole world will have to know that he supports the PLO.'

Mother retreated to fight another day. She and Adila returned to England. They reported the distressing news to the boy's family in Washington, whereupon the heiress and her son caught the next Concorde flight to London.

Mother brought the entire clan into the fray. She called all of us, detailed the story and sought our support. Telephone calls flew about to various corners of the earth. Asim, who was away on business, heard the news and threatened Adila: 'I will kill you!' He had married into a Saudi family and there was no way that he could sell them a Jewish in-law.

I hoped to keep any news of Adila's love life away from Mustafa but he realized that an international telephone marathon was under way and discerned the details. He reacted to the Jewish issue as negatively as Father and Asim, but I wondered whether he simply wanted to prevent Adila from marrying anyone. At any rate, he told me to spend the night at Mother's house, to convince her and Adila to avoid this great 'scandal'.

The intrigue ran very deep. In fact I suspected that the youngsters were ready to run off to the Regent's Park Mosque, marry and present the entire clan with a *fait accompli*. That evening, I confided my suspicions to my sister Rubina in Karachi.

Later that night Rubina called Mother and broke dramatic news: Father had suffered a heart attack! He was in an intensive-care ward. Mother and Adila must catch the next flight to Karachi. As Mustafa's exiled wife I, of course, could not go.

We all suspected (quite correctly) that this was a phony episode, but Mother and Adila could not call the bluff. They booked a flight the next day, leaving about noon. Then Mother called the heiress and her son at their hotel, briefed them on this latest news, and asked them to come over at 10 o'clock in the morning.

Mother recruited me for the dirty work. She told me that she was too distraught to meet with the young Romeo and his mother; I would have to talk to them. Mother detailed: 'You must tell them the whole situation, so that they will understand. If Adila marries this boy, she will lose all the support of the family. If the marriage does not work, nobody in Pakistan will ever marry her. She is burning all her bridges.' Mother was at her dramatic best when she reached the bottom line. She instructed me: 'Tell them they must put at least one million dollars into Adila's account for her security.'

'I can't say that!' I replied. I was always uncomfortable discussing money in general, but this was astounding. I thought ruefully: Adila isn't worth that much.

I went downstairs. The Americans waited in the study. They knew that Father's 'heart attack' necessitated an instant settlement of the matter. I delivered Mother's speech as best I could, but stopped short of mentioning a dollar amount.

'Adila will have all the security she needs,' the woman explained. 'My son has a job. He has just rented a two-bedroom apartment in New York. Adila will own his car and everything else he has.' She was beginning to run out of patience when she added, 'She will own his clothes, his socks – everything.'

The blood rushed to my cheeks as I asked, 'And what does he own?'

'He has about thirty thousand dollars in the bank.'

I explained, 'But my mother wants him to put up security for Adila, separately, in her own account.'

The American woman sought to make me understand. 'There is no other security,' she said. 'He will inherit from his grandfather, but all of that money is in trust. It's not for him to give away to anyone. He doesn't have anything to give away.'

I struggled to keep an expression of glee off my face. I knew what reaction this information would produce upstairs. I excused myself and went to tell Mother and Adila. They sat amongst a pile of packed suitcases and vanity bags, waiting in anticipation. With a dramatic air I announced, 'He only has thirty thousand dollars, and he's not prepared to give that. But she'll own his clothes – and his socks!'

Mother's mouth gaped and she slapped an open palm hard against her bosom. 'What!' she cried. 'He has *no* money?'

In an instant Mother and Adila realized that they were dreadfully late for their plane. Servants were called and, amid much shouting, the car was loaded. My mother and sister muttered hurried excuses to the two Americans.

'My husband is very ill!' Mother wailed.

'I have to be with my father,' Adila explained.

As they headed off for the airport, Mother fiddled with her prayer beads, imploring God to save her husband's life.

Indeed, Father's recovery seemed miraculous. In Karachi, he and Mother wasted little time in arranging a fine marriage for Adila. The boy was Rais Matloob, the son of a very respected landowner from Bahawalpur. His father, Rais Ghazi, had been hailed as the builder of the most beautiful and elaborate mosque in the area. In fact, once construction began the man had dreamt that, the day he stopped building, he would die; accordingly, he kept workmen busy for twenty-five years, adding every possible extra touch. Shortly after Rais Ghazi stopped construction, he did indeed die, which added greatly to the family's legend.

The marriage offered good prospects for Adila – he was a fine, charming young man – but the symbolism was obvious: Adila had shifted her affections instantaneously from a Jew to the son of a mosque builder.

'I wish you a marriage that I wanted,' I said to Adila in London as I helped her pack. 'I wish you no pain in your marriage. I wish for you all that I could not get out of life.'

Mother and Father were very happy.

I broke the news to Mustafa myself, watching carefully for his reaction. I knew that he had to approve, at least nominally. The ultra-conservative family was rich and revered, and hailed from the same region as Mustafa, the Saraiki Belt, which stretches across the south of the Punjab. Mustafa digested the news and then declared, with a distinct smirk on his face, 'It is a good match.'

Over time, Benazir's peevishness toward Mustafa had increased. She barricaded herself behind a burgeoning bureaucracy, and critical decisions were increasingly delayed by red tape. Her advisers fed her constant tales of Mustafa's impudence and ambition. By now, after two years of haggling over the future course of the People's Party, Mustafa was required to make an appointment to see her, and he sometimes had to wait for weeks.

Mustafa bristled. He believed that Benazir needed his experience to weather her first stormy years in politics. But she obviously felt that her head had grown large enough for the crown. Mustafa felt his power base slipping away, and he knew that other party workers sensed it. The Zia government was finally moving toward at least the appearance of democracy. In December 1985 martial law was lifted, and a party-less election was announced. Mustafa's natural political strength was eroded by upstarts – including three of his own brothers who stood for seats in the new National Assembly. Benazir planned for an eventual return to Pakistan, and Mustafa was shocked to learn that she was not considering him for the post of Party President in the Punjab. 'Too many people will disagree with this choice,' she explained coolly.

'I don't see how anybody can disagree,' Mustafa argued. 'I am the *only* choice. It is not something that you are doing out of the goodness of your heart. It is accepted that I am the leader of the Punjab.'

Other irritations followed. To the outside observer they were, perhaps, minor points of contention within the unfathomable world of Pakistani politics, but to Mustafa they were air and water. In frustration, he decided to resign from the Party, but he did not plan to give up without a fight. Along with his old political friend, Ghulam Mustafa Jatoi, he decided to form a new party, with a manifesto that claimed a return to the pure first principles of the People's Party. Their public goal was to attract the working-class elements among Bhutto's followers. Mustafa's private goal was to emerge as the logical successor to the Bhutto legacy.

Consciously trying to atone for his sins of the past eight years, Mustafa arranged for me to deliver our child in London's luxurious Portland Hospital. A large portrait of Princess Anne graced the lobby wall. This was where she delivered her children. Here, our son Hamza was born.

The delivery was not difficult, but Mustafa proved to be. He was scheduled to travel abroad in two days, to what he described as 'a warm country', and needed summer clothes. Thus, *one* day after the birth of my son I had to drag myself out on to the streets to shop for my husband.

The 'warm country' was India. Through Joshi, Mustafa had arranged a clandestine meeting with the new Prime Minister, Rajiv Gandhi. Mustafa spent six days in India and was treated with all the protocol of a visiting chief of state. He was lodged in a rest house to prevent the press from detecting his visit. He was taken on a big-game safari. Most importantly, he held long discussions with the Prime Minister. He returned to London with the report that Rajiv was ready to adhere to his mother's plan to come to the aid of Pakistan. 'We were unable to decide how we were going to implement it,' Mustafa said. 'But the policy remains unchanged.'

I reacted to this news with a surprising, to me, amount of disinterest, for I was suddenly overcome by an obsession of my own. I had dreamed that a great miracle had occurred: I was happy and was celebrating! In my dream, someone asked me how this miracle had taken place and a voice replied that it was due to the fact that I had visited the shrine of the great saint of Ajmer in India. I pestered Mustafa to talk to Joshi, to arrange for me to make the pilgrimage.

They met at yet another Wimpy Bar. Seated at a nearby table, I tried to appear inconspicuous – because I looked European – as Joshi arrived and greeted Mustafa. They spoke for some time; I knew that they were talking mainly about politics, but I hoped that Mustafa raised the issue of my trip. Finally they stood up, paid their bill and walked past my table. Joshi stopped, smiled at Mustafa and told him not to forget his wife. Mustafa grinned sheepishly and formally introduced me.

As the three of us walked out together, Mustafa told Joshi of my desire for the pilgrimage and the Indian replied that he would see what could be done. I could hear the voice of the saint calling me.

Two days later, as I prepared to catch an Air India flight, Mustafa instructed me not to pack any make-up – not so much as a lipstick – and he searched my luggage to make sure that I had complied. I was travelling alone for the first time, and he did not want me to attract any male attention. His paranoia irritated me. This is silly, I thought. I could buy make-up in India. How would he even know? My thoughts stopped short when I realized that he had probably arranged that too, through Indian intelligence!

Two men met me at the New Delhi airport, whisked me through customs and immigration – I did not have a visa – and drove me to the Taj Hotel, where they had reserved a beautiful suite for me. Ten minutes after I had settled in, a middle-aged woman came to the door and introduced herself as Mrs Singh. In a businesslike manner, she checked my itinerary. I realized that her job was not only to look after me, but to monitor my activities.

My two shadows reappeared and informed me in

officious tones that, in one half-hour, the Director General of the Agency would have tea with me. I asked Mrs Singh who the Director General was. She said that he was her boss, and a very important man, but she did not provide a name.

I carried a message for him from Mustafa: I was to report that the political situation in Pakistan was static – which was to say that Zia was still firmly in power. I was to preach Mustafa's message that Zia's policy of aiding and abetting the Afghan rebels would have disastrous consequences for the entire region. A withdrawal of Russian troops from Afghanistan would strengthen American influence and damage our common interests. Mustafa wanted once again to urge the Director General to convey to the relevant quarters that a move against Zia was now imperative. My instructions were to listen carefully to the Director General and report his words verbatim.

Over tea, the Director General said that he agreed with Mustafa's assessment and understood the situation. He assured me that he would convey the message to the relevant people and that he would, himself, contact Mustafa within the next two weeks. He indicated that he would be visiting London soon.

I also forwarded Mustafa's request for another meeting with Rajiv Gandhi. The Director General said that he would arrange the meeting and inform Mustafa through regular channels: Joshi.

Before he left, the Director General offered me advice concerning my visit. 'Try not to move about too much,' he cautioned. 'Somebody you know might recognize you. It could result in an embarrassment.'

The following morning I flew to Ajmer. My two shadows were at my side as I entered the shrine. Their Hindu presence disturbed my Islamic prayers. I wanted to be alone. I wanted to pray that God would restore sanity to my life. Here, of all places, my privacy should have been sacrosanct, but the shadows refused to fade.

Gradually the peace of the sanctuary took effect. All around me I heard the hum of others at prayer. Reality receded.

I asked God to curb Mustafa's bouts of violence and insanity. 'I want a normal home with peace and harmony,' I prayed. I asked that God would give Mustafa respect and end his exile. I prayed for further reconciliation with my parents.

I looked around and saw faded and torn women with naked children, women with pain exuding from their very beings. But like me there was a hope in their eyes that transcended their hopeless lives. I wept for us all.

My two companions shuffled their feet, destroying my tranquillity. They seemed restless – two Hindus, forced to stand in front of the mortal remains of the great Sufi saint who had done more to spread Islam in India than any general brandishing a bloody sword.

I turned and walked away with my head bowed. I felt revitalized.

In New Delhi, Mrs Singh and I lunched together, then went shopping. I bought a painting and a rug. When I asked Mrs Singh if she wanted anything from London, her eyes lit up. She would love a leather handbag, she said. But then her face clouded with fear and she explained that she was not allowed to give me her address. When I asked if there was an address in London where I could send the bag, she hesitated.

'Why this cloak-and-dagger stuff?' I asked. 'Why can't we be friends?'

'It's impossible,' she replied. 'Please never repeat this conversation. I'm not allowed to make friends with contacts. I'll lose my job.'

Finally, after furtive glances to the left, the right and behind, she slipped an address to me. The lure of the leather handbag was too great.

*   *   *

Mustafa was pleased with my report from the Director General, but my prayers went unanswered. Two weeks after my return from India, he once more hounded me for the legal papers that granted me the rights of divorce and child custody on demand. I chided, 'Mustafa, you should not have signed those papers if you did not agree. You were irresponsible. Now live up to the consequences. I cannot ask Asim for the papers; he will lose respect for you.'

He slapped me sharply, then went to the phone. He called my lawyer and said, 'My wife has agreed to revoke the agreement. Could you send us a draft specifying that the agreement stands revoked? She will sign it.' The lawyer said that the papers would be in the morning's mail.

I collapsed in fear. That agreement was my only protection, my last defence against this man's insanity. I knew that I had to do something, or I would be crushed under the weight of his re-established authority.

Mustafa was out the next morning. I waited anxiously for the mail to arrive and, when it did, I grabbed the envelope from the lawyer's office and, with the four children, headed for my parents' home.

Mother listened to Mustafa's tears on the telephone and once more attempted to persuade me to return to him, but I told her that I could never believe his promises again.

I wanted a divorce. I was resolute. My children were made Wards of Court; Mustafa was granted the right to take the three older children out every Sunday morning and ordered to return them by evening.

Soon after, I awoke one morning with a compulsion to cut my hair, to get rid of this talisman of Mustafa's desire. My hairdresser tried to dissuade me, wailing that my incredibly long hair was the key to beauty, but I was firm. I had not cut my hair since the age of fourteen and now, as the scissors snipped away, I felt as if Mustafa's evil spirit was exorcised from my life.

Mustafa soon heard, and understood its significance. He knew that I had finally decided not to return to him, ever again. Otherwise I would not have done away with what he loved most about me. Without my hair, he was a weak Samson.

11

It was high summer, the day before the celebration of Eid. Mustafa had made plans to take the three older children, Naseeba, Nisha and Ali, to an amusement park in Liverpool – he liked driving fast, so Liverpool seemed no great distance to him. When he arrived at my mother's house to pick them up, he handed out Eidi, the traditional monetary gift that marks the end of Ramadan, to them and to my mother's servants. He gave me my Eidi of £500. I was touched by the gesture, and felt sad about how things had turned out. As he piled the children into the car, he was a forlorn figure, fighting a lonely battle in exile.

The day passed quietly as I cared for my baby son Hamza. The older children were due home at 6.30 p.m., but Mustafa did not bring them back on time. By 7.30 my panic attack was in full swing. I phoned one of Mustafa's friends, who told me that he had taken the children to the countryside. The friend provided only sketchy details, and I sensed that something was wrong. But I did not know what.

A half-hour later the phone rang and I lunged for it. It was Mustafa. He reported that the car had broken down on the motorway and that he had walked a mile to a phone booth to call me so that I would not worry.

'Where are the children?' I asked.

'I've just come off the motorway. I left them in a roadside inn. They're fine – a bit tired and sleepy. They're having their dinner just now.' He added that his brother Arbi was with them.

I interrogated him: 'You said you had walked a mile. Walked a mile from where?'

'From the car, Tehmina.'

'But why? Isn't there a telephone at the inn?'

'No,' he said. 'There's no telephone there.'

'I find that hard to believe. This is England, not some godforsaken part of Pakistan.'

He stuck to his story.

'Can I speak to one of the children?' I asked.

'No. They're too tired. I'd have to walk back and carry them all this way. It's too much of a bother. Relax. They're fine. Listen, I'll go back now and see what I can do. I'll call you in an hour or so.' The phone went dead.

I paced. What is he up to? I wondered. Is he playing games? Could he be telling the truth?

At 9.30 the ringing phone again jangled my nerves. Mustafa was very composed as he reported, 'The children are fast asleep. I've just walked back to tell you not to worry. It was too much to carry them all this distance.' I found this completely out of character and doubted that he would have put himself through another mile-long hike simply to reassure me.

I asked suspiciously, 'Where exactly are you, Mustafa? I'll send a car for you.'

He muttered something about being on the M15, but he was vague, and he told me not to bother about a car. He would get his own car repaired and be home soon. His smug, controlled tone bothered me. Once more the clicking sound of the disconnecting phone line left me hollow.

I called a friend and asked if the M15 went towards the amusement park in Liverpool. No, she said, there was no motorway of that number near Liverpool.

Mustafa was lying, I thought. Then I realized that it did not matter whether or not I had caught him in a lie. He had the children! I was assaulted by wave after wave of terrifying thoughts. What was he going to do with them? Where would he take them? I forced myself to sit and breathe deeply. Think, Tehmina, I commanded myself. Think!

It was after 11.30 when Mustafa called once more and this time I asked my mother to speak to him; I did not trust my temper. Mother hinted diplomatically at my fears, but he coolly dismissed them as evidence of paranoia. He explained the nature of the car break-down in convincing detail and assured Mother that the children were all right. He embellished his story: 'I'd asked the servant at my apartment to cook *saalun* [curry] for us,' he said. The lamb curry was one of Naseeba's favourite foods. 'I've called him up and told him to wait. I had every intention to get back home by dinnertime. It is not my fault that the car broke down.'

As soon as Mustafa rang off, I called his apartment. Someone picked up the phone, but would not speak. I tried repeatedly with the same result. Finally, his servant answered. 'Farid,' I asked, 'have you cooked *saalun* today?'

'No, Begum Sahib,' he replied innocently. 'I was not ordered to.'

I put down the receiver and thought: Why is Mustafa lying about this? Where is he? Where are my children?

I phoned my father's lawyer, Mr Garret, awakening him. When I told him what was happening, he decided to alert the police. My father was in Pakistan on business and I called to inform him about the situation. We decided that strong threats were necessary to ferret out the truth.

It was 2 a.m. when I phoned Mustafa's apartment and once more spoke to the servant. He sounded very frightened. I chose my words carefully, to make sure that he would relay the correct message to Mustafa. I warned, 'Farid, I'm sending the police over. They will hang you upside down and thrash you till you tell them what's going on. Tell your Sahib when he calls to call me in five minutes or I'm going to send the police to every home where I suspect my children might be. Do you understand?'

The phone was barely in its cradle when it rang again. It was Mustafa, and he said that by coincidence he had called the apartment and spoken to Farid, who had delivered my ultimatum. The response had come so quickly that I doubted that this was true. Was he hiding in his own flat? I wondered. No, Mustafa claimed that he was still at the inn, waiting, and admonished me to curb my wild imagination and get some sleep.

The rest of the night passed with the aid of endless cups of coffee. My mother and my sisters Minoo and Rubina were with me. We spent the hours talking and thinking. At 5 a.m. we decided to contact the London station manager of Pakistan International Airlines – we could pull rank since my father had served as PIA chairman – to see whether my children might have been placed on a flight to Islamabad or Karachi. The manager had the records checked immediately and reported that three children bearing different names had boarded a plane yesterday at Heathrow, heading to Paris and then on to Islamabad. They were accompanied by a man and a woman, and I froze when I heard their names: the man was Ghulam Arbi Khar – Mustafa's brother! – and the woman was their nanny, Dai Ayesha! I knew that Dai must be an unwilling and terrified co-conspirator.

I realized that Mustafa must have secured false passports for the children. Then he had played for time, delaying until he could get the children out of the country. He had kidnapped Wards of Court. In a desperate gamble to get me back he had violated the laws of England, the country that had granted him political asylum for the past nine years.

In desperation I called my father in Pakistan and asked him to check with immigration authorities, to see if he could intercept the children. But it was too late. The flight had arrived, the passengers had disembarked and cleared immigration. Naseeba, Nisha and Ali were gone.

'I have taken *my* children,' Mustafa announced to my mother on the phone at 6 a.m. He was crying, but his voice was tinged with evil: 'I have sent them to Pakistan. There is no way that they can be brought back. The only way out is for Tehmina to return to me. I did this because I knew that she would never come back to me. This was the only way to get her back. I knew that she would not be able to live without her children. Does this not prove how much I love her?'

Then he spoke to me, and I found his words chilling: 'Please forgive me for taking the children away from you. I just can't let you leave me. Come back to me.' Once more he wept, but every sob heightened my anger. I did not want to believe his anguish. This man had abducted my children. He was holding them hostage. And the ransom was me!

I had two choices: return to Mustafa or learn to live with only memories of Naseeba, Nisha and Ali. Both options were unthinkable.

Mustafa was aware of the consequences. He had demonstrated once again that he was above the law, that he held legal niceties in contempt. Nevertheless, he knew that he was in a serious bind. He faced a jail sentence in England for kidnapping Wards of Court, yet he could not return home to Pakistan where he faced fourteen years in prison – or even the gallows. His options were as stark as mine. Mustafa the hunter became Mustafa the hunted. He went underground, flying first to Paris, then moving about the continent, dependent upon the People's Party network for his security.

Five days passed, during which I employed every strategy that I could devise. Mustafa Jatoi was in England at the time and I spoke to him on the telephone, hoping that he would funnel my message. I wanted Mustafa to know that he was no longer dealing with the old, passive Tehmina. He was locking horns with someone who had served a long apprenticeship under a masterful manipulator. I said to Jatoi: 'He has blackmailed me in the most cruel manner. Tell him that as he was a student of Mr Bhutto, *I* was a student of Bhutto's vile product. He is Mr Mustafa Khar, but I am *Mrs* Mustafa Khar. I shall fight him in his own spirit by his own standards.'

Jatoi listened to me carefully and I believed that he truly felt my pain. He was a feudal lord himself, but had always impressed me as being cut from a more luxurious cloth than Mustafa Khar. He seemed to revere the concepts of truth and honour. On a professional level, this episode occurred at a difficult time for him. He was currently travelling back and forth between London and Pakistan, where he had just announced the formation of the new National People's Party – Mustafa was his second-in-command. Jatoi found this scandal very embarrassing and counterproductive.

British tabloids picked up the story and I had to endure the sight of my children's faces peering out at me from news-stand displays. We also became daily front-page news in the Pakistani press. I worried constantly about the welfare of my three lost souls. They knew only their lives in England; now they were in a strange environment without their parents. Where were they? I thought that it was probably too risky for Mustafa to deposit them in Lahore or Karachi, and concluded that he had probably sent them to his primitive village of Kot Addu, where his extended family could rely upon the trappings of the feudal system to protect them from consequences. In Kot Addu, the Khars *were* the law.

What about their schooling? I worried. What about their diet? What was all this doing to their young hearts?

Minoo was at my side constantly. She had moved back to London from Boston. Her own marriage became strained, as during this crisis she reserved her priorities for me. My mother, who many times in the past had attempted to persuade me to return to Mustafa, was at last convinced of his evil nature. She supported me totally in my battle, and was determined to destroy

Mustafa politically. But her reasons were somewhat jaded. She was not as upset with the heinous crime as by the fact that Mustafa had taken the children from *her* home. This was a personal affront. He had betrayed her trust yet again. This was not how a gentleman was to behave, and it was not to be forgiven.

I provided Interpol with a list of telephone numbers for all the People's Party workers in Europe. Raids were made on homes in Paris, Brussels, Frankfurt and Geneva. To his embarrassment, police officers removed Mustafa Jatoi from the midst of a party at his Kensington residence and interrogated him in an adjacent room.

Through it all, Mustafa escaped detection.

My father contacted the highest authorities in Pakistan, and even went to see Zia personally. But no-one could or would help. Two of the children were girls, and the male mentality could not deprive a feudal lord of the right to control his daughters. What's more, Mustafa once more hid behind the bulwark of Islam. He proclaimed to the media that he believed his daughters should grow up in the Islamic tradition, rather than in western society, and this pandered to the vast number of Pakistanis who view the West as the citadel of vice and moral decay. The multitudes might be impoverished and illiterate, but invoke the name of Islam – no matter how erroneously – and they will rally. Mustafa's self-righteous stance made the issue very touchy. Zia worried that any move against Mustafa would further portray the man as an innocent victim and that any action he took might be viewed as harassment against a long-time political opponent; worst of all, of course, was the possibility that the masses might interpret it as anti-Islamic. Zia and other Pakistani officials took the public position that this was simply a domestic dispute.

While standing in a phone booth somewhere in Europe, Mustafa told me in composed tones that the solution to my dilemma was very simple. All I had to do was return to him and we would resume life as a complete family.

I was consumed by the sensation of total hatred towards this man as a husband, but now more so as a father. He had not even taken into account the trauma that our three little children were experiencing as he bargained and haggled for my return. Their disturbance meant nothing to him in comparison to his own whims. I spat out the words I had told Jatoi earlier: 'If you are Mr Khar, I am *Mrs* Khar. If you learned from Mr Bhutto, I have learned from you. If you blackmail me, I'll blackmail you. I will face up to the situation and fight you just as you are fighting me. I will not let you get away with it!'

The headlines blazed 'Khar vs Khar' as I swore out an arrest warrant for Mustafa Khar, formally charging him with the kidnapping. Since Nisha and Ali, born in exile, were British citizens, I contacted the British Embassy in Pakistan, asked them to help locate the children and return them to the UK. Interpol was prepared to extradite them.

I was discussing strategy with Minoo when I felt suddenly weak and dizzy. For a moment I blacked out. Very concerned, Minoo asked, 'What have you eaten today? You've got to keep up your strength.' I pondered her question and realized that I had not had any food that day. In fact, I had eaten *nothing* since the children were taken. For five days, food had simply not entered my thoughts. Minoo tried to feed me a bland lunch, but I vomited it out. Panic took hold of Mother. She had me admitted to Wellington Hospital, where they immediately began to feed me intravenously. I remained there for one full week until I was strong enough to begin eating again.

Meanwhile, Mustafa continued to shuttle about the continent, trying to stay one step ahead of Interpol. He contacted anyone who he thought might influence me to return to him.

Using his underground connections, Mustafa acquired a passport belonging to someone from the Pakistan Embassy in Belgium. While attempting to leave Brussels, he was detained by an immigration official who noticed that the passport photograph had been altered. He was thrown into jail with an assortment of drug addicts and other dregs of society. He spent two days there before his contacts obtained his release, and he was deported to Geneva before Interpol could catch up with him. Once more he had escaped the net.

I was still in the hospital when I heard the news of his arrest and temporary detention in Brussels, and I surprised myself by weeping for him. In my weakened state I grew very pensive and thought: he has become a common criminal in order to win me back. He had even thrown politics to the wind. I could not fathom the man. He was wholly to blame for the mess of our marriage. He had induced me to walk out on him; now he was trying to force me back. This man who could have gone back to his own country and assumed the dignified role of a political prisoner now endured a common jail with petty prisoners, because of me. The only thing one could expect of Mustafa Khar was the unexpected.

Mustafa varied his strategy between threats and supplications. During one phone call he told me in a serious and sinister tone, 'Tehmina, I'm not giving you up. I'll charter a flight and land in England. You'll be picked up and I'll carry you back to the tribal area where there is no law. You will live there with the children. You will cook and I shall hunt and fetch wood for the fire. I'm serious, Tehmina. I'll do it. Believe me.'

The moment he hung up, trembling with fear I called the police inspector and reported this fresh threat to kidnap me. I knew that Mustafa was capable of anything.

Six interminable weeks passed. We heard occasional rumours of Mustafa's whereabouts, but no hard evidence surfaced. I knew nothing of the fate of my three children.

My father goaded me into the distasteful task of writing a personal letter to General Zia, requesting his help. I found it repulsive to appeal to the man who was, for me and many others, a bitter enemy. I swallowed my pride and made a rather formal appeal, but there was no response.

It is a strategy used by negotiators to wear down hijackers and other terrorists: buy enough time, and the target will eventually succumb. Slowly my nerve depleted. Anger melted into helplessness and despair. I did not know how long I could endure the uncertainty.

Seven-month-old Hamza was, at the same time, a source of supreme joy and utter anguish. I saw all of my children in him and I thought: I have five children. Why is it that only one of them is with me?

My mind constantly displayed images of the children, accusing me of being selfish. How could life ever stabilize without them? How could I abandon them to an alien environment and begin a new existence? I knew that my guilt would never allow me to live normally.

Mustafa must have sensed that he was winning the war of attrition, and called once again. He was a masterful negotiator. Taking his time, he coolly placed my options on the table, chipping away at my spirit. Would I be able to give up the children for ever? Would I be happy living alone in England, with no word about the children? Was all of this fair to them?

Everything he said sounded false. I searched his words for innuendo and replayed the sentences in my head, trying to discover the hidden traps. What, indeed, was fair? As I weakened, he tried to re-establish his credibility. He told me that he was planning to return to Pakistan and asked me not to mention this fact to my mother. 'Your mother is jealous of you,' he contended. 'She cannot bear to see you get all the attention in Pakistan as my wife. She knows I have changed. She hates the desperation with which I want you back. She knows that I actually want to make up for all that I have done to you. She does not want this marriage to survive. She is not interested in the children's welfare. They are insignificant. All that matters to her is her bruised ego. She is more upset about the fact that I took the children from under her nose, from her bloody house! No man would risk everything and fight to get his wife back like this, don't you see?'

This was partly true. I knew it. And I knew that as my own resistance level fell, Mother had taken over the fight. Her tone was more strident and bitter than mine; she would not rest until she demolished the myth of Mustafa's vulnerability. This had a negative effect on me. I wanted to win my children; she merely wanted Mustafa to lose. Several times she said to me, 'Lose his children if you have to, but fight to the bitter end.' I could not accept that.

For me, winning became irrelevant. Nothing else mattered but the children. My mother could not understand this. She became angry and accused me of using her and the rest of the family. 'You want to back out after putting us in the forefront of this mess?' she shouted. We were at loggerheads. To her it was a matter of ego and pride. To me there could be no victory if it came without my children.

My father's response was cool and pragmatic. He advised, 'Turn your heart into stone and forget that you ever had any children. One day they will come back to you. Lead your own life. Restart it. If you cannot do that, then there is only one other option: Go back.'

They were parents themselves! Had they not experienced the same phenomenon as I – that, with each birth, a parent's capacity to love immediately and mysteriously expands to encompass more? With sadness I realized: No, they had not experienced that feeling.

*   *   *

One of my friends called with unexpected and wonderful news. My first husband Anees had been transferred to a job in America. He was moving there with his second wife, their three sons and our daughter Tanya. They had stopped in London on their way. Tanya was here! Now!

I rang up Anees's mother immediately and she granted her permission for Tanya to visit me. In fact, Anees said that she could now come to live with me permanently, since I had left Mustafa.

Tanya came to see me at my parents' house on 29 July 1986, which happened to be Naseeba's ninth birthday. She clung to me and we both wept. I stepped back to get a good look at this young thirteen-year-old. I hadn't seen her for nine years.

We went shopping. I bought her everything I could afford, as if this might make up for years of abandonment. As the day progressed, however, our laughter turned inexorably sour. I grew preoccupied and she grew sullen. She must have realized what I was thinking: my life was a tornado, and it would destroy her if she stepped into its path. It was better for her to stay with Anees, with a civilized father who loved her, at least until I resolved another crisis.

After we returned to my parents' house, I tried to explain. 'I don't know what is going to happen to me,' I said. 'I might have to go to Pakistan soon to find the other children. Mustafa might kill me in the process. I cannot involve you. It is better if you go to America with your father. He can provide security.'

Tanya clung to me and wailed, just as she had nine years earlier. She cried, 'I hate my stepmother!' Tanya had never felt her stepmother liked her, perhaps because her father loved her too much.

What was I doing? I wondered. One of my lost children had suddenly walked back into my life, and I was sending her away? How could I do this? Was I as heartless as my own mother? My mind spun through the ramifications, but each time it came to the same conclusion. I would never – ever – settle for anything less than all *five* of my children. That most definitely included Tanya, but we both had to sacrifice in the short term. I simply could not bring her back into my life at this moment.

It was futile to attempt to quell her tears, but I tried. I stared deep into her eyes and vowed, 'Tanya, I promise to take you back the moment that I can offer you a normal life. I shall bring you back to me as soon as things settle. I promise.' Once more she clung to me. Once more I pushed her away.

Later that evening, as I licked my fresh wounds from this encounter, the telephone rang. 'Hello, Mummy,' Naseeba said hesitantly. I nearly collapsed; Mustafa had granted permission for her to call me on her birthday.

'How are you?' I stammered.

'It's very hot here, Mummy.'

'Where are you, baby?'

'I can't tell you. I'm not supposed to say. We had to come a long way to call you. It is very, very hot.' I heard her cry.

'Do you have any books to read?' I asked.

'No.'

'Did you get any birthday presents?'

'Yes. I got a garland made out of rupee notes. It's horrible. I hate it. Mummy, it's so dirty and hot here. There are too many flies buzzing around. I hate them.'

I broke down completely. For many minutes, I could do nothing but sob into the phone.

Naseeba asked, 'Mummy, when will we see you?'

'Soon, Naseeba.' It was all I could think of to say.

'Mummy, why can't we come back? We want to come back to you. We want to come home. Please, please, call us back.'

'Soon,' I promised. To my ears, the pledge sounded vague and hollow.

Naseeba asked, 'How long do we have to stay here?' Then the connection went dead.

The following day, Mustafa called me from Geneva and I told him in a calm, measured tone that I would return to him. He overwhelmed me with thanks. His strategy had worked. Through his tears he proclaimed that this was God's will. He promised to be the ideal husband. He would make amends for his past behaviour.

Against the advice of my lawyers and the wishes of my mother, I dropped all charges against Mustafa. The arrest warrant was withdrawn.

Mustafa Jatoi played the role of special envoy. He flew from Pakistan to England to escort me from my parents' home to Mustafa's apartment in Holland Park. He promised me that the next time that Mustafa behaved badly, he would give up their personal and political friendship. I accepted his guarantee.

Mustafa, now free to return, rushed back to London. I waited for him in a daze. My mind had given up functioning, as if from severe mental fatigue. When he arrived at the apartment, I felt my skin crawl. I quickly averted my gaze. His demeanour was relaxed but the air held menace.

He maintained that he was a changed man. In tears, he vowed to live up to my expectations. I did not cry. I did not feel.

Over the next week, Mustafa grappled with a difficult decision. It was time to keep his part of the bargain – to reunite me with the children. Would we call Naseeba, Nisha and Ali back to England? Or would we take Hamza and join them in Pakistan? I followed his thought process as he calculated the risks. He was still, according to General Zia's government, guilty of various charges all boiling down to treason. He *could* be sentenced to execution, and he still faced a sentence of fourteen years of rigorous imprisonment – at a minimum.

Yet there were compelling reasons for Mustafa to end his exile. In Pakistan, Jatoi's new NPP was stirring interest. New faces were fast filling the vacuum created by the absence of Mustafa and his exiled 'comrades'. Remote control was not good enough; Mustafa had to be present to remain relevant. He had to fight the political battle on his own turf.

Mustafa would publicly maintain that his decision was patriotic and political, but this was not the case. My icy attitude unnerved him. He could see that I was no longer in love with him, and had lost respect for him. He was unsure of my intentions. If he brought the children back to England, I could easily leave him again and reinstitute criminal charges.

With the skill of a general, he executed a flanking movement and found my vulnerable point. He stopped being the repentant husband and evolved into the evangelical politician. He spoke with prophetic fervour about the future. Together, we would turn our shared dreams into reality. In truth, this theme now held far more interest for me than prospects for our personal relationship. He fed my idealism. I wanted to do something worthwhile with my life and, if politics was the answer, I was inextricably linked to him. Mustafa the husband no longer mattered to me. But the Lion of the Punjab could still command my respect and loyalty. He realized that Pakistan, not England, was the environment where I would be forced to view him as a statesman.

He made sure that I was aware of the risks because he wanted me to share the burden of responsibility. His eyes were intense when he said, 'Tehmina, I've been told by everybody not to return. My life will be in danger. I'm going to leave it to you. I want you to decide for both of us. I want you to decide whether you will be able to stand by me through all the trials I will have to endure. Will you be able to fight for me. And if anything happens to me, do you swear to take up my cause? If I am assassinated like Bhutto, would you remain loyal and faithful to me? Can you swear to dedicate your life to my cause and never remarry? Tell me. Do you think it is right for me to return? I cannot justify my exile any more. Martial law has been lifted. My people want and expect me to be amongst them.'

His words penetrated that secret area of my mind where my ideals were stored, where my hopes lay and where memories of my children were. I fell suddenly in love with a noble idea – the return of the exiled leader. My original love for Mustafa was replaced by faith in his mission. We had resolved our differences out of court; now we would take his case to the court of the people.

I promised that I would stand by him. I would fight for his cause. I would not leave him as long as I believed in his politics and respected his ideals. I wanted him to show me that his courage was genuine. I told him that it was time for him to face the dictator.

I discussed a serious embarrassment with him. In print, during our very public custody battle, I had called him names like 'Rasputin'. How was I to face the Pakistani press that had made a soap opera of our matrimonial wrangles? How was I to explain my capitulation to a man who had kidnapped my children?

'I should be embarrassed, not you,' he said with a smile. 'You left me. I forced you back. You don't have to explain your position. You've done the right thing. The people are like sheep. They will be led by anyone who seems to know the way.'

I began to understand that a politician must become used to having mud flung at him. He must shrug it off and get on with his business. Politicians breathe the oxygen of publicity; bad press is better than no press. Indeed, Mustafa reminded me that the incident had enabled him to draw a portrait of himself as a conservative man who was worried about the effect of western culture on his children's morals.

He advised me not to look back. Despite the prison sentence hanging over his head in Pakistan, he proclaimed that the future belonged to us.

*   *   *

I dressed with care, selecting an Yves St Laurent shirt emblazoned with tigers, as if it symbolized my allegiance to the Lion. A Louis Ferraud cape was draped over my shoulders to add a touch of decorum and elegance.

Standing before the mirror, I noticed how much I had changed from the young girl who had fallen in love with this controversial, much older man. The fact that I had used all my strength to live with him and then to leave him seemed to have sapped me, and yet there was a flickering light in my eyes. A long and turbulent exile was over and I was embarking upon a journey that somehow seemed to be taking me into the area where I could still function with Mustafa. There was a wisdom behind the sadness that glazed my eyes. I had learned to live in crisis and was trained to cope with uncertainty. The pain of life had dulled with the excitement of returning to my Motherland and to my children. This was the first moment when I realized the resilience of my spirit and its inextinguishable nature. In amazement, I shook my head at my image. I had always wondered about Mustafa, analysed and assessed him. But today the major neglected question surfaced: What was I all about?

Mustafa walked into our bedroom, sidestepping the luggage that occupied my attention. On an impulse, I asked, 'What would have happened if I did not come back to you?'

He disclosed the repercussions: When word of our separation reached Joshi, he had complained to Mustafa. 'How could you trust your wife, sir, when you did not have a stable marriage? The Indian government cannot afford to be implicated in an armed conspiracy to topple a foreign government. It must never be known that the Indian government extended material support to an opposition party to help it overthrow a government. A scandal of this nature would be disastrous.' I became a potential threat by leaving. I might talk irresponsibly. I was the weak link. Clearly, I knew far too much about the intrigue between Mustafa and the Indian government to be allowed to roam London untethered.

To save his political – and perhaps physical – life, Mustafa had had to swallow his pride. He had vowed that he would get me back, at any cost. Was it not, after all, for his love for me?

Mustafa looked me straight in the eye and answered my unasked question, 'I would have had to eliminate you.'

Part Three

LIONESS

12

During the extended flight, Mustafa insisted that I write an oath on the Koran promising to stay by him, even if he were imprisoned for fourteen years. I complied.

Apart from all the other considerations, Mustafa was excited over the prospect of a reunion with his mother. Through nine years of exile she had pined for him. Mustafa could plan on arrest and imprisonment, but he hoped desperately that he would be allowed to visit his ageing, ailing mother at least one final time.

As the plane began its approach to Karachi, I remembered how two of the most important men in my life had become prisoners. My father faced humiliation, and he had emerged from jail broken and shamed. But my politician husband would become a hero. Mustafa viewed his impending prison term as a source of pride. It was evidence of his bravery and loyalty to Bhutto and democracy.

Our arrival was anticlimactic. If Mustafa was surprised that no cheering throngs met us, he did not show it. We were led without ceremony to an office at the airport and told to wait. Soon, word of Mustafa's arrival spread, and the curious gathered to catch a glimpse.

We were served lunch and Mustafa ate quietly, with a look of defiant submission on his face; he had acquired the halo of martyrdom.

I was informed that Khaliqa Jatoi, Mustafa Jatoi's wife and one of my few close friends during my marriage, was waiting outside in a car. Mustafa asked me to go out and inform her of the developments. A guard attempted to prevent me from leaving through the outside door, but I brushed him aside, shouting, 'You have no business stopping me. Show me my arrest warrant.' He moved away to let me pass, and I realized that, as Mustafa Khar's wife, I could get away with sheer intimidation.

By the time I returned from speaking with Khaliqa, I found our bags opened and the contents strewn across the counter. The police took away Mustafa's clothes and books. Then they took away Mustafa.

From Karachi, I flew with Hamza to Lahore, where I was met by Mustafa Jatoi and several members of the newly-formed National People's Party. I was a fresh symbol, a rallying point. Tehmina Khar would make good press copy.

I was pleased to see the faces of the seven sacrificial lambs Mustafa had sent before him, years earlier. Choudhry Hanif, Sajid and the others had only recently been released from prison. They were happy, of course, for their own freedom, but worried that Mustafa was now in the dictator's custody. They looked to me as Mustafa's representative, but I could tell that they wondered about my continuing endurance.

The press surrounded me. I expected them to enquire about our notorious domestic battle, but they must have sensed my reticence and were kind enough to ignore that aspect of my life. A reporter asked, 'Will you fight for your husband?'

'Yes,' I replied without hesitation.

Asia in general and the subcontinent in particular have produced valiant women who have taken up the unfinished struggle of their menfolk. In most cases, their entry into politics began because of adversity and violence. Indira Gandhi, Cory Aquino, Benazir Bhutto and others stepped into the shoes of their fathers or husbands.

Only when Mustafa was imprisoned did I emerge.

I was a political animal now.

My children awaited me at my grandmother's house. Through the haze of tears, I saw that they looked well, but confused, and I realized immediately that whatever compromises had been forced upon me were insignificant.

'Did you think Mummy would never come back to you?' I cried.

'No,' Naseeba said staunchly. 'We knew that you would come to us. We just knew.'

In long conversations with my children, I learned the details of their ordeal. After Mustafa had picked them up from my mother's house in London, he had driven straight to the airport. He bought their co-operation by telling them that he was taking them to Disneyland. He explained that if I had known about the trip, I might refuse permission. At the airport, Mustafa took a very big risk, flying with the children, his brother and Dai Ayesha to Paris. Over the years, he had been careful to avoid PIA flights, believing that if the authorities learned he was on board they would arrest him on the spot, or even divert the flight to Pakistan. During the brief journey across the Channel, Mustafa kept telling the children how much fun it was going to be to shake hands with Mickey Mouse.

In Paris, Mustafa told the children that he had to leave them in order to attend to some work. Dai and their uncle would travel with them the rest of the way and he would join them later in America – in Disneyland! It was a cruel deception, and perhaps the children discerned it at this early stage of the plan, for they cried out their fears of abandonment. Nevertheless, Mustafa got off the PIA plane and returned on the next flight to London. That night it was from his Holland Park flat that he had made his numerous calls to me, stalling for time.

Next morning he informed Mustafa Jatoi about his actions. Jatoi was thunderstruck, particularly so due to the unfortunate timing. Their new party, still in its infancy, was thrown into disarray. But Mustafa had set his priorities and left Jatoi to make the necessary excuses.

My children landed in Islamabad on a hot July day. The temperature was well above 100 degrees. The dry, smouldering wind slapped them in the face. They were very surprised because they had not expected America to be so hot, or for that matter so apparently under-developed. The first thing that Ali noticed was the number of poor Pakistanis in dirty, shabby clothes who had somehow got to America.

The children were met at the airport by another uncle, Ghulam Murtaza Khar, the philanderer whom Mustafa had banished from Pakistan years ago for his affair with Safia. They had recently made amends. Murtaza was a Member of Parliament now. He whisked the children through immigration procedures without the formality of having their passports stamped; Mustafa did not want to leave a trail of evidence.

Next came the hot, uncomfortable six-hour drive to Mustafa's home village of Kot Addu. It was a terrible time for the children. Naseeba, the eldest, discerned that all of this was happening because I had left their father. She tried to put on a brave front, so as not to frighten her brother and sister, but as the car sped further into the back country of Pakistan, all three children felt increasingly alone and afraid.

They were hidden in the village, ensconced in a house with Mustafa's eldest son, Abdur Rehman. Little Ali was allowed to play outdoors, but Naseeba and Nisha could only watch from over the wall that surrounded the house. Naseeba was not quite nine years old and Nisha was only six, but their youth did not matter; girls had to remain indoors. They had to sit inside with the other females, all of whom seemed reconciled to the fate that life dictated for women in a remote Pakistani village.

Ali's lot was not much better. The poor village boys he played with were dirty. Stubborn flies and mosquitoes attacked him. The unpaved alleys in Kot Addu were generally muddy and the open gutters flowed with waste. There were no parks or playgrounds. Ali and the other boys whiled away their time in narrow lanes where mangy dogs sat about flicking away insects with their busy tails.

Mustafa's brother and co-conspirator Ghulam Arbi Khar soon drew back from the episode. He suffered from a bad conscience, and regretted his gullibility in acceding to Mustafa's plans. He heard that I was hospitalized in London and felt very bad about that. More importantly, he also realized that Mustafa did not have the children's best interests at heart; his motives were selfish.

Yet another brother, Ghulam Ghazi Khar, also a Member of Parliament, tried his best to help the children adjust. He was not on speaking terms with Mustafa, but he warmed to his nieces and nephew. He entertained all of them in his home frequently. He took little Ali on shoots; he bought him a pony and taught him how to ride. Ghulam Rabbani Khar, a member of the Provincial Parliament, showered the children with gifts and affection.

Television took over. The girls were entertained by a steady supply of Indian video films and were befriended by cousins, who were about the same age.

Once Mustafa learned that my father had contacted General Zia, and that we guessed that the children were in his village, he acted swiftly. The children were driven to Lahore airport. They were secretly excited, aware that there was considerable press coverage concerning them, and hopeful that someone would recognize them. Nevertheless, they had to maintain a low profile on their uncle's instruction. Whenever the car stopped at a traffic light, they were told to squeeze down in the seats and keep out of sight. The children's faces were well known, due to the extensive media coverage their kidnapping had caused. They were flown from Lahore to Karachi under assumed names. During the trip one of the attendants innocently asked Naseeba her name. She almost blurted out the truth but was stopped by the warning expression on Abdur Rehman's face.

From Karachi, the children were driven to Jatoi's village in Nawabshah, where they were the guests of Jatoi's son Masroor and his American wife Sarah. Sarah was a more conventional type of woman, as far as the children were concerned, and they liked her. They said that 'Jatoi house' was much cleaner than the others they had seen in Pakistan, and that Sarah even took them out boating – the girls as well as Ali.

This information was painful and disconcerting. All along I had been convinced that Jatoi was on my side – or was at least neutral. I was thankful that children are so resilient and have short memories. However, I shuddered at the thought of what would have become of them in the long term. I knew that they were very disturbed and unhappy during this period, but they were able to look back upon the events with a sense of humour. Like me, they were able to see the funny side of things.

The day after my arrival in Lahore, the National People's Party held its initial convention with great fanfare. Jatoi was chairman. Mustafa was the only political leader of note who was now in prison, and his absence made him – and by extension me – a great celebrity. I sat next to Jatoi on the dais and cautioned myself to compart-mentalize political and personal feelings. When the time came, I rose to present my maiden political speech, as Mustafa's voice. I was extremely nervous but managed to speak with conviction.

'Mustafa Khar is back!' I proclaimed. 'Unfortunately he has been denied direct access to you. His incarceration will strengthen you. He had the courage to return to Pakistan, although he knew that the generals would never allow him to play his destined role – a role for the uplift of the downtrodden people of this country.

'He is not made of the stuff that compromises or

breaks. He is here to fight. He will fight against martial
law and its injustices. We repudiate and reject the
verdicts of summary military courts and tribunals. The
generals cannot break our will or stifle our voices.
Mustafa Khar has returned to be with the unfortunate
victims of martial law. His presence amongst them puts
him into the category of the oppressed worker. He feels
proud to stand with the common man. He is a symbol
that the people of Pakistan do not accept illegitimate
rule.

'Mustafa Khar has directed all his comrades to unite
behind the leadership of Mr Jatoi. Your presence here
is an indication of your consistent belief in Mustafa's
leadership. With your support we will soon have him in
our presence, physically.'

Already I was beginning to understand how and why
the pursuit of power consumes men.

I had been in Pakistan for fifteen days before the
authorities permitted me to visit Mustafa. He had been
flown from Karachi to Faisalabad, where he was lodged
in the central gaol. In a cavalcade of cars, accompanied
by several workers and political aides, I made the
three-hour trip from Lahore to meet my husband in
the Superintendent's Office.

Although my life was now more uncertain and
abnormal because of Mustafa's incarceration, it was
different. I was without him for the first time since our
marriage. Driving to prison through the crowded, un-
disciplined traffic that included horse-driven 'tongas',
the old passenger carriages and noisy rickshaws, I looked
at our people, resilient in the summer heat, used to
hardships at every level of life. On bicycles or walking,
some barefoot, some huddled on donkey carts, they
presented an alarming contrast to smart Pajero Jeeps and
trendy, air-conditioned cars, mine included. I preferred
this mess to England's organized bliss.

Mustafa strode into the Superintendent's Office with

no sign of pathos on his face. I was taken aback. Perhaps I expected to see a 'prisoner' instead of a 'leader', but I should have known better. Mustafa never filled the bill of expectancy. Pakistan was his turf. He was a true leader here; he knew how to intimidate the authorities. In all our years in exile, I had never seen him so confident and so much in control.

I was allowed to visit every other week, and so we began a series of regular meetings. I was to be the conduit of information between Mustafa and the new party. In Lahore the days were long. I listened carefully to the arguments and counter-arguments of party workers, then fed them their 'daily bread' from Mustafa's point of view. The evenings were filled with press interviews. It was imperative that we keep Mustafa's name alive and in the limelight. Gradually, people began to realize that I had opinions of my own, which I was no longer afraid to express. They respected my analyses. I tried to pay special attention to my children before they went to sleep. Late at night, I collapsed into bed.

Activists campaigned fiercely for positions of power within the new organization. Many of them hoped that I would press their cases with Mustafa. It was a difficult time for the bosses. They would like to have accommodated all of the enthusiasts, but they knew that they would have to bruise some egos and inflate others. It was inevitable that they would create a reserve force of the disgruntled.

I reported that Jatoi was handing out key positions to his own people and alienating Mustafa's 'men' from the mainstream. That was, perhaps, inevitable. But Mustafa was not threatened. He felt that Jatoi was too much of a gentleman to play politics effectively at this gut-level. He could visualize the mess that Jatoi's accommodating nature would create. The new party would not reach deep into the masses; its manifesto and its store of pamphlets would end up amongst the many unread coffee-table books that were already neatly stacked in 'Jatoi house'. Mustafa was confident that he could relax in the relative comfort of his prison cell and wait for the call of desperation. By the time he emerged from prison, he would stand as the only person capable of organizing the party.

Mustafa was named President of the Punjab section of the party, although the day-to-day duties were assigned to a surrogate. From his prison vantage point, he adopted a strategy of disinterested neutrality. He cultivated an air of resignation. Many observers felt that the Lion of the Punjab had lost his bite, not realizing that he had adopted one of Bhutto's tried and tested tactics: set the fuse, but stand clear of the explosion; then walk through the smoke and pick up the pieces.

Our personal relationship was still tenuous. Mustafa knew that he had not won me over completely, and our brief visits did not give him sufficient time to brainwash me. He resented my freedom and was jealous of the time I spent away from him, although it was entirely dedicated to his work. He feared my vengeance if he became unreasonable, and realized his own inability to retaliate. I could see his mind working overtime, trying to find some way to spend more time with me. He could not suffer imprisonment alone.

I felt a measure of sympathy for him. His future was uncertain. He did not know how long he would have to languish in prison. He knew that Zia could order his execution almost as a whim. I did not want to do anything to aggravate his torment.

Months passed and I became weary of living out of suitcases at Arbi and Syma's house. I persuaded Mustafa to let me rent a house in Lahore, so that I could settle down with the children and enrol them in proper English schools. Fortunately, they did not seem to be suffering any ill-effects from their abduction – other than a plague of scalp lice, which only succumbed to a prolonged campaign of pest repellents and disinfectants.

It was at this time that one of our political workers brought a twenty-six-year-old woman to work for me. Shugufta came from a very decent and good family that had no source of income. She was underfed and very tired-looking. I took her into my service and put her in charge of little Hamza who, because of my long absences, became very attached to her.

Mustafa's brother who had been looking after his land provided us with some money. Our new residence was a spacious, five-bedroom house. I had air-conditioning and wall-to-wall carpeting installed and ordered beautiful furnishings. As I hung up wall paintings, I realized that I was in my element. One morning, shortly after we had settled in, I received a phone call from a journalist who told me that Mustafa had suffered a heart attack. Why had no-one notified me? Seized with panic, I called the Home Secretary and received special permission to visit my husband. Then I rushed to Faisalabad.

Mustafa was in a special ward of the local hospital, guarded like a fortress. His admirers stood vigil. Many NPP workers, men and women, sat around, solemnly reciting verses from the Koran and turning prayer beads.

I found Mustafa sitting on the edge of his bed, grinning broadly. 'This is Pakistan,' he explained. 'Anything is possible. I arranged this with the gaol doctor's connivance.' The British-based gaol manual allowed a hospitalized prisoner daily visits from his family, and henceforth, Mustafa decreed, I would come to see him every day!

At most, he was suffering from heartburn, and he was very content with his new routine. He began his day with yoga, balancing himself upside down, with his legs crossed, looking at the world from a different perspective. My own world was upside down, too. Each morning I had to endure the three-hour drive from Lahore to Faisalabad, lunch with my husband and ride back home in the afternoon. In the evening, I would have to meet the press to discuss the intricacies of the political situation as well as to issue the latest bulletin on the state of my husband's health. There was only a little time left for my children before I stumbled off to bed.

Even when I contracted severe 'flu Mustafa insisted that I make the daily visit. He was almost always unreasonable and insensitive, but I had no energy with which to fight. This routine continued for twenty days.

I received a message that Mustafa's mother was very ill. I flew to Multan and was driven to Kot Addu, where I found her laid out in her room. She was unconscious. Her grandchildren sat around the bed reciting from the Koran. No doctor was present and there were no plans to take her to a hospital. Everyone was waiting for her to die.

I insisted that we get her some medical attention, but Mustafa's brother Ghazi said, 'It's useless. She's dying. She is my mother – I shall decide.'

'Your opinion is not important,' I snapped. 'I'm here as Mustafa's representative. He's the eldest son and I shall decide in his absence. I insist that we call a doctor and have her moved to a hospital. We cannot allow her to die without maximum effort to save her life.'

Ghazi was furious, and shamed in the presence of his brothers, but my resolute tone carried the moment. A doctor was summoned and soon Mustafa's mother was receiving oxygen. Her blood pressure lowered slightly. She remained unconscious, but we were able to move her to Nishtar Medical Hospital in Multan.

Mustafa was transferred there immediately. Because of his 'heart condition', one complete hospital ward was converted into a sub-gaol, and he and his entire family used the facilities for their vigil. Party workers sent in great feasts. I argued briefly with Mustafa over these details. Why should we be allowed such privileges? 'What about the genuine patients?' I asked. 'Where will they go?' For once, Mustafa had no glib answer. He acknowledged that this relative opulence was out of character with his humanistic political philosophies, but he was willing to compromise his principles at the moment because of his preoccupation with his mother's condition.

He sat next to her comatose body for hours, talking, trying to cajole her back to the world. He assured her that he was home for good, and that he would never leave her side again. Each time Mustafa mentioned his name and said that he was with her, the old lady responded with a moan; sometimes a tear rolled down her cheek. There was desperation in his voice as he pleaded with her to open her eyes and gaze, just once, upon the son for whom she had so long pined.

This was a government hospital, the largest in Multan, yet I was appalled by the conditions. The physical plant was a mess and the sanitary conditions were obviously poor. Serious cases of post-operative infection were common. The electrical generating system was unreliable, prone to fail during the critical moments of surgery.

Feeling a need to do something constructive rather than sit around gossiping, I decided to visit the children's ward. I was appalled to find three or four children on each bed, varying in age from baby to toddler. Some were suffering from leukaemia, others severe diarrhoea or tuberculosis. There was no effort to separate those with contagious diseases from those with chronic illnesses or injuries. Unkempt mothers sat cross-legged on the same beds, attempting to tend to their children, but there were no supplies – none at all.

A woman sat on a bed holding her daughter on her lap. The girl appeared to be about three years old. The child's stomach was severely distended, and I asked a nurse what was wrong with her.

'Liver cancer,' she replied.

'What's being done for her?' I asked.

The nurse explained that it was the parents' responsibility to purchase the needed medications and supplies from an outside source. The girl's father was a labourer earning only thirty rupees (about 70p) a day. He would lose a day's wages if he took time off to search for medicine.

I pulled 500 rupees (about £11) from my purse and handed it to the woman, instructing, 'When your husband returns, give this to him and tell him to go and buy the medicine.' She looked at me warily, but accepted the money with gratitude.

When I returned the next day the girl and her mother were gone. I feared the worst, and asked the nurse what had happened to them.

'They've taken her home,' she replied. 'They have five other children to feed with your money.'

I shook my head in frustration and left the ward, determined to do what I could to change this appalling situation. I marched to Mustafa's comparatively luxurious 'suite' and buttonholed him and his brothers. I wanted donations of 10,000 rupees (about £225) from each of them to buy medicine for the children. This was regarded as a ridiculous waste of money, but in any event it was pocket change to these feudal lords.

That evening, beaming with the pride of accomplishment, I encountered the children's doctor and told him that I had raised 60,000 rupees (about £1,400) for medical supplies. He advised me not to hand it over. 'If the drugs and supplies are here,' he warned, 'they will just be stolen by the nurses and interns and wind up on black market.'

I was horrified and shot back, 'Why can't *you* supervise and administer them?'

He shrugged his shoulders and in a resigned voice said, 'It's just not possible.'

I refused to accept this reality and acted on my own. Soon I had 60,000 rupees' worth of life-saving medical supplies delivered to the children's ward. I pointed to the crates and admonished the nurses, 'At least see that these are not stolen.'

I never wanted to learn the fate of those supplies. I knew where they had gone but, like so many others before me, I turned my back and walked away from the hopelessness.

My mother-in-law remained in a coma and died without seeing her beloved eldest son.

Mustafa was granted permission to attend the funeral. As he walked out of the hospital gaol, people ran to him from all directions. He was gracious to them, but eased his way through the crowd to the car. He took his place behind the steering wheel like a child who has found a long-lost favourite toy. The chance to drive was a delicious whiff of freedom, even if jeeps full of policemen followed.

He told his brother Ghazi to sit in the back and asked me to sit in front. It was a progressive gesture, a break from tradition, a signal to others that I was now his equal. The women of the Khar family have always known their lesser place; Mustafa told the world that my place was beside him. Ghazi sat in the back seat with a glum expression on his face, obviously wondering how and why his brother had become so emancipated.

Swirling clouds of dust greeted us as we neared the funeral site at Kot Addu. It was twilight and the cows, coming home from pasture, stirred up the soil. Behind the screen of dust was an ocean of faces – as many as 60,000 – looking lost and desolate, like the souls that will gather on the Day of Judgement. The moment they recognized the Lion of the Punjab, returning home after eleven years, they cried out his name in ecstasy. They had gathered, ostensibly, to bury his mother, but their hope for the future lay with her son. Mustafa's presence signalled that deliverance was at hand. Torn, tattered and barefoot, the people lunged forward to catch a glimpse of their leader. They wept. They beat their breasts. Their moans soared to the sky.

The soil parted to receive Mustafa's mother. Then the crowds closed in to receive Mustafa.

He delivered his first public speech since returning from exile. 'I have yearned to be back amongst you,' he cried out to his people. 'Fate has played a strange game with me. It has been my prayer to Allah that I be given a chance to do something for you. I find myself here to mourn my mother's death. You have come to share my grief; I can give you nothing. I am still a prisoner of the dictator. I cannot serve you yet . . . Today, I make a pledge before my mother's grave. I shall return. I shall fight to return to you my people and together we shall overturn this corrupt and corpulent system. We shall build a system closer to your hearts' desire. Without you I am nothing. Mustafa Khar is your creation, born from your soil . . . I pray to Allah that he might grant me one chance to return your love and restore your faith in our beloved country.'

Pandemonium prevailed. People ran amok, sobbing and screaming for a chance to get close to Mustafa, even to touch him. Many were trampled. Mustafa stood quietly, resolutely acknowledging the outpouring of love.

During the return drive I could sense that, despite the loss of his mother, he was greatly relaxed. He knew now with certainty that his support had not crumbled during his absence. The people still saw him as a charismatic figure who could make their dreams come true. Now, he could be content to return to jail and wait for his moment.

Mustafa received permission to stay on in Multan for treatment of his non-existent heart problem, and he wanted me to move the children here. This made no sense to me. They had settled in a new house and good schools in Lahore. I pointed out that the schools in Multan were inferior. 'You are in gaol,' I pleaded. 'You have to learn to live in gaol, as a politician – with dignity.

Why can't you stop clinging to me? We have to put the children's lives in order. If you are in prison for fourteen years, are they also supposed to lead unsettled lives?'

'I knew it. I knew it!' Mustafa ranted. 'I knew you would do this. You promised to stand by me. You promised! And now you are doing this.'

As usual, Mustafa's arguments wore me out. His troubled condition as a prisoner blackmailed me. We sadly dismantled our house in Lahore and returned to Multan to set up life anew. The temperature was so high that heat burnt into our bones; even the air conditioners were ineffective in this cauldron. Our hosts, Sajid's brother and sister-in-law, were very gracious, but I was sure that they were uncomfortable with four children, Shugufta and myself. We seemed to have invaded their small, three-bedroom house; they had three sons of their own. My children were bemused and very confused when their new teachers asked them about the pronunciation and definitions of English words.

My hostess and I had little time together, due to the demands Mustafa put on me. Life was either about him as husband or as political leader. The stress made me for ever tired, and I was given constant vitamin B injections to help keep my nerves calm.

Six months later I discovered a small lump on my breast. Doctors advised me to have a biopsy.

'Have it done here, in this hospital,' Mustafa declared.

I refused point-blank. 'I'm going to Karachi,' I said defiantly. 'To the best hospital in the country. I may have cancer. I can't risk being operated on here. Don't do this to me. Isn't my life important to you? Do you want me to die?'

Mustafa lapsed into melodrama. 'At least I'll be with you,' he said. 'I'll hold your hand.'

I wasn't interested in having my hand held. I wanted the best doctor I could find.

Against Mustafa's wishes and despite the complaints

he lodged with his brothers about my stubbornness, selfishness and disobedience, I left for 'Jatoi house' in Karachi. My mother was in the city at the time, and I knew that she was aware of my pending operation, but she did not bother to call and ask about me. Rubina and Adila ignored me, too. Only Zarmina and Minoo called regularly.

Fortunately, the Jatois replaced my family. Khaliqa Jatoi waited outside the operating theatre at the Aga Khan Hospital during my surgery. She and her husband were at my side as I recuperated. Thankfully the cyst was benign, though the operation was very painful. The stitches were still fresh when a party worker called from Multan to report, 'I have a message from Khar Sahib to please come back immediately.'

This was incredibly insensitive. I responded, 'Tell Khar Sahib that my stitches have not been removed yet. I can't come.'

Mustafa had anticipated this. In a respectful, rather apologetic tone, the man said, 'Khar Sahib says that this is his order. The stitches can be removed in Multan.'

Jatoi was furious, and he nodded in agreement when I said, 'Tell Mr Khar I won't take unreasonable orders from him. He should not give me orders that he knows I shall not obey.' I slammed the phone down in anger.

The cyst may have been benign, but Mustafa was malignant.

When I was ready, I flew back to Multan. Even before I went to see Mustafa, I could sense the aura of apprehension among the party workers who had congregated to meet me at the airport; word of our domestic confrontation had spread.

The moment I walked into Mustafa's hospital room, he began to scream in fury. Aroused by my indifference, he grabbed me by the shoulders and shoved me against the door. 'It's too late now,' he grumbled. 'Just go away.'

I looked straight into his eyes for a moment, then turned and walked out.

For two days I left him alone, and he panicked. He inundated me with telephone messages, apologizing, until I relented and once again began my daily visits.

I felt we could no longer impose upon our hosts, and I asked Mustafa to find an alternative. He suggested that I talk to the owners of the Shezan Hotel, to arrange a discount rate. They were co-operative and my four children, Shugufta and I moved into a two-room suite.

Each day, after school, the children lunched with their father and then went off for private tutoring. I left Mustafa's room at 6 p.m., making up medical bulletins to hand out to the press concerning his phantom heart condition.

Six more exhausting months passed. I was depleted and suffering from mental fatigue.

Severe abdominal pain plagued me. An examination revealed problems in my uterus. Doctors believed that it was due to excessive child-bearing, aggravated by my constant marching up and down the four stairwells of Nishtar Medical Hospital at the beck and call of my husband. Once more I needed surgery. Once more Mustafa dictated, 'Have the operation here.' Once more I refused, but this time I compromised. If Karachi was too far away, I was willing to go to Shaikh Zayed Hospital in Lahore. The children were excited about the possibility of returning to Lahore for their school holidays.

Mustafa declared that he would never allow me to go to a male gynaecologist.

I told him that I never intended to; I assured him that I would find a woman doctor. He still refused to let me go, but I was resolute.

When I went with the children to say goodbye to their sulking father, he set strict requirements to combat my obstinate attitude. He made me write on the Koran my promise that I would return in exactly fifteen days. I did so, but I amended the oath to say that I

274

would return in fifteen days if nothing extraordinary happened.

'What's this?' he asked when he read my statement.

'Mustafa, I can't make an oath on the Koran that may not be kept. Anything can happen. I can't be so precise.'

'What can happen?'

'Well, I could die, for instance.'

'So what?' he growled. 'Even if you die, your body should come to me fifteen days from now. If you're sick, come on a stretcher – I don't care.'

I stared at the man, freshly incredulous at his nerve and insensitivity.

He changed tactics swiftly. 'OK, you can go,' he said. 'I shall keep Nisha and Ali with me.' Renewed shock crossed my face. He smiled slyly and explained, 'They'll be miserable here. So make sure you return on time.'

'Be reasonable, Mustafa,' I said, asking the impossible. 'The children want to go to Lahore. They've been looking forward to the trip. It's not necessary to separate them like this.'

'No. They'll stay here with me.'

'What will they do cooped up here? Don't do this. It's cruel. Nisha and Ali will be insecure and frightened. They'll feel helpless. They'll know that Naseeba and Hamza are having a great time in Lahore. Don't punish them because I've fallen ill.'

'I said *no*! They'll stay in the hospital with me. You should come back on time.'

Consumed by his own insecurity, he once more held my children hostage. I felt sad and sorry for this man who could not allow me to be happy with him. I pandered to his every whim, and he responded with extreme and increasing insensitivity. He seemed hell-bent on pushing me away from him. Perhaps he thought that his ploy would cause me to agree to have my surgery here in Multan, but I was now made of stronger stuff than he realized. I left for Lahore with Naseeba and Hamza.

*   *   *

Mustafa called a meeting of his brothers and sons to discuss my growing stubbornness, my headstrong nature and rebellious attitudes. He complained, 'When she wants to do something she can take any conceivable risk – at the cost of her life even. She puts the consequences aside for later handling.' His brothers suggested curbing me quickly before I 'turned' completely.

As the stretcher rolled towards the operating theatre I felt alone and abandoned by the man for whom I had severed my family ties. Against my mother's orders, my grandmother and Zarmina stood by me. In return for their kindness they were ostracized.

I remained in the hospital for a week, then moved to my grandmother's house to recuperate. I watched as she cried on her prayer mat to deliver me from the constant troubles I had endured since childhood. She fed me and loved me as if she might make up for the absence of all other relationships in my life.

The day that I was scheduled to return to Multan, the morning newspaper reported that Mustafa had been picked up in the middle of the night and transferred to Rawalpindi. This development was truly ominous. It was there that Bhutto had been hanged. Immediately the authorities returned Nisha and Ali to me in Lahore.

I called a press conference to condemn Mustafa's transfer. Having learned well the lessons of political rhetoric, I noted that my husband was a heart patient and complained that the long drive to Rawalpindi was dangerous for him. In fact, we discovered that the transfer was to the Adyala Jail, just outside Islamabad.

The following day, 2 August 1987, was Mustafa's birthday and the children and I – accompanied by other members of Mustafa's family – flew to Islamabad and met Mustafa in the Superintendent's Office. In my handbag, in an attempt to placate him, I had a photograph of myself as a birthday present, but Mustafa did not want it. He was furious with me, for whatever real and imagined reasons. He always managed to be the centre of attention. I had neither the energy nor the ability to calm him down, and was glad that we were in a public place.

Mustafa asked the Superintendent to allow us to accompany him to his room. Permission was granted and we all moved into his cell. Mustafa told his relatives and our children that he wanted to talk to me privately and asked them to wait outside. A bamboo blind on the outside of the barred door offered scant privacy.

He wanted to make love. The stitches were still tender. I pleaded that I was not well, and would need another six weeks to heal, but he did not care. To ward off his advances, I reminded him that his family, our children – and the police – were just outside. I could hear the family chatting behind the bamboo screen. 'I have to go out and face them afterwards,' I said. 'I can't.' He would not listen. 'Mustafa,' I whispered firmly, 'I swear on God, I swear on the Prophet, if you dare touch me now, I will never come back and see you. I will leave you. I will get a divorce!'

He forced himself upon me. The pain was worse than I had feared, and the humiliation was even more excruciating. Yet I suffered silently.

When I was finally able to push him from me, I growled, 'You are sick – so sick! You bastard!'

Instantly he tried to make it up. He stammered, 'Forgive me—'

'—It's impossible to be your wife.'

'Don't leave me here,' Mustafa pleaded. 'For God's sake. What will happen to me? You'll go away and I'll be locked up here. I'll have so many worries. You're the only person I love, who loves me. You're the only hope I have. If you leave me I'll have nothing else.'

I glowered at him.

'Give me your photograph, Tehmina,' he said, 'there could be no nicer birthday present.'

I took the photograph of myself out of my handbag. With deliberate movements, I tore it and scattered the pieces.

13

I was at my grandmother's house in Lahore, carefully composing a registered letter to Mustafa asking for a divorce. The doorbell disrupted my thoughts and I went to answer it. A lovely young lady stood outside, smiling at me.

'Tanya!' I shrieked.

We clasped one another and sobbed. My grandmother, Naseeba, Nisha, Ali and Hamza all heard our cries of joy and came to join in the celebration. The excitement of the reunion filled Grandmother's home. My eldest daughter was back! Why? I wondered. For how long? I had many questions, but waited for an appropriate time.

Later, Tanya and I discussed our futures. Mine, as usual, was completely unsettled, but she knew what she wanted. 'I hate living in America,' she said. 'I hate living with my stepmother.' She had come to Pakistan on holiday but she wanted to stay and live with me.

I was thrilled and apprehensive at the same time. I told her about the letter that I was writing the very moment that she arrived. 'I've no idea what's going to happen,' I admitted. 'But stay—' Her face beamed. '—at least for a while.' Her face fell. 'Tanya, I just don't know,' I explained. 'We'll have to see.'

Two days later, the superintendent of the gaol, while censoring Mustafa's mail, came upon my registered letter, and our troubles became public knowledge. News of the pending divorce hit the front pages of the papers, shocking everyone. Many condemned me as callous and inconsistent. My poor, ailing husband was suffering behind bars, and I was walking out on him. The more vicious rumour-mongers said that I wanted my freedom so that I could be with other men. A few days before I had been the crusading wife. Now I was the woman everybody loved to hate.

With each passing day the pressure grew worse. Tanya was accustomed to a quiet existence, with no hint of public scrutiny. Here, life was a series of telephone calls from insistent reporters and visits from political operatives, playing their assorted power games. Tanya craved normality. I had none to give.

Each moment that we spent together was more poignant than the previous. We both knew the outcome, but I was the one who had to drop the bomb: 'Tanya, you're in a good school in New Jersey. Your father loves you and can give you security. I can give you nothing – yet. I don't know what Mustafa will do to me. You must return to your father.'

Once more she clutched at me and once more I was forced to push her away. I wondered: How many times must we play this scene? Until we get it right?

Amid all this turmoil, Mustafa's younger brother Rehmani died of a heart attack. He was only thirty years old and I remembered him with affection; he had lived with us for a time, and he was always respectful and courteous toward me. When his body arrived from London, I flew from Lahore to Islamabad to pay my respects. Mustafa's brother Ghazi and his son Abdur Rehman received me graciously.

Mustafa was allowed to attend the funeral in Kot Addu, and I heard that he wept like a child. I wondered if the tears had been for his brother or for me. It was the first time since I had married him that I was not at his side during a time of special ordeal.

Nusrat Jamil – better known as Nuscie – is a journalist, working for the English-language daily *The Nation*. She phoned, introduced herself and asked for an interview;

she wanted to write a human interest story about the travails of a politician's estranged wife. I agreed to talk to her. Nuscie changed my life.

I found her to be beautiful, intelligent and articulate. She interviewed me at my home and then invited me to her house for dinner that evening. I went because I was now suing for divorce and felt suddenly no longer bound to Mustafa's dictates. The environment there was different from any other I had encountered in Pakistan. I categorized Nuscie's manner of housekeeping as 'stylishly relaxed'. She obviously cared more about substance than style. Her husband, known simply as J.J., was there, along with Yousaf Salahuddin, the grandson of the Pakistani poet, Allama Iqbal. I found J.J. to be a very liberated male, the most understanding I had ever met. We shared a fascination for Freudian and Jungian analysis. He believed in the talking cure, and he helped me make a tentative beginning at unravelling some of the mysteries in my mind.

Nuscie knew that mine was a conditioned life, that I had lived with a much older man rooted in a feudal mentality. My values were conventional, and yet she saw in me potential that instigated rebellion. She knew that I was underexposed to the modern world, and she decided that my initiation should be complete, but slow. She showed me that there was life after divorce. 'Social acceptability is insufficient reason to maintain a marriage that has rotted away,' she said. I was intrigued by this glimpse of another philosophical approach to life. These were people of my own age, but thought as I could not dare to think.

After dinner we drove to a roadside café to have *kulfi*, home-made ice-cream. My companions had relaxed me somewhat, but I still felt nervous and inhibited, like a truant from school. My new friends were in no hurry, and we lingered in the car outside the café past midnight. The late hour frightened and excited me at the same time. I felt deliciously naughty, alone with strange men, unchaperoned by Dai Ayesha, breaking Mustafa's curfew. It was almost as if he was present, scowling over my shoulder. He would find out about my night on the town; he always found out. But did it matter? Yes, it did.

Freedom was still not a simple issue.

My lawyer went to see Mustafa. The prisoner played the role of the jilted husband, professed his undying love for me and begged my lawyer to convince me to return. The bottom line was that he adamantly refused to grant me a divorce. I had no choice but to apply for *Khula* (literally, to 'disown' or 'repudiate'). *Khula* is a right of divorce granted to a woman by Islamic law as long as she agrees to rescind part or all of her property claims. Mustafa could not force me to continue the marriage, but he could leave me destitute.

I did not even think about money. Throughout my thirty-four years, money had simply been there. It had always been the man's consideration: first my father, then Anees, then Mustafa. All I knew at the moment was that there was sufficient money in our joint bank account to cover expenses for several months. What happened after that, who could foretell?

There was nothing left for me in Lahore. The publicity had ended my usefulness to the party and Mustafa had anaesthetized my passion for politics. My old friends had disappeared, and I realized the unpleasant truth that they were all Mustafa's allies and cronies – our social contacts were enmeshed in the net of politics. My father purchased a flat for me in Karachi and I settled in with the children and my maid, Shagufta. At first I was very bored. My life as the wife of an exiled political leader had overqualified me for a humdrum existence, for normality.

But before long Nuscie and J.J. arrived in Karachi and invited me to the village of Bhit Shah, in the interior of Sind, to join them in commemorating the *urs* of the great Sufi saint, Shah Abdul Latif Bhitai. (The *urs* is a celebration of a saint's death, and thus his reunion with God.) This was a religious holiday with political overtones. Since General Zia's assumption of power, and particularly so since Bhutto's execution, the *urs* at Bhit Shah had become a rallying point for the people of Sind. Here, under a canopy of mysticism, beneath a waxing moon, militant Sindis gathered and, through their music and dance, patterned a protest. The saint had been a master poet, whose subtle writings offered protection and release from an oppressive order.

In the interior regions of Sind, respectable women cover their faces with a *chader*, leaving only the eyes and brow visible. For this occasion Nuscie and I used *ajruk*, a traditional Sindi cloth dyed with vegetable pigments.

It was carnival time in Bhit Shah. Sullen yet proud faces peered through the windows of our car. The village was abuzz with activity, and the festival was unlike anything I had ever seen. All norms were abandoned, all standards put on hold. We strolled amid crowds in the makeshift bazaar, sidled our way past fortune-tellers and dismissed the spiels of the *bhang* (opium) sellers. I had heard of opium, of course, but had never seen it. It was against political law and perhaps against Islamic law, but the latter was an arguable point. Many of the mystical *faqirs* contend that opium enhances their religious ecstasy.

We peeked into sleazy cafés where eunuchs, clad in golden, skin-tight body suits, danced lewdly and made seedy assignations. One of them strutted like Michael Jackson as he screamed out an Urdu version of a rock-and-roll tune. These half-male, half-female performers comprise one of the most enigmatic classes of our society. No-one seems to know where they come from. They are visible to the public only on special occasions. One seldom sees a very young eunuch or an extremely old one. It is said that they live in segregated colonies where social intrigue runs deep, and where they conduct their passionate love affairs in their own mysterious manner. The hypocrisy of our male-dominated society was thrown into broad relief by the spectre of men who adopted the feminine role. I craned my neck to view the grotesque, wicked scene. I thought: This is a dream that Fellini might have had.

We took in a circus, complete with a big top and a few flea-infested, bored elephants and lions. The trapeze artists were eunuchs who wore frilly bloomers over their leotards. We indulged ourselves with music, and watched the gyrations of the whirling dervish Soong dancers in their saffron-hued robes.

That night we stayed at a rest house in Bhit Shah with a few other of Nuscie and J.J.'s friends. I was surprised and somewhat shocked when I realized that six of us – male and female – would 'crash' in one room. I could not believe that I was to sleep in the same quarters as three other men, none of whom was my husband. But my companions were nonchalant about the arrangement, and I scolded myself for being such a prude.

Very early the next morning we visited the shrine of Shah Abdul Latif, one of the most beautiful in the East. Supplicants, exhausted from the previous night's revelry, lounged in the courtyard; their famished eyes were a thousand begging bowls. *Faqirs* sang an eerie chant in harmony, pleading for dawn to break upon the nation. One of them, his hair braided into dreadlocks, danced in an intoxicated frenzy.

Standing before the great saint's grave, I wondered: What should I pray for? My mind spun like the Soong dancers. I was overcome by a sudden sense of guilt. How could I pray for myself while my husband languished in prison? Through the veil of my *chader*, I uttered silent prayers for Mustafa's release.

After two days in Bhit Shah, when the full moon began to wane, ending the festival, we drove back to Karachi. I sat in the back seat of the car, between J.J. and another man. Throughout the ride, however, I was very self-conscious lest I inadvertently touch either of the men. Everyone was amused at this.

Nuscie and J.J. invited me back to Lahore for a round of parties celebrating the 1984 World Cup cricket tournament. I was again excited and apprehensive at the prospect of partying without a husband. The children and I left for Lahore to stay with my grandmother. I was determined to enjoy myself. In Nuscie's crowd I met confident young girls who twirled on the dance floor in tight jeans and miniskirts, openly cavorting with men who were not their husbands! It shocked me that they exposed their legs – this was Pakistan, not London – and it shocked me further that no-one else was shocked. This was the generation that had grown up in Zia's time. Their idols were not Che, Mao or Sukarno, but Madonna, Iacocca and Trump. Poverty meant a flat without air-conditioning. The deprived drove Suzukis. The effects of the Afghan war and the drug explosion had filtered in. The poppy fields on the borders of Afghanistan and Pakistan had become more productive, the traffic quite legalized, and refugees unlimited. It was as if many centuries had been traversed in an instant. Modern women had moved so far ahead that their sisters in the hinterlands had been reduced to fictional characters.

I understood, then, that I had been caught in a time warp and was still mentally trapped. For the first time in my life, I began to believe that I was strange, that the world held other, perfectly normal souls who were unwilling to suffer in silence and would react to injustice. My views on life and marriage were outdated and restrictive. I realized that Mustafa and my family had drawn me into their world and shut all the windows.

I enjoyed my role as a detached spectator, but I remained on the sidelines. The music was so loud that it drowned out conversation, and I was not about to indulge in intimate whispering games. My idea of a party remained a sit-down dinner where everyone gets to know everybody else. Still, I enjoyed the glamour.

I went to my first cricket match and savoured the game vicariously, through Nuscie and J.J. When they stood up and cheered, so did I. When they were silent and tense, I plastered a glum expression on my face. There were frenzied and delighted screams at the end: Pakistan had beaten the mighty West Indians and was now favoured to win the entire tournament.

At the height of cricket fever, I walked into Yousuf Salahuddin's *haveli* (a traditional-style home in the 'old walled city' of Lahore) and found a few men sprawled in the central courtyard. None of them rose to greet us. How strange, I thought. In my world, a gentleman always rose when a lady entered. Yousuf reclined on a marble divan and surveyed, with a hint of royal disdain, the host of miniskirted women who flitted about, displaying punk hairstyles. Outside, the walls were plastered with posters calling for the restoration of democracy. Inside, Yousuf was a replica of a Mogul dynast, the epicure personified.

I was introduced to one of the bodies on the floor, Imran Khan, the great cricket idol. Trying my hand at some cricket talk, I blurted out, 'I saw how you batted the West Indians out.' His small, narrowed eyes glanced at me with irritation, and I realized that I had probably not phrased the statement correctly. I also met a man named Mubashar, who told me to call him by his nickname Moby. 'Moby,' I asked, 'are you a cricketer, too?' How was I to know if he might not also be superstar material? I met the dashing Omer Farooq and his wife Minna. Omer was known by various nicknames, such as 'Goldi' (for 'Goldfinger'). Due to his financial acumen, it was said that everything he touched turned to gold. Others referred to him as 'Mario Falichi', which seemed to be a reference to his ambience as a sort of Mafia-style tycoon, which he consciously embellished with well-cut designer suits.

Over time I got to know all of these people better, and I liked them. I found Imran to be a highly principled man, combining his sense of honour with a fiercely competitive nature that served our country well. Moby was the strong, silent type, who had an ability to communicate through silence. Goldi was reliable. Yousuf was full of fun and games. It was a major achievement for me to create new relationships not imposed upon me by Mustafa. These people saw me as myself, not as the extension of a politician.

I realized that although the details of their stories varied from mine, each of these people was a survivor. Everyone in this group had been through points of adversity and struggle, and emerged stronger. The critical element of the healing process was that they had analysed their lives and corrected deficiencies. These were concepts that infused me with hope about my own existence.

But who was the person *I* wanted to be?

I was driving my grandmother out of her mind. Sometimes I asked her to pray for Mustafa's release from prison; sometimes I asked her to pray for my release from him. She frequently threw up her hands and screamed in exasperation, 'Should we love him or should we hate him? Make up your mind. Even the Almighty is confused with what you want. You give Him no time to answer your prayer. When He begins to answer, the request has changed again.' On her prayer mat, she cried out to Allah, begging him to settle my restless spirit.

It was true. I was horribly confused. A new life beckoned to me, but the old ways still had me in their grip. What was I to do? What did I want to do? I did not know.

A change of scenery was in order, and I decided to take my children back to our London flat, to give me time to patch my shattered personality. When I had to postpone the trip in order to settle some paperwork, my lawyer advised that if I delayed too long Mustafa might hear of my plans and obtain a stay order, preventing my children from leaving the country. The better strategy was to send my three older children on first, and then join them later. Hamza, the youngest, would stay with Shugufta at my grandmother's house.

I called my sister Minoo in London and asked if she would meet the children at the airport and care for them for the few days until I arrived. Minoo agreed immediately, eager to help and excited about the prospect of seeing my children. We both knew that our mother would be furious to learn that Minoo was doing anything to help me. There had been no contact with Mother since my last reunion with Mustafa.

Naseeba, Nisha and Ali were already on the plane, en route to the UK, when Minoo called back with a frantic message. Our mother had learned of the plan and had ordered Minoo to have nothing to do with it. It was Mother's contention that this time I had kidnapped the children, and she was determined to punish me. Once more, my children were pawns.

What was I to do? Who would meet the children at the airport? I still had many friends in London, but I did not want to involve them in my domestic dispute; most of them would be very reticent to side against Mustafa anyway. On an impulse, I phoned Minoo and suggested that she call the PIA manager and ask him to meet the plane and send the children to her home by taxi. 'They will show up at your doorstep,' I explained in a conspiratorial tone. 'You call Mummy and tell her that the kids are there and you can hardly turn them away.'

When my children left the plane at 10.30 p.m. and their aunt was not there to meet them, they were frightened. Fortunately the PIA manager took charge. He put them into a taxi and handed the driver a scrap of paper with Minoo's address scrawled upon it. The driver got lost. He scolded my petrified children for not knowing where they were going. Naseeba feared that he would simply leave them off somewhere in the dark, unfamiliar streets. All three children sobbed in terror.

Finally, the driver found the house. Minoo took in the three waifs and offered comfort. Then she called our mother to report the 'unexpected' arrival. Mother exploded with rage and ordered Minoo to put the children on the next flight back to Karachi, but Minoo's husband Ali declared that he would not be a party to such crass and callous behaviour.

Mother called back early the next morning and declared that, if Minoo and Ali would not co-operate, *she* would send the children back to Pakistan immediately. Frantic, Minoo called me with a report. Mother had threatened to disown her unless she complied. The children had to be removed.

Nuscie came to the rescue. She called her sister Chinni in London and asked her to care for the children until I could arrive. Poor, bewildered Chinni could not fathom my family's irrational behaviour. She had children of her own to care for, but she graciously granted temporary sanctuary to mine. By long distance I arranged for a wonderful woman from the Pakistan Embassy to care for them during the day, while Chinni attended her college classes. The children felt unwelcome and were traumatized by having to stay with strangers. They were aware of Chinni's discomfort over their presence.

Within a few days I flew to London on a six-month visa, with Hamza howling for Shugufta because we had to leave her behind, and set up house at our Holland Park apartment. I found a boarding school for the older children in Kent. It was a Lebanese institution run along Islamic lines. This provided ammunition against Mustafa's old charge that the children were being exposed to a degenerate western lifestyle.

Mustafa's soul stalked me. His brother Arbi called me to report that Mustafa was broken and distraught, crying ceaselessly for me and the children. 'He'll die in gaol,' Arbi prophesied. 'He doesn't eat or sleep. He's obsessed with you.'

The message from Mustafa's son Abdur Rehman was more sinister: 'He's planning to make any compromise necessary to obtain freedom. He'll come to England and take the children again.' I was petrified that he might send someone to London with instructions to murder me.

I was a fugitive. How far and how long could I run?

The mirror reflected hollow, lifeless eyes, with traces of anger and defiance. These were eyes that had forgotten how to dream; eyes that pursued me through my London flat, taunting me for my lack of endurance, mocking me for turning my back on an unfinished task; eyes that glowered at me and accused: You had become a part of the struggle for the people of Pakistan, determined to help them rise from indigence and squalor. Like everyone, you have betrayed them.

I suffered sleepless nights, bedevilled by the image of Mustafa languishing in prison. Leaving him did not bother me, but the timing did. I had kicked him when he was crippled.

Mustafa Khar had ceased to be my husband, but he remained my political leader. I still wanted to transform our dreams into reality, but I was ill-equipped to return to my country and make a political stand on my own. For that, I needed the platform that Mustafa provided. I pictured him alone, broken and deprived of hope. It was his own nature that had led him to this forlorn state, his own nature that had pushed me away. Yet I could not escape the truism that he needed me. I did not want to go down in history as a woman who had aborted a dream.

I could not shake the message of Faiz Ahmad Faiz's humanistic masterpiece of poetry:

Do not ask me for the same intensity
with which I loved you once . . .
I turn, I turn again and again to the pain.
You are still beautiful, so beautiful –
but – the pain.

Had I bartered the happiness of the masses for my own
peace of mind? I was secure in my British cocoon – but
– the pain.

I thought of the children in that horrible ward at
Nishtar Medical Hospital in Multan. I tried to convince
myself that I had done my part by raising money and
delivering medicine, but I knew that I, like everybody
else, had walked away from a hopeless situation.

I began to paint again, and my paintings showed me
the way. Almost trance-like, my hand recreated my
experiences among the wretched of the earth. I painted
urchins, with ribs struggling to break out from the
confines of taut skin, whose past, present and future lay
in overflowing garbage heaps. I painted the expressions
of mothers whose breasts had gone dry. I painted old
men and women sitting in an alley, their heads bowed
in exhaustion. I painted in blacks, beiges and browns.

Another Faiz poem crept into my canvas:

I bequeath my life to the lanes and alleys of my land,
where the ritual of silence stalks.
Where no one holds his head up high.
And Fear takes nightly walks.

I painted women with their hair loosened, as though in
mourning. Ordinary people with limited wants penetrated my mind and appeared on my canvas.

Images of gaol flooded my brain. I had seen women
in prison who had been raped by the staff. Some were
later taken away by frightened gaolers who forced them
to abort their pregnancies in order to eliminate proof
of the crime. Others bore the bastardized offspring of

'justice'. I painted them, mothers and children together behind bars, fearful of release into a hostile and uncertain world.

Each brush stroke brought me closer to a decision: to return. The words I had written on the Koran haunted me: 'I will stand by Mustafa through his incarceration be it for life.'

After only a month in London, I began to pack.

14

We landed at Islamabad airport. Mustafa was in court
under police custody that day when I sent the children
to see him. Press photographers gathered around to
record the tearful reunion of the Lion and his cubs.

I visited him the following day and noticed that he
had lost a visible amount of weight. We were tentative
with one another until finally he broke the ice. 'Let's
give our marriage another chance,' he implored. 'I'll try
and understand you. You must try and understand me.
Let's forget what happened.'

Mustafa told me that he had been miserable while I
was away, spending his days on his prayer mat, weeping
and wailing so loudly that the guards were overcome by
his grief. They, like I, had been devastated to see this
powerful man bent and broken with grief.

Pictorial images of the Prophet and his companions
are forbidden in Islam. The ban was ordained to prevent
idolatry. But for the Shias (a Muslim sect), especially in
Iran, it is customary to keep a painting of the Prophet's
cousin Hazrat Ali, who is revered by all the sects.
Mustafa had such a painting in his cell. Hazrat Ali is the
great intercessor, the symbol of strength and protection,
to whom Muslims respond in adversity with passion and
fervour. Mustafa told me that whenever he was overcome by feelings of helplessness, he turned to this
portrait of Hazrat Ali and begged for his intervention.
'If it hadn't been for my faith I would have broken,'
Mustafa contended. 'His very name exudes a great
power that has sustained me.'

He admitted that his introspection had been painful

but necessary. He now realized that he had done terrible things to me, and was chastised by the memories of his violence. Often, he said, my tormented face visited his dreams.

He spoke of the Adila episode, and was convinced that the Devil had entered him. He knew that he had imprisoned me in loneliness, and now, he believed, God had punished him with imprisonment while I was free. He had thought that he had lost me for ever, and all he had was this room and God. He now realized what it must have been like for me at the time of Ali's birth when I was isolated and alone. He had been very distressed by the fact that I was young and attractive and could easily meet another man and begin a new life. He had heard rumours about my days of freedom and was insanely jealous. 'At last I understand your pain,' he said, 'by the experience of my own.'

He promised to change.

For the first time I sincerely believed him. But could I risk acting upon that belief? It was impossible to know. Yet I had made up my mind when I bought the airline tickets back to Pakistan. I did not care what anyone else thought. When the press asked me to justify my inconstant behaviour, I remembered what Mustafa had taught me about the art of confidence – the people are sheep; they will follow if they feel you know the way – and I responded, 'It was my decision to leave and my decision to return. I shall continue to campaign for the release of my husband with the same zeal.'

We had an emotional reunion with Shugufta and Dai Ayesha. Shugufta was now a trendy young lady. She had begun to dress like me and her confidence was soaring. Mustafa often said I was like the Empress Noorjahan, who was renowned for improving the fashion sense of her maids. Dai Ayesha was a little chagrined by Shugufta's closeness to me, but I understood that.

* * *

During each visit Mustafa regaled me with stories of prison life. 'There's a black market operating here,' he disclosed. 'You can get anything for a price. The gaol establishment is like the Mafia. The superintendent is the don. I'm aware of all that goes on here, and I am going to pull it out from its roots.' Other prisoners were of course treated very differently from important ones like Mustafa. But he viewed the other prisoners as his family; he was the paternalistic feudal lord, taking up their causes with conviction. The eyes of the other prisoners haunted my dreams. I could see that they looked to Mustafa as the repository of their hope.

Mustafa disclosed, 'The superintendent takes protection money from all the prisoners. The amounts are paid out weekly. Any prisoner who will not or cannot pay this extortion tax is punished. They're either beaten mercilessly or placed in fetters. Many prisoners are deprived of their meals because of their inability to pay. Entire families have had to pay the price and are groaning under the burden of debt.' He knew all the methods of torture, and some of them were too terrible to describe.

Mustafa's eyes took on a faraway look as he complained, 'Tehmina, the superintendent is a bloody parasite. He lives off human suffering. He thrives on pain. He collects fifty thousand to eighty thousand rupees a month from the wretched of the earth. A part of this money is distributed like booty amongst his subordinates. This isn't a prison where you reform. It's a slave camp where criminals are being created by injustice. This is the reason I'm in politics. I'll not rest till this inhuman system is razed to the ground.'

My own anger mounted as I witnessed some of the atrocities myself. I saw women prisoners – many whose babies were incarcerated with them – abused and assaulted. I saw the pleading eyes of innocents who were convicted upon false testimony. If there was hell on earth, this was it.

Mustafa appreciated my empathy and he joked, 'Let

me come to power and I'll make you the minister of gaols.'

'I'll hold you to that,' I replied, somewhat seriously.

One day we were interrupted by a wrenching shriek. I said to Mustafa, 'It sounds as if someone's soul is being ripped from his body.' I plugged my ears with my fingers in an attempt to drown out the horrible wails, aware that we could offer no help.

Mustafa's eyes burned with anger. He waited for a time, then bolted from his seat. He marched to the padlocked door of his cell, banged loudly upon it and commanded 'Kholo!' (Open!). A frightened guard promptly opened the door and saluted. Mustafa brushed him aside like an insect and strode toward the sound of the screams. I raced after him, trying to keep up. The guard followed at a distance, afraid of the consequences.

We came to a large outdoor compound, where many prisoners were sitting on their haunches, forming a large circle, receiving a brutal lesson in deterrence. One of their fellow inmates was in the centre, spreadeagled on the ground. Several policemen were kicking him and beating him with staves. He was bleeding profusely and was only semi-conscious, but continued to emit terrifying shrieks. I winced in sympathetic pain as two of the guards grabbed the prisoner's legs and stretched them apart as far as possible. The man shrieked once more. His pupils disappeared into the upper eyelids. Then there was a terrible, deathly silence.

Mustafa shot like a lightning bolt toward the deputy superintendent with fire in his eyes. He grabbed the prison official by his collar and slapped him sharply, several times. The deputy was stunned, but dared not react. Mustafa Khar may have been a prisoner, but he was not a man to be taken lightly. In a voice like thunder Mustafa roared, 'If I ever hear a scream again, I will beat you to a pulp!' Then he released his collar-hold and pushed the man so that he fell back upon his buttocks with his legs in the air. Mustafa turned and strode back to his cell. If the other prisoners had dared, they would have applauded, but they confined themselves to signalling silent admiration with their eyes.

Soon the deputy superintendent arrived at Mustafa's cell, accompanied by three policemen. He murmured quietly, 'Sir, you should not have slapped me in front of all those prisoners. I have lost their respect. We have to control them, you know that.'

'You don't deserve their respect,' Mustafa retorted, in a powerful and dismissive tone of authority. 'You cannot rule through fear and violence. I shall have you dismissed from your job. You will not be spared, you bastard. Leave us! I won't waste time talking to you. I shall deal with you when the time comes.'

The hapless deputy superintendent mumbled an apology under his breath and walked away, shattered.

I was very proud of my husband. I asked, 'How did you decide to do what you just did? You are their prisoner, but you turned the tables on them.'

He told me a story, gleaned from his early readings under Bhutto's tutelage. 'Napoleon Bonaparte once kicked open his prison door and announced to his stunned captors that he was Napoleon! This was enough. His reputation preceded him. Remember, politics is based on conviction. What I did was right. I had the upper hand in moral terms. If my confidence had wavered even for a second, the deputy would have retaliated. We can learn a lot from the confidence trickster. He plays on his victim's gullibility by keeping a straight face and coming across as sincere and genuine. We cannot afford to display any chinks in our armour.'

Mustafa's act of defiance soon became prison folklore. The superintendent's hatred for him grew, but was made impotent by the strength of Mustafa's burgeoning popularity. The authorities knew that, with a single word, like oil on a smouldering fire, the Lion of the Punjab could detonate a riot.

My political education began in earnest. Mustafa realized that it was the lure of politics that had brought me back, and he gave succour to the idealist in me. He encouraged me to ask questions and I sensed that, at times, I forced him to formulate answers to issues he had never addressed. He was on his best behaviour. He understood that – hopefully – we were grooming one another for a spectacular re-entry into Pakistani politics, and he knew that it was important for a leader to be exemplary. He taught me his craft, explained strategy and indoctrinated me. It was a meticulous cloning process. He coached me for the role of playing *him* on the stage of the outside world. His release would be assured by a combination of his brains and my total commitment to the cause.

He detailed for me his vision, built through years of quiet contemplation. I had absorbed bits and pieces of it over the years, but now he weaved it into a coherent mosaic. His starting point was the people. The aspirations and expectations of the common man had been bartered away by self-seeking politicians. He spoke of exploitation, of the unholy axis that had been forged between the civil and military bureaucracy and the feudal and urban lords. It was the power of the people, he proclaimed, that was the soft underbelly of the current crop of politicians.

Mustafa emphasized the need for organizational work at grass-roots level. He looked forward to a political system where power flowed upward. He advocated a return to the early principles of Islam. He argued about Marxism, pointed out its defects and admired its universal appeal. He reconvinced me of the need to cut the size of the military establishment. 'We have to direct our scarce resources away from this monster,' he preached. 'Our people need food, shelter, clothing, medical facilities, potable water and education. The army has gobbled up our national wealth. It is a waste of manpower. If I come to power I will use the army for the construction of roads and bridges. It is also a constant threat to constitutional rule.'

He was a fervent advocate of fraternal ties with the Soviet Union. He repudiated Zia's stance which opposed the Russian invasion of Afghanistan and was opposed to the resettlement of Afghani refugees in Pakistan. 'Zia is sacrificing our future for short-term gains,' he contended. 'He doesn't understand the terrible spillover of this unnecessary involvement. The Russians will never forget our role. Gun culture and the drug trade are natural spin-offs of this conflict. The generals are myopic. They have been dazzled by the dollar diplomacy of the Americans. The Americans are unreliable allies. They'll use us only until they've accomplished their own designs.'

In fact Zia had made drug-trafficking legitimate. While Afghanistan was the major grower, the poppies were processed in Pakistan. It was said that labs had been set up by US Mafia connections – no border, free movement, no control, quick money. *Allegedly*, the Inter Services Intelligence (ISI) had a hand; even the war was financed through the sale of opium and heroin. When aid dwindled, the Mujahadeen used drugs as a source for funds.

The Soviet Union apart, Mustafa was convinced that Pakistan had to distance itself from the power blocs. The country had to become more insular, at least for a period, in order to foster a sense of independence. 'Look at China, look at India,' he said. 'They are developing their own indigenous technologies. They don't go around with a begging bowl in their hands. They have great national pride. We have taken the easy way out. Everything is imported – even our ideas.'

He was the natural heir to the politics of his mentor. Bhutto had left behind an uneven legacy. He had been a populist with the right slogans to galvanize the people, but he had lacked the time to implement the necessary reforms. Mustafa believed that the opportunity was now in his hands.

I felt that, finally, the man I always wanted to see emerge had done so. Here was a selfless politician who was inviting me into his mind and showing me the truth. To me, at that time, there was a messianic quality about him that his prisoner status only served to enhance.

In a very subtle way, Mustafa prepared me for public life in a country where appearance, especially that of a woman, matters. He used his sharp sense of humour, without malice, to tease me about my appearance, and to guide me toward altering it in the most effective ways. On a number of occasions he complimented me by saying that I looked like a model who had just stepped out of the pages of a fashion magazine. That was great, but he laughed, pointing out that my appearance was a bit incongruous for my role as the wife of a noted political prisoner. Once, to his amazement, I added copper, gold and ash-coloured highlights to my brown hair. He was so astonished that he burst out laughing, and suggested that I go back to the 'long brown tresses that had imprisoned' him fifteen years earlier. He was further shocked when I had my hair permed and appeared with long corkscrew curls. 'What's this? Have you grown springs on your head?' he asked.

One day I entered his prison cell immediately after attending a political meeting in Gujrat. I was buoyant; the meeting had been a great success. I was wearing traditional, black baggy trousers, a black-and-white knit shirt with red collar and cuffs, and a long red cashmere cape draped over my shoulders, my hair freely cascading down my back. Mustafa took one look at me and said, 'You know what you look like today? You look like Margaret Thatcher in a *chader*. Where was your meeting? In Birmingham or Southall, or was it in Gujrat?' I grinned, sheepishly acknowledging that I should have dressed more appropriately for the occasion.

Another time he shook his head when he saw me coming into the prison yard without a *dupatta* (veil). 'I had to see this day,' he moaned. 'My wife walking into a prison, with all these men around, uncovered by a *dupatta*.'

'I forgot it,' I said with a shrug.

'Is it something you forget?' he asked sharply, but with a view towards education and not malice. 'You've forgotten a very basic thing. It represents your *sharam* [shame] and your *haya* [feminine modesty].'

I cringed. Mustafa had made a basic point: freedom does not mean licence.

Colours had always fascinated me; then one day something snapped inside me and I decided that, from now on, I would wear only simple white cotton. When I told Mustafa of this decision he was not shocked. In fact, he seemed to have expected it. This is what he wanted so that I did not look attractive to the male society in which I now moved. But he knew that he could not force it upon me. For my part, I felt as if a great burden had been lifted. My white cotton would not be a mere symbolic gesture; it was the culmination of a long and painful process of self-discovery. My over-indulgence in clothes and the need to look beautiful was a legacy from a childhood spent as my mother's wardrobe mistress. I used them in my adulthood to maximum advantage. I had enticed and entrapped Mustafa with my appearance and been caught in my own trap. I had tried to keep him with the help of clothes and Adila had tried to snatch him away with hers. I had used clothes to make a public impression – the glamorous wife of a political prisoner had emerged to replace the conventional drab, covered image. The need to impress with either my belongings or my appearance dissipated. I had come to rely upon my personality and beliefs – the priorities stood converted. Now I realized the contradiction: the indulgences of vanity separated me from the people I sought to represent.

Throughout his long sojourn in prison Mustafa wrote me politically instructive letters, which were always hand-delivered. He taught me not to betray my true feelings during negotiations. 'Keep an expressionless face,' he advised. 'Keep your opponent guessing about your reactions.' He told me to be polite but firm, to enquire but not inform. He cautioned me about the pitfalls of stirring up unnecessary controversies and tutored me on the art of fielding tricky questions at press conferences.

His letters were embellished with romance as well. He explained his unreasonable attitude of possessiveness and insecurity by saying, 'All the great legends of love end in tragedy . . . their love was intense, not practical and balanced. You cannot find balance in love, which is why you have to be prepared to carry its burden if you want love.' He reached out to the woman in me. He told me how much he needed me and how proud he was of me. 'Without you I cannot achieve anything,' he declared. 'I feel that I can achieve anything when you are at my side. I can take the greatest of risks. I would gladly die today, if I knew that you would remain committed to me.'

From time to time, I suggested that Mustafa clarify his philosophies on paper, so that we could publish pamphlets and distribute them. I predicted that this would set the imaginations of the deprived on fire. But Mustafa said, 'Our people are illiterate. They have no interest in pamphlets. They want a leader who can articulate their demands, who can feel their needs. You have to go out amongst them and speak to them in a language they understand. If I write down everything I want to do, the people in power will eliminate me. They will be the first to sit up and take notice. Why should I serve notice? I will attack them in the field, not in column inches.'

When he explained it like this, I had to agree. He was proRussian, anti-military, anti-feudal, anti-industrialist and anti-bureaucratic corruption. The forces in power would never accept such a socialist reform platform. The blueprint had to remain in Mustafa's mind. Only when he was free, when he was in command of the masses, could he reveal even glimpses to the public. Until then, he had to lull the reactionary forces.

We often spoke of the future, and of how the prison experience had forced us to reorient our priorities. The future was not what it used to be. Power was no longer a goal in itself. In fact the acquisition of power, under our current political strategy, would force us to lower our social standing. We vowed to live simply, fear God and serve the people. 'We shall live in our present small house,' Mustafa decided. 'We have to set an example. We have to become role models for the people.' And I believed him.

One day my reflection in a mirror caught me by surprise. I thought: Who is this woman in white? Can it really be me? Mustafa had moulded me into a serious person with a sense of mission. I had packed away my designer clothes and mothballed my vanity. I was ashamed of my collection of shoes, which seemed to rival that of Imelda Marcos. My beautiful matching handbags remained empty and unused. I wore only silver jewellery, like the poorest of Pakistani women.

My metamorphosis was complete. Mustafa knew that I was attractive, but he had no choice other than to let me fight his battle in this male-dominated society. He became secure in his trust only when he was convinced that he had created a political being whose loyalty and mission were beyond reproach. He knew that as long as I was convinced of the righteousness of his cause, I would never stray. I had to believe him to love him.

And I believed him.

I had four children to raise, and they were still too young to comprehend why their father was imprisoned. They did not know how to cope with the taunts of their classmates. I explained as best I could the distinction between a common criminal and a political prisoner, and tried to paint a word picture of their father as pure goodness combating evil darkness. My daughters, being older, were able to understand this better than my sons, but they still found it very difficult to convince their friends, who came from apolitical bourgeois and feudal backgrounds, that their father was in prison simply because of his opposition to martial law. Seven-year-old Ali got into a few scraps, trying to prove that his father was not a murderer. Little Hamza was hopelessly confused. He was only eight months old when his father went to gaol. He only knew Mustafa as a 'big man' who, for some inexplicable reason, could not come home. Every time we left the prison after a visit, Hamza asked, 'Why can't we take him home?'

They needed a father to identify with, and to love. I built him up in their minds by recounting anecdotes, and underplayed my present strange role as his protector. I explained that I was merely carrying his fight forward and that when he came out of prison he would protect all of us. They learned to admire their father for his courage against the dictator. Gradually, even Hamza developed pride in his father's incarceration. He came to view Adyala Jail as his father's palace and Mustafa as the great prince who lived there under police protection.

I was obsessed with getting him out. Here was a man whose experiences had sculpted him for this moment in history. He had a decisive and critical role to play, I thought. A mind such as this should not be left to rot in gaol.

I was also desperate for a normal life. We had spent our entire marriage either being hounded by the abnormality of exile or the constraints of prison. We had never lived without the strain of opposition politics. I thought that without the pressures Mustafa might have behaved very differently I ascribed much of his abnormal behaviour to abnormal circumstances.

Since Nuscie had been a friend I had made when I was separated from him, Mustafa refused permission for me to see her, J.J. and my other new friends. 'When I come out you can see them again,' he declared. 'Until then, I cannot permit it. The subject is closed.' Any mention of Nuscie aggravated the situation. And he kept me so busy with political work that I had little time to socialize anyway.

At public meetings, I heard Mustafa's voice emerge from my mouth, and I saw the crowds respond to me as they had done to him. Through me, Mustafa had scaled the prison walls.

I had to proceed with great care. Powerful forces were arrayed against him. If they perceived him as a threat, they could, and would, liquidate him.

Our old friend Taj-ul-Mulk offered me the annexe of his mansion in Lahore to use as an office. It was at a dance there that Mustafa had proposed to me. Punjabi workers from the National People's Party flocked to see me. As Mustafa had predicted, they had grown disillusioned with the leadership of Jatoi and his henchmen and sought a new focal point. Sajid, who had worked with both Bhutto and Mustafa since 1967, moved from Multan to offer guidance and to help me carry out Mustafa's strategies; he became my chief aide. Others, who had been student leaders in the early days of our marriage and who had now matured, joined our cadre.

I persuaded our group that the time had come to mount a sustained media campaign. We contacted financial backers who provided funds for posters and print advertisements demanding Mustafa's release. I found that, just like Mustafa, I could draw the party workers to me, orchestrate their actions and keep their morale high.

Rival party leaders resented my growing popularity and spread rumours. They warned workers that Mustafa did not trust me; they criticized me for leaving him and accused me of actually conspiring with the military to keep my husband in gaol. 'She wants him dead,' they charged. 'She wants to take over.' Some of the workers were quite shaken by these nasty attacks, but when Mustafa heard about the smear campaign against me he issued a strong statement to the press: 'My wife represents me. Everything she says and does is what I want her to say and do.'

God gave Mustafa one more glimpse of His reservoir of power. His brother Ghazi died suddenly. Zia granted permission for Mustafa to attend the funeral and, because time was tight, loaned him the use of the air chief's official plane. The aircraft, with Mustafa on board, flew to Lahore to pick me up. Then we took off for the funeral in Multan.

During the trip I could tell that Mustafa was very shaken by the fact that death was now raiding his own generation. He confided to me, 'I have prayed very hard to God for a chance to visit the holy shrine in Taunsa Sharif. I wonder when my call will come.' He knew that, as a prisoner, there was no way for him to make the pilgrimage. But when we arrived at Multan, we were surprised to learn that the funeral procession had already left and we were instructed to drive to the city where Ghazi had desired burial – Taunsa Sharif! Mustafa immediately prostrated himself and thanked God for this miracle.

Although my head was covered, my face was not. It was unheard of for a woman to enter the holy city of Taunsa Sharif without covering herself completely, but Mustafa abandoned tradition. The only concession he made was to ask me to wait for him in the car.

A huge crowd of mourners was electrified when they heard the sound of sirens, announcing the approach of our official convoy. They surged forward and almost crushed our car. Mustafa managed to extricate himself and disappeared into the mob. I caught brief glimpses of the funeral bier amidst wave after wave of the distraught crowd. There was a strange juxtaposition of elation and grief; another Khar was being buried, but their leader was among them!

I thought: The Sufis have it right. They believe that the death of a saint must be celebrated, because it is the moment that his soul achieves union with the Eternal Being. Death and reunion seemed to go together with the Khars.

As we drove towards the aeroplane that would carry him back to prison, I could sense that Mustafa felt more strongly than ever that supernatural forces were on his side. His personal sense of manifest destiny was re-inforced.

15

Over time, Mustafa's situation in Adyala Jail became even more comfortable. He was their most important prisoner, and – who knew? – in time to come he might be of use to the generals. And so he was allotted seven rooms. His main cell was air-conditioned against the infernal summer heat. Another room held a refrigerator and a deep-freeze. He was allowed to have a television set and had unlimited access to reading material. He was eclectic in his reading habits and could skip easily from an account of Mao's Long March to Caliph Omer's reforms. He told me that he was quite willing to accept some of Hitler's contentions, declaring, 'Any programme that elevates suffering but pursues ultimate progress is acceptable.'

In the mornings, he practised yoga on the veranda alongside his almost constant companion, a tame talking partridge. He had a small compound of land at his disposal, which he converted into a chicken farm. A few of the other prisoners were assigned to keep his house in order and tend his flock. Mustafa supervised the work and then relaxed by cooking his own meals. He was a great chef, capable of conjuring gastronomic delights, but here he was content with a simple diet of lentils and vegetables.

Gaol rules did not allow him private visits, but whenever I went to see him he dismissed the guard with a wave of his hand.

I found all of this somewhat confusing. Part of me felt that a true political leader should suffer, in order to cleanse himself, but I was able to dismiss these thoughts as hangovers from the catechism lessons I had endured in convent school. I had to remind myself that Mustafa was a political prisoner, not a criminal. The authorities had to be aware that today's political prisoner is tomorrow's leader. Mustafa's time was likely to come, and his gaolers had to protect themselves against future retaliation. He brooked no insolence. His manner was that of a monarch who was only temporarily deposed. Everyone remembered his past. Nobody could ignore his future. His present paled into insignificance.

Among the inmates were four Palestinian freedom fighters who had hijacked a Pan American World Airways Boeing 747 in Karachi in September 1986. Although Mustafa disagreed with their actions, he was obsessed with their cause. Yasser Arafat was a member of the pantheon of leaders who inspired Mustafa. The head of this group of prisoners, a boy named Ali, sent a message of distress to Mustafa. Being imprisoned in a foreign land was in itself a tragedy. The Palestinians could not speak our language and they had to suffer the unfamiliar prison food, which was short on nutrition and long on spice. Mustafa empathized and began to send them food from his own kitchen.

After Mustafa told me about the Palestinians, I wrote them a letter telling them that I, too, believed in their cause. I ended with a prayer: 'I hope my children can be as brave as you, and fight at the risk of their lives for their Motherland.'

Jatoi and others constantly pressed Zia to release Mustafa, but nothing came of their efforts.

At Mustafa's direction, I had meetings with leaders across the spectrum of Pakistani politics and asked them to lobby for the release of all political prisoners. Mustafa was the only leader, but hundreds of party workers still languished in prisons, and they needed a voice. We held seminars in Lahore and Islamabad on this issue. They were well attended and received good press coverage, but nothing seemed to move the ruling élite. We concluded that we needed to do something more dramatic.

Mustafa and I came to a momentous decision. A part of my heart wished that he would carry the fight to the gallows, as Bhutto did. But another part recognized the uselessness of another martyr and acknowledged the need for Machiavellian strategy – to serve the people practically, by first obtaining release. We rationalized the matter and agreed that we would have to compromise some of our earlier, extreme principles and attempt to woo the military leaders. Mustafa, who had once sought to overthrow the military regime with violence, now sought a secret alliance.

Early in 1988 I was granted an appointment with General Akhtar Abdur Rehman, Chairman of the Joint Chiefs of Staff. He was Zia's right-hand man and had been the ISI chief during our coup attempt; he was also in charge of the Afghan Mujahadeen war strategy which was run entirely by the ISI. Mustafa coached me carefully. No-one was to know of our attempt to negotiate with the military junta; such knowledge would drive away legions of Mustafa's supporters.

The meeting was held under stringent security procedures. I was told to be in the lobby of the Holiday Inn in Islamabad at a certain hour on a certain date – wearing dark glasses. I would be met there by Brigadier Khursheed, who would take me to see General Rehman.

We spoke for ninety minutes at the general's office. It was a difficult session. My aversion to the generals and their martial law was deeply ingrained. I did not like the idea of negotiating with Zia or any of his representatives. I hated begging for Mustafa's release, and I did not have much to offer in exchange. I tried to sell the idea that Mustafa realized that the army was indispensable to the political process; he had concluded that the Turkish form of government – where the politicians and the military share power – was feasible for our country.

General Rehman interrupted. He pointed out that

Bhutto had made a similar agreement with his generals, and then reneged. How could I guarantee that Mustafa would not do the same?

'Mustafa is not Mr Bhutto,' I said. I reminded him that Mustafa had openly opposed many of Bhutto's ideas, and I promised that Mustafa would honour any and every commitment he made. Then I launched into a well-prepared speech. Mustafa had told me to play upon the army's fears about the intentions of the current leaders of Bhutto's People's Party. I predicted to the general that, in any future election, the People's Party, led by Benazir Bhutto, would prevail, bringing about an emotional resurrection of the Bhutto myth. The people – most especially the Sindis and Punjabis – were waiting for an opportunity to take on the forces that supported Zia. At this point in time, I argued, the army would need a buffer, a man who was accepted by the People's Party workers, a man who could persuade them not to vent their wrath against the military. They needed a leader with roots in the Punjab, who understood the realities of power politics and behind whom a huge percentage of the People's Party workers would rally. Only one person had the capacity to do this, I proclaimed: Mustafa Khar.

The fact that the general asked me to return for another meeting was proof that I had struck a chord. But I came away from the first meeting with no positive or negative impression. I realized the general's training as an intelligence man disallowed even a slight revelation of his real feelings. He remained expressionless.

Several additional meetings ensued. I discussed these with Mustafa and returned to the general with fresh comments and proposals. Each time, the general spoke more. Each time, I found him more caring and sensitive, at least concerning my situation. My hopes grew.

In May 1988, the Ojhri ammunition dump in Islamabad, the semi-secret staging front for supplying clandestine

weapons to the Afghan rebels, was blown up. Missiles
flew off in all directions, leaving hundreds of innocent
civilians dead and injured. The city was paralysed with
grief and horror.

As it happened, Mustafa's son Abdur Rehman was to
be married the next day, and Mustafa had been granted
a twenty-four-hour parole to attend. Along with the
children and Nuscie, I greeted him at Lahore airport and
joined him in a secure caravan of cars, heading toward
the bride's home with sirens blaring.

The bride was dressed in traditional red, the fairy
lights flickered and the guests had already started to
arrive when Mustafa surprised everyone with the
declaration that, because of the tragedy at the Ojhri
Camp, the wedding had to be postponed. He said
that it would be wrong to rejoice at a time when so
much pain had encompassed the nation. We were in a
quandary; everything was upset.

The bride's family reacted with shock. The bride, coy
and bejewelled, listened solemnly as Mustafa tried to
explain that she was marrying into a special family. 'I
am a politician,' he said. 'I have responsibilities to my
people. They will question me about this wedding if it
is held on such an unpropitious day.' The media praised
Mustafa's noble gesture, and placed him in sharp contrast with the dictator who now made a huge blunder.
Fearing an inquiry into what qualified as a sabotage
attack on the Ojhri ammunition dump, Zia dismissed his
hand-picked Prime Minister, Mohammad Khan Junejo,
as well as the lower house of Parliament, and installed
a caretaker government.

In my fifth meeting with General Rehman in August,
I sipped tea as I presented Mustafa's assessment of these
developments to both the general and his wife. The
problem was not solved, Mustafa predicted. Zia had only
created a vacuum. The caretaker government would
prove ineffective and the People's Party would move into
the gap. Mustafa suggested that he be permitted to play

his role as a free man to thwart the People's Party. He needed time to curtail Benazir Bhutto's rise to power.

The general promised to discuss the matter with General Zia.

I was proud of myself and the success of my secret negotiations. I was certain that Zia and his advisers were now ready to accept this reasoning.

A week later, on 17 August, a C-130 military transport plane mysteriously exploded in the air over Bahawalpur. General Zia, who had presided over the nation's destiny for eleven years, was on board. My first reaction was extreme happiness. The dictator was dead! Then I remembered that there were other people on that aircraft whom I had known. One of them was my new friend General Rehman, who had seemed so close to engineering Mustafa's release. The other was Brigadier Khursheed, who had frequently transported me to and from the meetings.

But I had to banish all thoughts of the human tragedy. Zia's sudden death changed the entire equation of politics in Pakistan. The Chairman of the Senate, and Zia's close ally, Ghulam Ishaq Khan, was sworn in as President. 'We must not do anything at this stage to provoke the army,' Mustafa advised. 'The best course is to wait and see.'

We decided to draw maximum attention to our predictament via peaceful protest. Our brave party workers launched a hunger strike in front of the Senate, while it was in session. The authorities arrested the first batch immediately, on charges of attempted suicide.

We tried to march to the Senate, carrying placards denouncing martial law and calling for the release of political prisoners, but police swooped in and arrested the marchers.

Two senators invited me inside the Senate building and introduced me to several of their colleagues. I caused quite a stir when I walked in to urge someone to raise the issue of political prisoners. I said to one senator, 'If your wife was here and Mustafa Khar was in your place, he would have definitely responded to the issue.'

Our hunger strikes continued. We created enormous media interest but the government continued with business as usual, unabashed and unmoved. Seeking an even more dramatic venue, we chose the Faisal Mosque in Islamabad. We felt that a government that paid constant lip service to Islam might shy away from arresting hunger strikers within the holy precincts of the mosque. And if they did, the press would vilify them. Either way, we would win our point.

The hunger strikers were seated in prayer when the police gathered. I confronted the authorities and proclaimed that they could not arrest the workers while they were praying. The police hesitated, and waited for the prayers to cease. But the prayers droned on without end. Crowds gathered, wondering which side would crack. The workers never faltered but the police did. They finally moved in and dragged the praying men off to jail as they shouted slogans against the government and in support of political prisoners. We, and the press, made sure that the entire nation heard about the desecration of the mosque by the functionaries of a so-called Islamic government.

Further strikes followed, all at very public locations in Islamabad: again at the Senate, at the President's house, at other mosques – even at shopping centres. The capital city was suddenly the scene of peaceful protest, with me centre stage.

By this time I had decided that the leader's own family had to make sacrifices. So far, it had always been the poor workers who offered themselves for arrest. I persuaded Mustafa's two sons, Abdur Rehman and Bilal, to participate in one of the hunger strikes. They were arrested outside the Senate.

We were moving, creating agitation. The press reported favourably upon our peaceful attempts to force change, and the repressive tactics of the police. More and more, we could tell that the crowds were on our side, cheering the strikers and jeering at the authorities. But still Mustafa and thousands of other political prisoners languished in jail.

How could we break the impasse?

I suggested to Mustafa that I would go on a hunger strike myself. I was aware, of course, that the momentous decision could lead to my death because I could not withdraw from it, but I was confident that my action would arouse such national and international media interest that the government would realize that it could not let me die – and would release the political prisoners. I knew that the press would treat me kindly. My role as a wife struggling for her husband's freedom played well in the newspapers, and reporters were increasingly eager to know what I would be up to next. I had made the acquaintance of a new breed of well-educated journalists who were committed to the cause of justice in Pakistan. Although in this modern world they used word processors, someone had coined an appropriate term for them: 'typewriter guerrillas'. I knew that they would be on my side.

In addition, both Mustafa and I knew that my father would be galvanized into action to save me. He had many influential friends in the army and in the Senate, and he would surely bring immense pressure to bear on them.

We made the arrangements. A team of doctors would be ready to attend to me when I was arrested. Mustafa included Dr Sultan, a physician attached to the Adyala Jail, so that he could remain fully informed of my condition. Dr Sultan briefed me: 'Within twenty-four hours you will feel the strain. As time progresses it is possible that the key organs in your body could be damaged – your kidneys, for instance. If it goes on too long, your brain could be damaged and you could go into a coma.' He added, 'But we won't let you die.

You'll receive intravenous fluids and we'll give you milk!'

I was very frightened, yet determined to go ahead. But there was a sudden anti-climax. Fortunately for me, the president announced the release of some political prisoners. Mustafa was not included, but the process had begun. We put my hunger strike on hold.

I talked to every politician and general whom I could corner. The words of one of them conveyed the prevailing feeling: 'Mustafa is a traitor! I cannot help a traitor to my country.'

The sense of chaos heightened when elections were announced. Without notice, our old friend Mustafa Jatoi joined the IJI – the alliance of parties that had been bred by Zia and currently held power – and presented Mustafa with the same option. If he took it, the doors of his prison cell would open instantly. Mustafa was desperate to emerge and play his role in the elections, and he contemplated striking a deal.

A host of callers descended upon me, trying to convince me to persuade my husband to cast his lot with what was, at the moment, Pakistan's political establishment. One warned me that Mustafa would never be released from prison if he did not join. 'He'll rot there for ever,' he predicted. 'You don't want that, do you?'

I had evolved. After all those years of marriage, I was no longer Mustafa's programmed robot; I was a thinking person capable of independent actions. I rejected all the arguments that I heard in favour of Mustafa joining the IJI, and told him why. If he joined, he would be repudiating everything he stood for. These were the parties that had stayed in power by bowing to Zia; they were the unnatural political growths that had fed on Bhutto's blood. To ally with the IJI would be to negate his fight against martial law and his long struggle for democracy. His years in exile would count for nothing. Beyond that, the move would be humiliating because the IJI was headed by Nawaz Sharif, a man whom Mustafa had long portrayed to the public as a political pygmy. I told my husband that I would lose every scrap of respect for him if he sold out now. I contended, 'It's better to be respected in gaol for ever than to be free and humiliated.'

Mustafa weighed his options. He could be out of prison within twenty-four hours, or he could retain his honour and his wife. He decided to reject Jatoi's pragmatic offer and complimented me for my counsel: 'It's your strength that allowed me to take this decision. I'm glad I took it. Short cuts to power are dishonourable.'

I made a press announcement on behalf of Mustafa, rejecting Jatoi's stand and breaking away from him to form 'Khar Group, NPP'. I declared, using Nelson Mandela's words, 'Prisoners Cannot Negotiate. Mustafa is not a free man.'

We decided that Mustafa would run for parliament from his prison cell. Under Pakistan's electoral system you can stand for as many National and Provincial seats as you wish. However, at a given date after the election you have to withdraw from all except one: you can either be a member of the National Assembly or the Provincial Assembly. On the other seats you forfeit, you can nominate your own candidate, and after the election a by-election is held in those constituencies. Mustafa would file nomination papers for two National Assembly seats and three Provincial Assembly seats and decide, during the heat of battle, where to concentrate his efforts. The most notable confrontation was predicted to be in Lahore, where he would challenge Nawaz Sharif, the sitting Chief Minister of the Punjab. With the announcement, Mustafa was once more cast in the role of the brave, courageous Lion of the Punjab, roaring from behind bars.

But it was not to be easy. Mustafa's own brothers had found they could cash in on his absence, and decided to run against him in his home constituency of Muzaffargarh, and they lined up support from powerful government groups. I filed the papers necessary to launch Mustafa's five campaigns, but I knew that we faced tough odds.

I set out on the campaign trail as Mustafa's surrogate. In Muzaffargarh I faced the task of speaking to a confused crowd of people. Mustafa had sent a woman to speak for him? Why had he not sent a brother or a son? Mustafa had foreseen this difficulty, and had armed me with the proper argument. I waved my arm and noted, 'The *Sardars* ['chiefs'] of all these areas hide their wives from the poor, oppressed people of their villages. They place them behind the *chader* so that you, who come from their soil, cannot set your eyes on their "honour". But in the cities they let their women remove their veils and mingle with aliens. Mustafa has asked me to inform you that he is not from that breed of men.'

The crowd applauded loudly and raised slogans for Mustafa.

I continued: 'He has, by my presence in front of you, given proof that you are the people who can behold his woman, because for you I am a daughter, a mother or a sister. You are his family. He will not hide his woman from you. He is breaking false and hypocritical tradition today – for you!'

This argument won a multitude. The crowd roared its approval and prayed for Mustafa's release – and his success in the election.

His brothers rallied strongly against me, saying I was a disgrace to their father's honour. Some said I wished to send Mustafa to the gallows.

In Lahore I held numerous meetings with party workers. They were unanimously happy with Mustafa's decision, but we knew that it left him without the backing of any major political force. We discussed the possibility of other alliances. Should we rejoin hands with the People's Party? Should we contact the dismissed Prime Minister Junejo to seek a coalition?

Mustafa asked me to speak to Benazir Bhutto. I contacted one of her aides and enquired about the possibility of Benazir and her People's Party offering support to Mustafa. The aide came back with the enigmatic message: 'I think we should wait for Mr Khar's release.'

This statement made me realize that Benazir did not expect Mustafa to be released and that she did not want to support a man to whom the army was opposed. Perhaps she wanted her old 'uncle' to remain in prison and conveniently out of the way?

Running the election by proxy was too much responsibility for me. Mustafa said that the only way for me to gather enough support in his absence in the key district of Lahore was the time-honoured tradition of door-to-door canvassing. People would feel touched by his wife's personal request for support. But I found this embarrassing. Unlike the emotional, illiterate crowds of Muzaffargarh, the electorate in Lahore did not know me well enough; they received me with confusion. I sensed that, as far as they were concerned, I was not a suitable proxy for my husband, especially against the chief minister in his home constituency. We desperately needed to have Mustafa out of gaol, so that he could have the impact needed for such a victory.

I contacted Inter Services Intelligence, seeking a meeting with its chief, General Hameed Gul; but his second-in-command, Brigadier Imtiaz, said that he would see me instead. Our meeting at the ISI head office turned into a five-hour marathon. It was a sophisticated interrogation. The brigadier had a comprehensive dossier on Mustafa and his ill-fated Indian connection. In the face of this evidence, he viewed my husband as a traitor. I tried to paint a picture of Mustafa as a different kind of patriot, but the brigadier was not convinced. When I told him of my meetings with General Rehman he was very surprised. The ISI knew nothing about them!

We met on several occasions before I was finally

granted an audience with General Hameed Gul, and flew to Islamabad to see him. I knew that this was our last, best hope. It was a difficult meeting. The general listened carefully to my arguments, but I could not gauge his response. Finally, in desperation, I pleaded with him to meet Mustafa face to face. I was confident that Mustafa, by employing his gift of the gab, could talk his way out of prison. I was surprised and ecstatic when General Gul agreed. I also realized that this was evidence that our country was in a state of flux; it was very unusual for a man so highly placed to visit a prisoner.

No-one was to know – not even Mustafa. I was driven to Adyala Jail by the brigadier at midnight. In the Superintendent's Office I met General Gul. Then a very surprised Mustafa was brought in to meet us.

To my dismay, Mustafa came across as sheepish and phony. It was as if he realized that the man sitting opposite him knew the secrets of his heart. The general was charismatic, articulate and forthright; Mustafa was mediocre. My husband, my leader, shrivelled before my eyes.

Come on, Mustafa, I thought. You must say the right things. You must say the things that will make them release you. It's your only chance. Your last chance.

But as the meeting ended the general's aide made it apparent that they had already made their decision. He nodded towards me, smiled, and said to Mustafa, 'You couldn't have found a better ambassador.'

With deep intensity Mustafa said, 'Without Tehmina I could never have made it!' After he composed himself he added, directly to me, 'If ever I write my auto-biography I shall say that you were my wisest political adviser.'

The following day, the courts decreed Mustafa's release, after more than two years' confinement.

Joy and sorrow came hand in hand. It was at this very time that I received a disturbing call from my sisters

Zarmina and Rubina: Father was in love with another woman! Mother was distraught. The other woman was Sabiha Hasan. She had worked with my father when he was governor of the State Bank. My sisters wanted to call a family conference to try to salvage our parents' marriage. Mother was ready for me to return to the family fold, to help her through this terrible time.

I was bewildered by this strange combination of happiness and grief that had come together at the same moment. My life was like a kaleidoscope in the hands of a fidgety child.

16

The 6.30 a.m. flight from Lahore to Islamabad was the one I had taken every Sunday for more than a year. But today, 4 November 1988, was different. I was charged with elation as I walked confidently with my four children toward the airport gate. The annoyances of having our papers checked and submitting to body searches were brushed aside by a sense of achievement.

The airport staff greeted us with smiles. Once we boarded, the flight crew sought us out to offer its congratulations. As I fastened my seat belt, settled in and perused a newspaper, a passenger leaned towards me and said, 'Your husband must be very proud of you.' I smiled graciously, aware that our struggle had only just begun.

During the flight I stared out of the window, into the distance. A stray speck of cloud, anchored in nothingness, seemed to blush as the sun's first rays sprayed it. I could feel my excitement mounting. Two epochs of my marriage were over. First, exile, which brought with it betrayal and violence; I had felt trapped in the eye of a storm, struggling constantly to survive. Then Mustafa's imprisonment, which for me held frustration, loneliness and fatigue, but also brought practical political training and maturity, an independence that had been thrust upon me by necessity.

Now Mustafa and I were entering a new period, one of freedom and trust. We had survived adversity and were, for the first time, confronted with normality.

Islamabad Airport was awash with jubilation. Faces that I had seen through the years, wearing determined expressions, were now wreathed in smiles. People moved toward me, then stopped at a respectful distance. I wanted to thank them for their support and hug them, but they were all men and we were conditioned by Islam, stifled by tradition; a woman does not demonstrate affection towards a man who is not her father, brother or husband. I tried to appreciate them with words, but these were inadequate.

Soon we were in a car, leading a motorized cavalcade along familiar roads. A festive atmosphere prevailed. Drivers honked their horns; pedestrians shouted encouraging slogans. We passed the site of the Rawalpindi Central Jail, where Bhutto was hanged. General Zia, before his recent death, had ordered it demolished since it now served as a shrine to the memory of a martyr.

We passed the Army Headquarters, and the sight of the tank outside the gates made me smile. In the past this tank, the symbol of military rule in Pakistan, had intimidated me. Today it seemed powerless. The power of the people had prevailed over the dictate of the gun.

The convoy turned on to Adyala Road. Thousands of spectators lined the way, impeding our progress. Our car crawled down the long ribbon that led towards the gaol. Faces peered in through the windows of the car, flattening their noses against the glass. Some people flashed the 'V' for victory sign. Others thumped on the hood of the car, expressing exuberance. These were the masses, about whom Mustafa and I had so frequently spoken. It was their destiny that we had to help shape. Not so long ago these people were an abstraction to me, the topics of endless drawing-room discussions. Today they were real; they mattered. They did not depend on us; we depended on them. The downtrodden people of Pakistan, trampled for centuries, had begun to rise, just as the clouds of dust rose about our car.

I did not dare roll down a window. Repeatedly I raised my hand to my forehead in traditional salutation, and the crowds waved back.

Adyala Jail appeared fragile and no longer impregnable before the swarm of humanity that converged upon it. The towering walls, which had always filled my heart with foreboding, were not frightening today.

Mustafa's friends and colleagues from all over Pakistan were here in a show of loyalty against the remnants of the Zia regime. Many of them had suffered imprisonment on far harsher terms than Mustafa. In their darkest hours, this had been the moment for which they dreamed.

The frenzy of the crowd increased as the moment neared. Groups of young men danced the *bhangra* and the *luddie*, Punjab's most popular dances. The resounding drumbeat intensified.

Then suddenly, there he was, emerging from prison: Mustafa Khar, champion of the underdog, courageous Lion of the Punjab, political Messiah.

Even at this unique moment my mind wandered. I worried about my father and mother. My marriage was ready to resume; theirs was breaking apart. I worried also for the inmates of the prison, who were losing their resident protector. Life is not fair, I lectured myself, and forced my attention back upon Mustafa, who would return to them one day with reform. I had often questioned why, although so many political leaders were incarcerated and had true insight into the inhuman conditions of ordinary inmates, none had taken up their issues – not even when they gained power. Mustafa had promised not to forget the plight of those condemned to imprisonment.

A pathway was cleared through the crowd for me and the children to leave the car and join him at his side as he waved, acknowledging the general adulation. Our children finally were able to understand my lectures: their father was not a criminal; today, he was a hero. He personified hope. He was the man who stood against a morally bankrupt society where injustice, corruption, exploitation of the weak and abject poverty had become the norm. He had suffered for his people. He had spent years watching exiled sunsets. He had been incarcerated, but he had not bowed down.

As we slowly made our way towards a jeep, wrinkled old men elbowed their way to the edge of the crowd to kiss his hand, touch his face and weep. Words were unnecessary.

We stood in the jeep, our torsos emerging through the open sunroof. The vehicle inched forward, nudging aside the ecstatic crowd. From all sides people reached out to touch Mustafa. From every rooftop and every window faces peered out for a glimpse. Rose petals fluttered down, drenching us in their aroma.

Mustafa turned to me, clearly overwhelmed, and said, 'Tehmina, you know I would never have been here if it wasn't for you.'

We stopped at the National People's Party headquarters in Rawalpindi where Mustafa spoke to the people on the crowded road. In an emotion-filled voice he outlined the programmes that he had discussed with me so often during these past two years. His voice broke frequently, sending his listeners into empathetic spasms of fresh tears.

As Mustafa spoke, I found myself busy signing autographs. Young boys passed scraps of paper, notebooks – even rupee notes – to me for my signature. I realized that I had acquired my very own army of groupies. They had a collective crush on me! I tried to tell them to stop chattering and listen to Mustafa's speech, but they were not interested.

We headed for Islamabad, and finally arrived at the residence of Siddique Butt, one of Mustafa's political colleagues, which had served as my headquarters during the past tumultuous months. This evening the house was illuminated with a myriad of fairy lights. Another crowd awaited us here, along with another contingent from the press corps. Mustafa spoke once more and fed the hungry crowd inspired words, knowing that he would make the front pages of all tomorrow's newspapers.

That night, we fell into bed exhausted but euphoric.

Early the following morning, we headed out again. Our destination was Lahore, normally a five-hour drive, but we were to make several stops along the way. The children would not hear of travelling separately by air – even little Hamza rebelled. I gave in to their insistence. After all, they were well trained, unlike others of their class, for rough and extraordinary situations.

The sleepy little town of Gujar Khan was shut down for business, its streets converted into a stage for Mustafa. They knew him well here, and adored him, but their love was not blind. This was a politically astute crowd, and it was willing to support Mustafa only if he made his peace with the People's Party. By now it was clear that Benazir Bhutto's party was emerging as the real power in Pakistan. The people of Gujar Khan wanted Mustafa in the National Assembly, but not as a dissenting voice from a minor party, and not as an opponent of Bhutto's popular daughter. Banners waved at us, voicing support for the People's Party, Benazir Bhutto and the Lion of the Punjab. Men jumped on to the running-board of our jeep and pleaded with Mustafa to rejoin Benazir.

In Jhelum we encountered a similar sentiment. Mustafa moved his listeners with inspired words, but they put their message across just as well. It was clear that the people wanted Mustafa back in the Bhutto fold.

By the time our cavalcade crawled into Gujranwala it was already dark, but our welcome was sparkling. We were three and a half hours behind schedule, but the people had waited eleven years for this moment. Mustafa had to wade through the sea of frenzied supporters who pushed and jostled just for the privilege of touching him. When, finally, he was able to emerge on to the speaker's platform, the crowd exploded into a joyous cheer. As Mustafa regaled the audience with yet another speech,

I signed more autographs. By now I had grown accustomed to this new phenomenon.

Very late that night, after the long day on the road, we entered Lahore, the city that Mustafa once ruled. It was the city that rallied behind him when he took on Bhutto. We were exhausted. My white clothes were stained red from the abundance of rose petals that had been dropped upon us throughout the day. The grime of the road had mingled with the perspiration on our faces. When we arrived, Mustafa wept like a child.

We mounted a truck. Loudspeakers blared. Cheer-leaders led a chant to welcome him. Banners were all over the place and I blushed when I saw one that proclaimed:

LIONESS – CONGRATULATIONS
YOU HAVE SUCCEEDED IN FREEING THE LION

We halted at the shrine of Data Gunjh Buksh, the Sufi saint who was also a mystic poet and who, the people believe, protects the city of Lahore. Revered by all faiths for his humanism, his shrine stands majestically near the old bed of the River Ravi, near the entrance to Lahore. A rally was held here, and all around us the now-familiar demand echoed: 'Rejoin the People's Party. End the tension that is dividing the hearts and minds of the people.' Loyalists had erected a huge portrait of Mustafa to excite the crowd, and others had placed one of Benazir, equally as large, alongside. The symbolism was clear. Press photographers insisted that Mustafa hold up Benazir's portrait, and he did so, to resounding cheers. I sensed his unease; the crowd was forcing him to accept as his leader a little girl who still called him 'uncle'.

He spoke in a conciliatory tone: 'I will do whatever I can for the people, for the workers who have kept me politically alive. The People's Party is my party. The workers of this party are my brothers. I have nothing against the party or the workers. I have differences with the party leadership. These differences can be overcome.'

We had another pilgrimage to make that night, to the sanctuary of my grandmother's home. She was not feeling well, but her eyes lit when she saw us. She had spent much of her life praying for my happiness; throughout the past two years she had spent countless hours in her home, prostrate, weeping, begging Allah to free Mustafa from prison, so that I could live a normal life. At last we were home. Mustafa was free in his own country. Nothing else mattered.

Only twelve days remained until the election; there was no time to waste. Early the following morning, Mustafa and I visited the constituency where he was to take on Chief Minister Nawaz Sharif in electoral combat. I was daunted by the enormity of the task ahead of us. This was the area that I had tried to canvass door-to-door, with little success. Now the people whom I had not been able to mobilize responded overwhelmingly to Mustafa.

The news of his arrival spread like warm butter. The people gathered, and Mustafa was in his element. He chatted easily, as if there had not been an eleven-year break in his relationship with these voters. With no hint of arrogance or distance he achieved an easy camaraderie. He did not have to ask the people for their votes; they offered them along with their hugs. His handshake confirmed the agreement.

Here Mustafa made what came to be a famous statement: that he was a servant of Bhutto. Mustafa knew that this district was full of diehard supporters of the People's Party, and the danger was that he and the People's Party candidate would split the vote, allowing the mutual enemy, Nawaz Sharif, to win the seat. Mustafa hoped that his rhetoric would dissuade the People's Party candidate, but when, under Benazir's directive, that gentleman refused to withdraw, Mustafa did so instead. He told me that he was merely post-poning his inevitable confrontation with Sharif.

Mustafa still had other races to consider, and we left for Multan, en route to Muzaffargarh. We would concentrate on campaigning in the outlying southern districts of the Punjab.

In Multan, with me at his side, Mustafa predicted to the press, 'I will change the direction of politics in this country . . . I intend to liberate the Punjab – with the support of the people – from a man who has bought it with corruption money from the generals.'

We arrived at Muzaffargarh in darkness. Thousands of silhouettes danced, clapped and cheered, illuminated by the flickering flames of lanterns and torches. The people had emerged from their hovels to show us, beneath their tattered clothes, their rich hearts. I knew at once that these were the faces of despair that had stared from my paintings. I had bequeathed my life to these men, women and children; this was the crowd that justified my return to Pakistan, to Mustafa.

He was truly home. He greeted many faces in the crowd with familiar names. I was moved to see how many women broke convention to greet him. The menfolk did not mind; Mustafa was everyone's father, brother, son. Their acquiescence was their return gesture to the message I had brought earlier.

We set up election headquarters in the home of Mustafa's late brother Ghazi, but Mustafa was so confident of victory here that he did not campaign in the traditional sense. Wherever he went throughout the area, people ran from all directions to meet him. He disdained formal speeches and concentrated on quiet conversations with the simple, honest folk. He made a point of visiting even the most remote reaches of his constituency.

Three of the candidates here were Mustafa's own brothers. Murtaza was the direct enemy, but Rabbani and Arbi were also rivals. Mustafa sent me into the field to campaign against all three. The rural crowds responded to me with the same fervour and excitement as they did to Mustafa. I was his Lioness, and therefore an object of great reverence.

My theme was betrayal. I vilified the Muslim League as Zia's creation, and told the crowds that Mustafa's brothers had betrayed their blood ties. In 1985 they had joined the enemy camp. They had compromised with their brother's captives. I reported to my eager audiences that Mustafa's brothers had not even bothered to make regular visits to him in prison. It was left to me, a woman, to emerge from my home and fight my husband's battles. I declared that a vote for the Muslim League would be an endorsement of the regime that had kept Mustafa away from his people for eleven years.

Election day was devoid of suspense. I remained up to watch the results on television, but Mustafa fell asleep. He was sure that he would win by a large majority, and he did, qualifying for all the seats he fought for in the National and Provincial Assemblies. Even Murtaza's own servants voted for Mustafa.

However, despite Mustafa's tremendous victory as an independent, most of the Punjab supported the Muslim League, assuring that the Chief Minister's post in Lahore would continue to be held by Nawaz Sharif who had filled the vacuum during Mustafa's absence, and whom the People's Party candidate had failed to dislodge. But the People's Party swept to victory in the North West Frontier Province and in the Sind – even Mustafa Jatoi lost his seat. This meant that the federal government in Islamabad would be headed by a new Prime Minister, the daughter of the martyred hero of Pakistan.

The elections made Benazir Bhutto the most powerful person in Pakistan. For many, it was as if Zulfikar Ali Bhutto had been resurrected.

*   *   *

I had not been in contact with my parents since my return to Pakistan. I was still smarting from the manner in which Mother had treated my defenceless children in London. But now I tried to put a lifetime of pain behind me. Mother was experiencing her own, very deep agony: another woman. This was the ultimate loss of face for a woman who lived on appearances. I could not forget Mother's callousness toward me in the past, but I was able to find forgiveness somewhere in my heart. I felt drawn to her. Before the National Assembly convened, we decided to visit my family in Karachi.

Rubina met us at the airport. Adila and her husband Matloob were also there with their two children, Leena and Mohanad. I had not seen my youngest sister since her marriage.

We arrived at my mother's home and found her grief-stricken. Her poise and commanding demeanour had crumbled. She broke the news that our father had married the other woman.

The words came as a great shock. Despite the problems that had plagued our family, our parents' marriage had always seemed to be built upon a sturdy foundation. Now we realized that they had simply concealed the warts from their children, just as they had concealed ours from the world.

It was always a great mystery to me how successfully Mother's personality had controlled Father's. He was naturally affectionate, yet he seemed forced to keep strict control on his emotions, with Mother and with us. Like us, he also had to live by her rules: no late, unexplained evenings, and no drinking – ever. His relatives were simple people, and we all adored them, except for Mother who found them uncouth. They were allowed only short, formal visits to our home. All through their marriage Father had spoiled Mother. She had never wanted for anything; in fact, she overspent his hard-earned money and never seemed to give anything in return.

It had been difficult to watch this powerful government official submit to constant nagging. Sometimes, at night, I would hear my parents argue behind closed doors; she always sounded aggressive and he always sounded apologetic. Mother even extended her domination to his office staff; if the refrigerator or the air-conditioner at home broke down, Mother was on the phone to the office, demanding that someone come to fix the appliance immediately. The office staff, like us, appeared to be petrified by her.

Once I saw Father's valet, Amir Khan, bring him a Pepsi. He gulped it down quickly and asked for another. He went off to the dressing-room for a few moments and I could not contain my curiosity. He returned suddenly to catch me touching my tongue to the contents. I was surprised to realize that the Pepsi bottle was filled with an alcoholic drink. His tone took a conspiratorial edge as he said, 'I can trust you. You won't tell Mother.' That was true, but the realization filled me with sadness that such a strong and powerful man had to hide a drink in his own home.

I was sure that one day he would break under the strain, and now, apparently, he had.

When I had a chance to speak to my father, he set out his reasons for me. He complained that my mother had cramped his personality. He said that life with her had been a continuous masquerade for him. With a sardonic smile he proclaimed that his new wife, Sabiha Hasan, accepted him for who he was. 'I don't have to be the Great Man that your mother made me,' he said. 'I wasn't a great man.'

I understood the simplicity of his words and concluded that he was going through a late-life crisis. However, I felt that it was irresponsible of him, now that he had raised his own family and had eighteen grandchildren, suddenly to take a second wife.

I weighed the evidence and instinctively sided with my mother; I could empathize with a wronged woman despite the fact that this latest development seemed like a manifestation of divine justice. Mother was somewhat luckier than I, since the other woman did not cause her to lose her entire family. Yet she still had to experience the shattered ego and fear of public humiliation, just as I had. The temptation was great to flaunt the experience in my mother's face, but I realized that I wanted to support her, to demonstrate the difference between right and wrong.

Father was unmoved by my sentiments. 'You want me to spend the last few years of my life living a lie for the sake of an image,' he said. 'My life has at last become important to me – not what you all think about me. I have reacted only once in sixty years, you know.'

The only positive feature of this very depressing visit to Karachi was Adila. I found in her the little sister I had always wanted. She showered affection on me and fussed over me. She told me that she wanted to be as close to me as Zarmina and Minoo were. She frowned over my new image and could not understand why I had put all my 'lovely' clothes away and wore only white cotton and silver jewellery. She insisted that I make up my face and paint my nails red. Her attitude toward Mustafa was one of sisterly affection; she subtly maintained a proper distance from him.

It was refreshing to realize that my family now viewed me as Tehmina Khar, the woman who had fought a relentless and ultimately successful battle to free her husband. I had developed a presence that they found impressive. They had to notice the change in Mustafa too. In front of them all, he lavished appreciation, respect and love on me.

We returned to Lahore, leaving my family to sort through its new mess. After his first meeting with Chief Minister Nawaz Sharif, Mustafa offered his opinion of the man: 'He was very nervous of my presence. He offered me the earth. They want me to support the IJI.

They're afraid I'll join the People's Party. But what can they offer me? The only post I would be interested in is his own. They know that.'

In fact, Mustafa was now leaning towards the IJI. He had no confidence in the 'chit of a girl' who had become Prime Minister on 'the strength of her surname'. He laughed at Benazir's first televised speech and predicted: 'She's never going to make it. She hasn't managed to rouse any emotion for the dead prime minister. What an opportunity she has lost!'

I tried to wean him away from what I saw as opportunism. My suggestion was that he distance himself from *both* parties. I advised him to address the pertinent issues of the times, to pinpoint the defects in the political structure and to attack the follies of both party lines. It was apparent that the two major parties were on a collision course and Mustafa, elected as an independent, was perfectly positioned to play a positive role. All he had to do was speak the truth and present his own solutions for changing the unworkable and corrupt system that still remained as our legacy of British rule. I knew that this stance would catapult him to renewed popularity and, even more importantly, provide him with unassailable credibility.

To my dismay, I came to realize that Mustafa was not interested in being the conscience of the nation: all he wanted was power, and he wanted it now.

After the general election Mustafa had to vacate one of the two National Assembly seats that he had won, and he decided to offer Mustafa Jatoi as the by-election candidate for his seat from Kot Addu. I was shocked, because Jatoi was an IJI candidate and we had just won elections by condemning the alliance. This would be an uphill struggle. Jatoi was a Sindi – a rank outsider in the Punjab. Mustafa would have to work hard to motivate people to vote for his alien friend.

The Jatoi candidacy was an obvious pressure tactic – in connivance with the IJI bosses – aimed at unsettling the People's Party government. I sensed that it was also Mustafa's riposte to the party leadership for not accepting his extended hand of friendship. He was sending a signal: I am capable of having a Sindi elected from the Punjab; I am sending him into Parliament as a viable alternative to you, Ms B–h–u–t–t–o.

It was not all that long before I began to sense Mustafa's resentment towards me and my fresh image. Whenever a reporter asked him about me and my future in politics, an uncomfortable look crossed his face and he found some way to parry the question. I was no threat to him – quite content to return to the shadows – but he seemed to view our political lives in a competitive sense. This became most apparent following one press conference, when a foreign journalist jokingly commented, 'Your wife is very articulate. She gives even a better press conference than you do, Mr Khar.' If looks could expel, that reporter would have been on the first plane out of Pakistan.

In his dealings with the press, Mustafa consistently ignored the role that I had played in bringing him to freedom. He wanted me to fade from the nation's memory. I was not the only one who noticed; several party workers and journalists commented on the fact that any mention of me or my achievements irritated him.

I decided to give Mustafa the space he needed, and began to absent myself from political appearances. I saw weaknesses developing in his style. He had begun to compromise quite blatantly. He knew that I was against that. An increasing number of opportunists – faces absent for the past thirteen years – appeared around him. His brothers, who had first dissociated themselves and then fought viciously against him, and whom he had compared to the evil brothers of Joseph in many press statements, were suddenly allies once more.

He pushed away many of the dedicated workers who had supported me in my campaign to release him. Sajid,

335

Choudry Hanif and many of the other veterans of our long struggle exchanged sad, meaningful glances with me. We all began to distance ourselves from the man for whom we had waited so long.

17

The Jatoi campaign began amid great fanfare. For the political neophyte, this was fine spectator sport. Jatoi was cast in the role of the powerful opposition leader to Prime Minister Benazir Bhutto and Mustafa was emerging as the kingmaker. Among those who wanted to witness the fireworks first-hand were my sister Adila and her husband Matloob, whose brother was related to the Jatois by marriage.

Despite our recent reconciliation, this development put me in an uncomfortable spot. Too many people whispered about Adila's past involvement with Mustafa – even though it was a taboo subject. I did not want her in my life on a day-to-day basis again, and I spoke to Zarmina by phone about this, suggesting that it would help if she and her husband Riaz also came. Zarmina said that Riaz was opposed to her participation because there would be too many men around, and I suggested that she try to dissuade Adila with the same argument.

But Adila was adamant. In fact, she insisted that Zarmina and Riaz came along as well. She said that we three sisters would find much to talk about as the men were out campaigning. Beyond that, she wanted to spend time catching up. She wanted to tell me all about Matloob and his family and learn more about my own incredible experiences. Unwilling to let her notice my hesitation to accept her extended hand of friendship, I nervously gave in to the pressure.

She arrived at midday, with her hair freshly styled, wearing chiffon. She sported the current craze –

337

coloured contact lenses. I was taken aback by her appearance, but tried not to show it.

Matloob quickly involved himself in the campaign, and life assumed a routine. The men set out in the morning to garner votes. Throughout the day, various women from Mustafa's large family joined us for endless discussions of marriages, children and domestic crises. One evening we dissolved into giggles as we playfully debated the wisdom of slipping each of our husbands a Valium, so that they would leave us alone to talk all night.

Late every afternoon Adila retired to her room. Then, just before the men returned for dinner, she emerged transformed – her face painted, her hair done, her coloured contact lenses in place. She was dressed for an evening out, even though our dinners were very simple at-home occasions. Throughout the evening she pandered to Mustafa, who was full of political stories and full of himself.

I told Adila that she did not have to go to such effort for our dinners. 'It's good to dress for dinner,' she responded. 'You should do the same. Mustafa must see you looking beautiful. You've started looking too matronly.' Gradually I began to make a conscious effort to look better. It was taxing. I was unused to it – this was a phase of my life that I thought was over – but I did not want Adila to upstage me.

In a casual conversation I told Adila about the new friends I had made and added that Mustafa was irritated at their mention. 'He hates them,' I admitted. That evening I was in an adjacent room when Mustafa enquired about our day's discussions. Adila 'innocently' repeated our conversation. Later, Mustafa growled at me, and I felt a familiar chill run up my spine. The old days were returning. I could sense it.

Mustafa noticed my fear and his initial response was calming. 'I think she's trying to make trouble between us,' he admitted candidly. 'She wants us to fight. Let's not.' But, as the days passed, my suspicion deepened. I noticed every little move that Adila made in the direction of my husband's heart. Then I noticed him making small sallies toward hers. Politics and adversity seemed to have built a strong foundation for our relationship, but that was crumbling. My disillusionment with both his attitude towards principles and myself had caused me to draw away from active participation in his ambitions. Adila again attacked the only other area of marriage left: our personal relationship.

Mustafa began to mock my plain white clothes. I could not escape the feeling that he was succumbing by the minute to Adila's unsubtle seduction. The signs were fleeting but discernible. Others noticed them as well.

It was mornings that began to bother me most. Adila appeared in our bedroom quite early every day. She sat on the bed chatting with me, apparently oblivious to Mustafa's presence as he did his yoga. I was encompassed by an eerie sense of *déjà vu*. I tried very hard to forget the past, but it seemed to be slowly encroaching upon the present. I was irritable, depressed and confused. Increasingly I sought out the calming effects of Valium.

On a few occasions we accompanied the men on their political campaigns. I watched Mustafa on a platform in Kot Addu, flanked by Zia's protégé Nawaz Sharif and IJI candidate Jatoi. Amidst these publicly proclaimed political enemies, Mustafa was promising an improved future for the downtrodden masses. He declared that, in order for the voters to keep his respect and honour, 'Mr Jatoi must not get fewer votes than you gave me'. The words sounded hollow to me, but the crowd still responded with cheers.

Mustafa constantly badgered me to address groups of women, but I removed myself from the political scene. Once again I sought refuge in painting. A familiar-looking woman began to appear on my canvases. Under the subconscious strokes of my brush, she moved away from the centre of the scene and cloaked herself in shadows. With a start, I realized that I had composed a self-portrait.

On election day, against my wish, Mustafa insisted on driving us around to visit the polling stations. Matloob was at his side in the front seat; Adila and I sat in the back.

At the polling stations I saw a different Mustafa. He was displaying his power and charisma for Adila's benefit, but he tried too hard, like some struggling understudy who is anxious to cram everything into one performance. Nevertheless it worked. Adila's eyes lit up as mine went dim. She was captured by the glamour and excitement; I had just struggled free from its power. I could also feel Adila's contempt for the boring, powerless Matloob.

The drive home seemed to take for ever. I wanted to curl up and hide from the present world that was sucking me into the past. As soon as we arrived home and had a moment alone together, Mustafa asked angrily, 'What's wrong with you? You're always in a foul mood. You're always grumbling and complaining. You're never happy.'

'That's not the point,' I retaliated. 'I didn't like the way you behaved. I'm not a fool. I can tell. I'm unhappy and I have sound reason to be.'

He eyed me suspiciously for a moment and then stomped out of the room.

Dinnertime was approaching, and I went to my room to make myself more or less presentable. But instead of standing in front of the mirror, as I knew that Adila must be doing at this very moment, I fell upon the bed and began to cry.

Moments passed – I did not know how long – before Adila entered quietly. I glanced up to see that she was wearing a fresh, bright satin outfit. The contact lenses were like masks over the guilt in her eyes. We had no chance to speak before Mustafa entered to inform me angrily that guests had arrived. I growled at him, told him to tell them to wait and demanded that he and Adila leave *my* bedroom. Mustafa retorted with hostility: I had no business to tell anyone to get out of our room.

'Why not?' Adila asked sarcastically. 'It's her bedroom—' she paused for dramatic effect, then added, '—isn't it?'

Both of them stared at me, their grins visible under the camouflage of straight faces, mocking my anguish. After all the pain over all the years, this was the moment that shattered me.

Somehow, I collected myself and managed to make polite dinner conversation with our guests, even as a storm brewed in my heart. The clouds were dark and ominous. Those around me remained oblivious to my mental state.

At dinner I was suddenly aware of Mustafa's voice: 'Tehmina, really, you look like a nun in those white clothes.' Did his use of the word 'nun' have sexual connotations? Was he saying to Adila: As far as Tehmina is concerned, I'm celibate?

After our guests left, Adila remained behind to witness our brewing fight. Mustafa declared in a somewhat stilted tone, 'Tehmina, I can't live with you any more. You're ruining my life with your sulking. I'm miserable with you.' This was not vintage Mustafa. I realized that he was saying these words for Adila, not for me, transmitting the message that he was ready and willing to resume their affair. His words hung in the air as he left the room.

The drums began to beat and cheering rang in the air. Jatoi had won the election by 60,000 votes. This was the exact victory margin that Mustafa had achieved, and it was a powerful vindication of the hold that the Lion had on his people.

After a brief, very strange moment of celebration, Mustafa sought me out once more, making sure that

Adila was not around. Suddenly he was grovelling. 'I'll never misbehave,' he cried. 'This was your moment. Without you none of this would have been possible. I'm nothing without your support. Mr Jatoi would not have triumphed. It's your victory. I owe everything to you. Forgive me. I was upset. Maybe it was Adila's presence. Perhaps the sinister past had re-entered our lives. It reminded us both of the horror. Let's get rid of this woman – she's evil. Let's restart our lives.'

He sent for Adila. When she arrived, he sat at my feet and begged for forgiveness. Turning to Adila he said, 'I owe everything to Tehmina. Nothing can make me forget that.'

What was I do to? Which Mustafa should I believe?

My decision was instantaneous. I had spent many, many years with this man, endured his abuse and his follies. I had borne four of his children. I had laboured tirelessly to extricate him from prison because, if I did not believe in the man, I most fervently believed in his message. His commitment to that message was growing hazier by the hour, but mine was still resolute. Could I cast it all aside? Could I risk the futures of my children?

This last question brought shudders. If I left Mustafa now – after everything – what was to become of the children? I had seen what he was capable of doing in opposition to English law, and here we were in Pakistan, where popular sentiment holds that a man owns his children. All around me were signs of his power. I grasped at the last straw of hope. I would try my best to believe the petulant Mustafa, because I could not leave.

Celebrating victory, we all left Kot Addu for Multan the following day. Mustafa and I were guests at the house of Sajid's brother and his wife Shahida, where the children and I had lived for many months. That evening, despite the fact that her baby was ill and we had all seen enough of each other, Adila insisted on joining us again. I was sitting on a sofa in our bedroom and Mustafa was

342

lying on the bed, when Adila marched in, dressed in a green satin outfit that matched the emeralds that hung about her neck and dangled from her ears. Mustafa complimented her profusely. 'You're a woman now,' he pronounced.

Adila informed me that my sister-in-law wanted to see me outside.

I asked Adila to call her into the bedroom.

Adila said that she had done so, but the lady insisted that she needed to talk to me alone.

I did not want to leave Adila and Mustafa together in the bedroom, yet I did not want to make my fear obvious. I walked out, found Shahida and sent her in quickly, as an unofficial chaperone. But it was too late. In the short span of time that Adila and Mustafa were alone, something had happened. Shahida's entry was met with an abrupt silence.

Later that evening, I happened to misplace something. Mustafa reacted as in the past, raising his voice with that old dictatorial authority. I cringed as he heaped profanities upon me, but kept my silence – at least for the moment.

Once Adila was gone I lost my temper, but Mustafa declared that he did not want to hear any more of my 'nonsensical complaints'. He screamed, 'I'm under a lot of pressure, Tehmina. I've serious work to do and can't be distracted by a hysterical woman.' He switched off the bedside lamp and turned over to sleep.

I was heartbroken and greatly confused. Locking myself into the bathroom, I cried until I reached a saturation point. What was happening? I did not know how to handle this chameleon of a man. I thought that I had changed. I thought that *we* had changed. Now, suddenly, the old Mustafa was back, and I was not prepared.

A cold war ensued. On the aeroplane back to Lahore the next day, Mustafa was once more the miserable husband. 'You're mistrusting me again,' he complained.

'I can't live like this. I want a peaceful life with my wife.'

'How can you have a peaceful life when you create unnecessary trauma?' I asked. 'You know I'm unhappy. I can't trust you. You don't let me. Your actions are all suspect.'

'You *can* trust me,' he said sweetly, grasping my hand. 'Do you know what Adila said to me when you left the room last night?' I gaped at him, unsure that I really wanted to know. 'She said that I should not eat anything you gave me,' he continued. 'She said that you intended to poison me.'

I was flabbergasted. As Mustafa expanded upon the story, I realized that Adila had distorted our innocent conversation during the campaign when all the women – Adila included – had joked about slipping Valium to our husbands. Adila's wily charms were at work again, and Mustafa was weakening. After all that we had been through, Mustafa was still giving her room to manoeuvre. It disgusted me.

Back in Lahore, I withdrew more and more into the shadows of my painting, especially when he decided to fire Shugufta because he had no hold over her, as he did over poor Dai Ayesha. I sent her to work for my mother in Karachi. We were all heartbroken, especially little Hamza; but at least I knew that Shugufta was going to a home where she would live amongst civilized people with great style.

My mother's heartbreak continued. Minoo was in London, but my other three sisters and I decided to visit Sabiha Hasan, the new woman in our father's life, to see if we could settle anything. Zarmina and I flew to Karachi and were met by Rubina. As we waited for Adila to arrive at Rubina's house, we discussed what had transpired during the election campaign in Kot Addu. We were all disgusted by Adila's behaviour but, in retrospect, not greatly surprised.

We waited long enough for our youngest sister. We

tried calling her at home, but the line remained busy.

On an impulse, I tried to reach Mustafa at home in Lahore. That line was busy, too.

Two and two made four.

One and one added up to a sordid couple.

Still, we had to conduct the business of the day. Adila arrived and as we drove to see the 'other woman', I thought: How ironic that I'm going in the company of the 'other woman' in my life to plead Mother's case. Nobody – certainly not Mother – had ever pleaded mine.

During our meeting with Sabiha Hasan, Rubina, Zarmina and I tried to convey, diplomatically, that she was about to break the home that our mother had worked so long and hard to maintain. But Adila was rude, trying to provoke Sabiha into taking a hard line.

On the ride back to Rubina's home, we all shouted at Adila. Her convoluted plan was becoming ever more clear to us: If Father walked out on Mother, Adila would have an excuse to resume her affair with Mustafa and break my marriage. She would explain it as revenge. She would say that she owed nothing to our father and was justified in creating havoc in the family that he had abandoned. Why should she care for family honour if he didn't? We knew that Mother would take Adila's side. She would never mistrust Adila's motives. Adila was the only daughter whom Mother could depend upon as an ally against our straying father. Father would be the target, and I would be caught in the crossfire.

It was all so strange. Our family, full of intrigue and deception, backbiting and backstabbing, was a microcosm of Pakistani society. The rule was simple: Do whatever you want to do, just blanket it.

Under the surface, everything was colliding and falling apart.

Presidential elections were held. The two candidates were Ghulam Ishaq Khan and Nawabzada Nasrullah Khan. The former was the acting president and a reactionary bureaucrat with long ties to the Zia forces. The latter was a genuine progressive who believed in democratic ideals and had been extremely supportive during Mustafa's incarceration. When Mustafa returned from voting, he assured me that he had cast his ballot for the Nawabzada.

The phone rang. The caller was Ghulam Ishaq Khan, thanking Mustafa for his vote. Mustafa had lied to me, but the more important point was that he had compromised principle once again. The incident further eroded my belief in his political vision.

We left Pakistan to travel to Saudi Arabia in the company of the Jatoi and Khar clans – a horde of brothers and wives. The mission was to visit Mecca and perform *umra* in gratitude for Jatoi's success in the Kot Addu election.

But I had my own prayers. I cried to Allah about my continuing problems with Mustafa. I pleaded that I did not have the strength to cope with further betrayal and abuse, and begged for mercy.

Following the pilgrimage, Mustafa and I flew to London to settle a thorny business affair. Mr Garret, the lawyer who had represented me against Mustafa during the kidnapping episode, was suing us for his fee. My parents were supposed to have paid him, but had reneged when Mustafa and I were reconciled. Garret had billed us for £50,000 and had threatened to foreclose on our British properties – the city flat and the country home – if he was not paid.

I watched as Mustafa sat across the desk from the attorney, haggling as if the man were a bazaar trader. 'I'm paying you for nothing,' Mustafa said at first. 'Can't you see the irony? Your client is sitting here with me. You could not get me extradited or arrested, nor could you get her children back to her. She had to return to me.'

Garret held firm and reminded Mustafa that the law was in his favour. If we did not pay, he could sell our

346

properties out from under us. Mustafa demanded a discount, considering Garret's 'failure' to win the case. They settled on a sum of £25,000.

Although the money came out of my pocket as well as Mustafa's, I found supreme enjoyment in the reality that Mustafa had to pay something for all the trouble he had caused. At last he was held accountable in some manner. Inwardly I laughed that he had to pay for the warrant for his own arrest!

As he wrote the cheque, I thought: how reassuring to know that I am worth £25,000 to this man.

Upon our return to Pakistan we learned that my grandmother was dying of lung cancer. She had perhaps two months to live, and everyone gathered at my maternal Uncle Asad's house in Lahore, where the matriarch of the family awaited the end of her days.

Adila had no sense of occasion. Even as our grandmother's life ebbed away, Adila primped and preened, making sure that all her accessories matched. Her presence bothered me but, for a time, I could find no specific objection.

One day, Mustafa was scheduled to collect me from Uncle Asad's house at 5 p.m., but he called to say that he had been delayed by important political business. It was only then that I noticed Adila had left an hour before in Grandmother's car. Zarmina and I questioned the driver, who had returned without her. He said that Adila had been dropped off at a bookshop, and that she had asked him not to wait; she would return on her own. This was very odd. Even those of us who lived in the city of Lahore would never move around without transport. Zarmina's eyes met mine.

I disappeared into the bathroom and gulped down two tablets of the tranquillizer Lexotinal. Adila returned at about 7.30 p.m. and Mustafa arrived shortly after that. I could not face them.

My father told me that I looked doped. My sick

347

grandmother sensed my disturbed state – she was the only one who could decipher my carefully concealed emotions – and asked me what had happened. 'Pray for me,' I asked. 'I need your prayers. I don't know what's happening.'

Suddenly my grandmother looked greyer and more frail than ever before. She knew. She felt it in the air – Adila was back!

I sensed that Mustafa was waiting for my grandmother to die. He would then systematically attack and destroy the person I had become over the years. Mustafa Khar simply could not live with an adult woman who was capable of taking charge of her own life. He would reduce me once again to a neurotic, frightened girl. Adila was the perfect young and attractive instrument who could make me retreat into my old position. I had to be undone.

Grandmother slipped closer and closer to death. My marriage drew closer and closer to an end.

Grandmother was moved to the hospital. I sat in her room, trying to let her know how dearly I loved her, watching her struggle against her pain. When I called home, I somehow got a crossed line. I could hear Mustafa's voice, talking to someone, but I could not hear who it was. 'Somebody is on the phone,' Mustafa said to this person. 'I'll call you back again.' I immediately sent Zarmina and Riaz to their house, where my mother and Adila were staying. They sneaked upstairs and picked up the extension. I continued to sit with Grandmother, rubbing her back, praying that my suspicions were not correct.

When Zarmina returned, she sat by me and said that the caller was not Adila. But she quickly looked away, and her face paled. Speaking in whispers behind our grandmother's back, I pleaded with her to tell me the truth. 'It's true,' Zarmina at last confirmed, clutching at her stomach. 'It was her. They were making plans to meet this very evening, even as our grandmother is dying.' Then Zarmina rushed into the bathroom to vomit.

But their plans were disrupted. Sensing that her time had come, Grandmother summoned the family and, in the presence of everyone, declared, 'Whoever causes Tehmina pain, it is my prayer to God that He punish them with ulcers that will grow on their hearts. They will suffer like they cannot even imagine.' She glanced up at the ceiling – beyond the ceiling – and cried out, 'I am leaving Tehmina with you, oh Allah. Don't let me down. She has nobody left to protect her. Even I have been called away and I come to You willingly, but my soul begs an assurance that Tehmina will be protected by You.'

She beckoned for Mustafa to come close, took his hand and spoke bluntly: 'Tehmina has been very unhappy with you, but she has struggled and stood by you throughout your days of ordeal. Today, I'm asking you for a favour. Please be good to her. Be a good husband. She must never be unhappy again. This is my last request to you. It is my last request to anybody on this earth.' Her voice grew weaker as she struggled with her final few words: 'If you walk alone without Tehmina, each step you take thinking it shall bring you honour shall dishonour you. You shall look for fame and power and respect, but you shall get nothing but shame. If she is with you, God will make you reign supreme. This is my prayer for you.'

Mustafa whispered in response, 'Don't worry. I shall look after Tehmina. I promise.'

Grandmother lapsed into a coma. We took turns sitting with her, one at a time, throughout the bleak night. Each one of us had something special to say to her, regardless of her state of consciousness. When it was my turn, I wept and told her softly, 'This time you won't be there. This time I won't have your prayers. This time I won't be able to come to your home. Where shall I go? Where?' Her expressionless face held no answer. Grandmother was leaving me alone to face the most painful situation I could imagine. I knew that I would get no emotional sustenance from my parents; they would be more concerned with maintaining whatever social image they had left. I doubted whether Grandmother heard me, but I continued, 'You are going away from me, just when it is starting again. I am so alone. Why must you go? Why?' I cried hysterically.

Suddenly, huge tears rolled from my grandmother's eyes. I forgot my own pain and realized that, in her last moments, I had caused her more grief. My words had penetrated her comatose mind.

I tried to pacify her. 'Don't worry,' I whispered. 'Please don't cry. I'll cope. I promise. I'm strong. You know I'm strong.'

Slowly I pulled myself away from the only family I had known.

After me, it was Adila's turn to say her goodbye. But my youngest sister was in the room, alone with Grandmother, for only a few moments before she came rushing out, screaming, 'Something has happened to her. She is moving her head about. She's struggling. It's horrible. Come and see.'

I knew what had happened. Even in a coma, Grandmother could not abide Adila's presence.

Soon after that, she died. I was an orphan in my parents' lifetime.

I reverted to my old self, without realizing where I was heading. I spent my days picking up the telephone extension, sniffing his shirts for her perfume, checking for signs of lipstick. Once more I returned to the prayer mat.

I hated him, but I tried to keep him. Was it my heart breaking or my ego shattering? Amid the intense pain I could not differentiate.

One day Adila and I happened to be with the rest of the family, and I watched her squirm. I suspected that she had arranged a meeting with Mustafa. She paced the floor, and tried one excuse after another to leave. Finally, pleading that she was supposed to meet a friend – some 'Sara' who was coming in from Karachi – she rushed off.

I spoke to Tasneem, Adila's sister-in-law. Adila was staying at her home. 'She hasn't mentioned any friend arriving from Karachi,' Tasneem said. 'In fact, there is only one "Sara" whom she mentions often and she's abroad.' To my surprise and relief I realized that I had an ally. Tasneem said that she knew what was going on. 'Your husband picks her up here and drops her off,' she reported. 'I can't tell my brother. He won't believe me.'

Mustafa arrived home after 10.30 p.m., soaking wet with perspiration. Shocking pink lipstick smudged his shirt. He said that he had been at a public meeting where 'it was so hot, even my shoes are drenched'. With that explanation he fell asleep.

I lay awake at his side for some time, wondering what to do. Then I slipped downstairs, called Tasneem and asked her what time Adila had returned. 'At about ten-thirty,' Tasneem acknowledged. 'She was soaked wet. She ran up to avoid me, in case I suspected something. But I saw him drop her off in a beige Pajero.' Our car!

I returned to bed numbed.

Mustafa woke at 3 a.m. and took a bath. Then he spread out his prayer mat and began to say his prayers.

He did not realize that I was awake – still – and my voice jolted him when I taunted, 'I thought you were making an idiot out of me, but you're not. You're trying to fool God.' He ignored me and continued his prayers, but I raged on: 'You're facing Him after you have gone against everything that He commands you to adhere to. You've done something today that He has expressly forbidden and you've begged forgiveness for. You've betrayed *Him* again. What are you saying to Him now, Mustafa? That you're sorry again? Do you really think you can fool Him? Do you? Huh? If you think you can fool Him, I must be nothing. I don't even want to fight with you any more. He needs to take on this fight. It is His insult much more than mine—'

'—Stop this nonsense!' Mustafa commanded, breaking his prayers. 'You're going mad. There's nothing that I've done. You've become mental. You're imagining things.'

Tears assailed me, and I reached out instinctively for the picture of my patron saint, Hazrat Ali, and clutched it. This was the same protector who had sustained Mustafa throughout his incarceration. Although Mustafa had conveniently forgotten about him from the moment of his release, he knew that my faith was not a passing fancy.

Mustafa strode toward me and snatched the picture from my hands. 'This!' he growled, glaring scornfully at the saint's image. 'Is this going to save you?' He tore the picture into shreds and stormed out of the room.

I cried out to God for forgiveness as I gathered together the bits of consecrated paper.

From then on I was chasing Mustafa all the time. Nuscie and I talked on the phone when he was out, planning how to catch them red-handed. Because I was not free to go out and unable to drive myself, Nuscie became a detective. She was shattered by my weakening condition; instead of breaking away from the marriage, I was consumed and embroiled in its toxic mess, trying desperately to put together the shards of glass; the effort left me cut and bleeding. No advice was relevant, no other option acceptable. I could do nothing until I had proof.

Any other husband, knowing that I was supremely suspicious, would have grown cautious. But not Mustafa. He left the house at 7 p.m. the following evening, telling me that he would be back at 9 p.m. As soon as he was gone, I phoned Tasneem and confirmed my suspicions that Adila was scheduled to be out from

7 p.m. to 9 p.m. I rang again. This time she reported that Mustafa had picked up my sister.

I could not locate Nuscie. Quickly I recruited a cousin for moral support. We drove towards Tasneem's house and parked at a corner, where we could keep the site in view. It was 8.45 p.m. when a beige Pajero pulled up in front of the house. Mustafa was at the wheel. Adila jumped out of the passenger's seat – my seat – and rushed into the house. I spotted Tasneem at the window, peeking out from the edge of a curtain.

My cousin and I sped home, arriving before Mustafa. That evening I did not have the strength to confront him. I did not want to hear his denial and I did not need to hear confirmation.

We flew to my mother's ancestral village the following day for my grandmother's *chelam* (the ritual ending of the forty-day mourning period). I decided to tell my mother everything. Mother was very disturbed and later talked to Adila, without revealing the source of her information. Adila admitted that she had been out with Mustafa three times, but she contended that 'nothing had happened' and Mother believed her.

'What does she mean nothing happened?' I raged, when Mother reported back to me. 'How could you accept it? How could you sit there and listen to her justifying her date with her sister's husband? How can you be so normal and so passive? You know she's had an affair with him. You know it's started again. And yet you believe her, in spite of the evidence I gave you? I'm astonished. She has transgressed again and she has the gall to say she hasn't *done* anything? Would you believe Sahiba if she went on a date with your husband?' Mother had different standards for herself. That had always been clear.

There was no end to my tears. Everyone noticed, but they thought that I was crying for my grandmother.

In Mother's presence I finally confronted Adila. I told her that I knew everything. Then I declared, 'I want you both to know that you have successfully broken up a home that I have tried desperately to keep, despite your efforts. You have broken up not only my home, but the home of my four children, and I warn you both that this time you've taken on the wrong woman. Perhaps you're under the misconception that I'm still the worm you knew in London, the one you nearly crushed. There's a great difference between "Tina" and "Tehmina Khar", and I shall fight your injustice – even if I have to die.'

Unshaken, Adila tossed her long hair casually and asked, 'Do you know what I've done for you? You wouldn't call me a sister; you'd call me an angel – if only you knew. I am responsible for saving your marriage.' She declared that Mustafa was pursuing her and wanted to marry her, but contended that she was unwilling to break up my home.

Could it be true? My contention was that she should never have allowed him to approach her. Why was she negotiating if there was nothing to negotiate?

I tried to warn Mustafa of God's wrath. 'He's testing you, can't you see?' I asked. 'He's checking whether your appeal for mercy against this sin was genuine in prison. *Tauba* is a contract with God for the future. You cannot treat it so lightly.' I pleaded with him not to hit his own feet with a hammer. 'You'll destroy yourself, the wife you fought to regain, the children you profess to love – even politics will suffer. I'm known publicly for my role in your life. The people will not spare you.'

Nothing had effect. His eyes and ears were shut. He would sometimes comfort me for my 'growing insanity' and sometimes brush me aside for 'hysterical insecurity'. He said that I was suffering from middle-age crisis. 'It happens to women who cannot accept growing old,' he said smugly.

Mustafa regressed to his youth. He went back to T-shirts and blue jeans, safari suits and crocodile shoes.

I looked into a mirror and told myself sadly that

354

perhaps I had to change too. I must look like her. I must dress like her. I must change my whole personality to resemble hers. It's the only way. Maybe my marriage would work then. Look at you, in your white clothes and your high ideals. You are not his kind of woman. Adila is. And yet he says he loves you. He says so all the time.

The mirror stared back.

In my mind I heard Mustafa's sinister voice: 'No other woman can be like you. But I want you to be like a sixteen-year-old. I want romance again.'

I recoiled. I can't do that, I thought. I'm not sixteen. I'm a mother of five. I'm thirty-six years old. How can I have romantic notions with a man who's having an affair with my own sister? How?

I reached out to God. I visited shrines. I prayed any and every way I knew: 'Please stop my home from breaking up. Please stop my children from ruin.' I wept and begged.

Only silence answered.

I must not crack up, I lectured myself. I must not. I had to go away for a while. To look at things from a distance.

I could have accepted another woman. I would have handled her and emerged stronger. But not my own sister. Not Adila.

I knew that I had to leave Mustafa, but I did not know how or when. I needed proof. Despite knowing everything, my family clung to Mustafa and Adila's version and insisted I was imagining things. They insisted I was insecure and was losing my sanity. I was a vegetable again.

One night Mustafa wanted to make love, and I knew from his attitude that he would not accept a refusal. I had to let it happen. I controlled my hatred by alienating myself from the moment. I stared over his shoulder and begged God to punish him. This is incest, God. You have forbidden a man to have a relationship with two

355

sisters at the same time. It is in Your Koran. If You have made this rule, then You will never allow this to happen to me again. Never allow this man to touch me again. Never let him have the audacity to disobey You. I cannot do anything, but You can stop it.

A miracle occurred. From that night on, Mustafa stopped touching me. Each night he climbed into bed, put his head down on to the pillow and fell asleep. It was divine intervention.

18

June 24, 1989. Mustafa prepared for the hunt. He was
wearing the same attire as the day I had fallen in love
with him: khaki trousers tucked into Wellingtons, a
camouflage jacket with a bullet bag hanging at his side,
and a Mao cap on his head. I watched him as he selected
a gun from his large collection. I sat silently as he turned
toward me with a smile to say goodbye. I kept watching
his back as he moved toward the door and strode out of
my life – much as he had come into it.

I held a long and painful discussion with my children,
explaining the situation to them as best I could. There
had already been too much drama in their young lives
and I could not bear to put them through another
kidnapping; I wanted them to be able to live as normally
as possible under these terrible circumstances. They
cried tears of desolation when I told them of my decision,
and I knew that it would take them much time to
understand. I also knew that I would never be satisfied
until they, as well as I, escaped from the prison that was
Mustafa. But I had to go first.

I delivered my children to the care of Mustafa's
sister-in-law. Then Zarmina picked me up, and I left
Mustafa Khar's house for the fourth and final time.
There had been too many false starts towards freedom.
This time my decision was irrevocable.

Once more my life was reduced to newspaper headlines. Once more everyone branded me as inconsistent.
The press was inquisitive, but failed to ferret out Adila's
role in the saga of one of the nation's most famous
political marriages.

To my dismay, I discovered that Mustafa had anticipated my action and had withdrawn all the money from our joint bank account. I had never had to face poverty; it humiliated me when suddenly I was forced to rely on the charity of relatives. My Aunt Samar and Uncle Akhtar took me into their home and tried to give me the kind of support that my grandmother would have provided.

At first I was able to build a small amount of resilience against my weak position, but my mother's reaction mobilized the entire family to attempt to force me to change my stand. One by one my supporters began to move away, and I found myself falling deeper into a hell of betrayal, injustice, poverty and anguish. My desolation became so frightening that I reached a point of numbness. There was no present and no future – only the past, which invaded and enveloped my whole being.

Now Mustafa refused to let me see the children. After fifteen days he took them to Karachi to discuss the situation with my parents. Adila was also there, and the fact that my parents did not send her away during his visit shocked me further. My children wandered about the house bewildered. I was furious to learn that they played innocently with their Aunt Adila, even as I was refused contact with them. Mustafa tried to persuade my father to intervene in our dispute, to convince me to return. He claimed that I had concocted the Adila story. He said that the only reason I wanted a divorce was that I had become used to freedom and was influenced by the new friends I had made during his incarceration. Despite her own knowledge of the details, Mother sided with Mustafa – and Adila. She wanted to evade the issue of divorce at any cost, because there were too many fingers pointing at the reason for it. The scandal loomed overhead and, to divert it, my life was a very small price to pay – perhaps no price at all.

But my father knew better, and told Mustafa to

contemplate giving me a divorce so that the matter would die silently.

Naseeba called on her twelfth birthday. She cried into the phone, begging me to be with her when she cut her cake. Since Mustafa was away I decided to attend the party. A number of Mustafa's brothers and friends were there, with their wives and children. Naseeba was thrilled, and as she gripped my hand firmly as we cut the cake together, I realized that her little hand was not letting go. In her innocence, she was looking for strength from that which was so weak.

Mustafa arrived unexpectedly – at least to me. We greeted one another in a civilized manner. He approached and asked quietly, 'Can you come upstairs? I need to talk to you.' There were many guests in the house, and I did not wish to create a scene at Naseeba's party. Reasoning that Mustafa would not dare misbehave with so many people around, I agreed. I followed him upstairs and walked into what had been our bedroom. When, behind me, I heard him quickly turn and bolt the door, I knew I was trapped.

'You can't leave now,' he confirmed, in a tone full of menace. 'You're going to live with me for two months, in which time I'm going to make sure you stay with me for ever. Your mother has said that you should be with me. I'm taking you back to the village tomorrow.'

Panic engulfed me. In the past, he had abducted my children. Now it was to be me. When would this madness stop? I tried to hide my fear and face down this bully. 'Mustafa!' I commanded, 'you open that door now, or else I'll scream the house down. Why do you forget that you are dealing with a very different kind of woman?'

'Scream, I don't care,' he said. 'Bring the country down if you like.'

The shriek began low in my throat and emerged in a loud, high-pitched call for help.

He was on me instantly. Grabbing my wrists, he pushed me into the bathroom, slammed the door and locked me inside.

I continued to scream, hoping that my cries would penetrate someone's conscience – the servants, our neighbours, his friends and family.

Mustafa's daughter-in-law Marikha rushed upstairs, followed by others. I heard her yell, 'Daddy, you can't do this!'

'Get out of the room!' Mustafa raged. 'Nobody should interfere in my private affairs.' Marikha scampered away.

I waited a few moments, trying to compose myself. This was a serious threat. He could and would spirit me off to the tribal areas adjoining the remote village of Kot Addu, where I would live as his prisoner until – who knew when? For ever, perhaps. Nobody would be interested in rescuing me, save Nuscie, Zarmina and Minoo – and what could they do? There were numerous women who lived just such lives of imprisonment and despair. In that environment he could easily coerce me into rescinding the divorce. I spoke through the locked door, trying to be firm but reasonable. 'Mustafa, you cannot do this to me,' I shouted. 'My lawyer will have you arrested.'

'I can. And I will. Your parents are behind me.'

'Let me speak to them. Let them tell me that.'

'No.'

My aunt and uncle were growing concerned because I had not come home from Naseeba's party. Uncle Akhtar called. 'Tehmina isn't coming back,' Mustafa told him. 'She's decided to stay here.'

Uncle Akhtar smelled a decomposing rat. Just then, my sister Minoo happened to call him from London and he told her of this latest event. Minoo swung into action. She phoned the Chief Minister's house in an attempt to get the government to intervene. Then she contacted the press. Soon word of my 'imprisonment' reached my lawyer, Asma Jehangir. She wanted to delay action until the following morning, when she could have warrants served against Mustafa charging illegal confinement and attempted abduction.

I had no idea what was going on in the world outside Mustafa's house. All I knew was that, even now, his son Bilal was making arrangements for our departure to Kot Addu.

Mustafa opened the bathroom door. I was sullen, wary and scared, but pretended not to be. He picked up a bottle of Valium 10, extracted two tablets and offered them to me. I tried to resist, but he utilized the same method he had employed with his dogs. He overpowered me, pushed the pills into my mouth and forced water down my throat, holding my nostrils until I was compelled to swallow.

Adrenalin warred with Valium and emerged victorious. After some minutes, I felt more hyper than ever. But Mustafa had great faith in the pills and, when he believed that I had calmed somewhat, he allowed me to call my mother. 'Tell her you have consented to stay,' he ordered.

I nodded.

When I heard Mother's voice on the other end of the phone, I raged, 'If you force me to stay with this man, I'll commit suicide. What sort of mother are you? I'll tell the whole world that you drove me to death.'

She said, 'I don't know what you're talking about. What is he saying to you?'

Mustafa snatched the phone and spoke into it, 'I need your co-operation. She will be fine when I take her away.'

After the call, I sat him down and tried stern reasoning. 'Listen carefully,' I said. 'Don't use tactics on me that have been tried in the past. I am aware of their zero value. Try your games on somebody who hasn't played them.'

He shook his head at me and muttered, 'What have you become, Tehmina?'

I returned a confident smile and chided, 'I have become *you*, Mustafa.'

Someone banged on the door. Mustafa opened it and the room filled with brothers and sisters-in-law. They tried to convince Mustafa to let me go. 'Don't interfere in my marriage,' he ordered.

'What marriage?' I shouted. 'Your marriage, according to the Koran, was over years ago when you slept with my sister. I have been living with you in sin. The contract stood null and void long ago.'

Mustafa was called to the phone and dismayed to find a reporter on the other end, asking difficult questions. None of us knew how the word was spreading.

I was desperate to get out. Nothing in this house that I had decorated with such loving care interested me. All my possessions, collected over the years from various remote areas of my country, now seemed distant from me. Every single thing in this house had held some meaning, yet nothing was meaningful enough for me to want to stay – but then, had not Mustafa held meaning? With him had gone my love for the surroundings that I shared with him. I forgot the ordeal that I had already begun to face as a divorcée: the saying that it is easier to wash the dishes in your husband's home than in the world outside was turning truer by the minute, yet paled into insignificance now. Nothing was left of the marriage. Nothing was left of the man.

While Mustafa was out of the room, I scrawled Aunty Samar's telephone number on to a scrap of paper and smuggled it to Amna, Mustafa's fifteen-year-old daughter by his earlier wife, Sherry. 'Please go somewhere and call this number,' I begged. 'Ask them to come here and save me.'

Amna was unused to espionage. She stumbled toward the door, petrified by the intrigue, looking extremely guilty. Mustafa encountered her in the doorway and was immediately suspicious. 'What are you hiding?' he demanded. His eyes pierced hers. He pulled her hand forward and tore the note from her clutched palm, glanced at it and screamed at his daughter. Sobbing, she looked back at me, as if to say, 'At least I tried.'

My father called and Mustafa handed the receiver to me. Father said that there had been a terrible misunderstanding. Mustafa had told them that, given an opportunity, he could convince me to resume the marriage. They were supporting him only as far as that. I screamed into the phone that Mustafa was forcing me to stay against my will. Father asked for Mustafa and spoke firmly to him, saying, 'Let her go. Now.'

Mustafa's response shocked me. He agreed.

As I walked out, he remained in the room with his family, dialling a telephone number. I was halfway down the stairs when I realized that in my haste to leave, I had forgotten my bag inside the room. As I returned and opened the door, I stopped. Mustafa was talking to my mother. 'She has some severe problem with you,' he said. 'She feels insecure because I respect you so much. You and Adila have become her monsters. It has nothing to do with me.'

I interrupted this conversation by striding into the room. I picked up my handbag, turned to Mustafa and, making sure that my voice was loud enough to be heard over the phone line, said, 'You are a very dangerous and sick man. And, my poor mother, you have made such a fool of her.'

My father arrived to end the marriage before it exploded in Adila's face. Mustafa demanded custody of the children and ownership of all of our properties – the country house in England and our London flat, which were jointly titled, and the house in Lahore, which was in the names of my daughters. My father accepted these provisions with the cavalier pronouncement: 'Leave her penniless. She doesn't need anything from you. I can support her.' Another condition, mutually important to the men in my life, was that I make a press statement citing incompatibility as the reason for our divorce; we both also signed a statement declaring that neither of us would speak to the press further on this subject. The final point of our contract was that I would be allowed to see my children daily.

The next morning Mustafa arrived to sign the divorce papers. He disgusted me by calling all our children into the room. With tears streaming down his cheeks, he said very intensely, 'I want you, my children, to bear witness that I don't want your mother to leave. I want her to be my wife. I love her. But she wants to leave me.'

I thought with a smile on my face: What a great actor you are, Mustafa.

He signed the papers and handed them to me as the children cried and pleaded with me not to break up our home.

My face remained expressionless, my eyes dry, as I signed.

A great burden lifted from my shoulders. I was no longer Tehmina Khar.

I stared at Mustafa and said, 'You've stripped me of everything. But from today, you can never say that Tehmina is your wife. You lost me in the bargain.'

In fact, the divorce would not be final for three months. Islamic law provides for this period, called *Idat*, so that the parties involved have time to consider their decision carefully and retreat if possible.

Mustafa used the three months to wage a systematic campaign to pressure me to return. He called me, crying for forgiveness. 'I can't live without you,' he proclaimed. 'I was mad to lose you. I've not forgotten your support, your patience. Don't punish me so severely. Give me one last chance.'

'No!' I shouted. 'I am not your kind of woman any more. I am not a victim any more. It will *never* work, not for one day.'

Soon after that, he arrived at Aunt Samar's house with

364

a family delegation of brothers and sisters-in-law to plead with me to return for the sake of the children. I stared into his eyes and dared him to tell his family the true reason that I had left him. He remained silent, of course, so I detailed the story.

'It's your imagination,' he interrupted.

I stood up, pointed toward the door and told him to leave. My fury unleashed, I said, 'Return only when you have the guts to admit every single detail of your relationship with my sister. Otherwise, don't cross my path. I'll stamp on you like you cannot even imagine!'

I strode upstairs, leaving Mustafa and his clan gaping in shock.

The press printed a lurid account of Mustafa's relationship with Adila. They attributed the story to me but I denied being the source, and I told a painful lie for Adila's sake. I said that I loved my sister and that this was just malicious gossip. I had no intention of ruining her marriage.

Mother was beset on all sides, and frantic to preserve her family's reputation. She asked me to meet Adila's husband Matloob and his family and convince them that I was so desperate to leave Mustafa that I had concocted the Adila story as an excuse. Mother warned me that if I did not do this, she and my father would not support me financially. I refused to lie any further for the sake of 'my poor baby sister'.

I was homeless, destitute and scared. Even as I tried to rise from my crawling position, Mustafa manoeuvred himself into further prominence and power. Benazir's hold on the government was tenuous. Her Achilles' heel was the Punjab, controlled by Nawaz Sharif and the Muslim League. Mustafa was the only man who commanded enough support in the Punjab to spearhead a viable 'get Nawaz' campaign. Now the opportunity was at hand. A seat in the Provincial Assembly had become vacant and a by-election was announced. The People's

Party desperately wanted their candidate to win it, and they wooed Mustafa. They wanted him to rejoin after all these years, manage the campaign and send a message to Nawaz that Bhutto's legacy was alive and well in the Punjab.

Mustafa had the audacity to call me from Islamabad and ask me to pray for him. He was about to announce his decision to rejoin the People's Party. 'You should be with me at this time,' he said. 'This is your success more than mine.' I did pray, with sincerity and without deception, that God would show him the right path.

The public announcement that Mustafa was rejoining his old party was received with jubilation. Party workers felt the strength of the Lion in their blood. Mustafa was now the second most powerful leader in the party, next to Benazir herself. He had successfully moved to a position from where he could reach towards the very top.

Jatoi, now seated in the National Assembly thanks to Mustafa's support, had been appointed leader of the opposition. The IJI attempted a 'no confidence' vote against Benazir which, if successful, would install Jatoi as the constitutionally elected Prime Minister. But Mustafa discarded his old political ally and played a significant role in the failure of the 'no confidence' vote, thus straightaway demonstrating his effectiveness and loyalty to Benazir.

Uncle Asad goaded me to return, saying, 'You have lived with him through all his difficult times. It is now your turn to reap the fruit. You must not be stupid. For your children's sake, go back to him. The worst is over.'

But just as I had found it impossible to leave a fallen, struggling man, I now found it impossible to return to a free man on the rise. There seemed no justification any more for going back to a marriage that had lost everything. I clung to my beliefs, while everyone around me tried to snatch them away.

Uncle Asad was under severe pressure. He was

hoping, through Mustafa's influence, to be given a People's Party ticket for the coming by-election, and was embarrassed that anyone on his side of the family supported me over Mustafa. When all else failed, he ordered his sister, my Aunt Samar, to get me out of her house. 'Let her go to her father's relatives,' he said. 'Just get her out at once.' But Uncle Akhtar refused to turn me out. 'I shall book you a room in a hotel,' Uncle Asad offered. 'I don't want my family to have anything to do with you at this point.'

'I don't need you to do me any favours,' I snapped. 'You represent the mentality that cripples women. You've just given me the reason that condemns women into bad marriages. Your attitude stinks of dishonour.' And then, with the determination that was by now taking over, I added, 'You've won this round, but let me tell you that I shall win the final round.'

I decided not to embarrass my hosts. For a few weeks I shifted to the home of another uncle. During this time, Mustafa came to see me for an earnest discussion. With only God, his conscience and me as witnesses, he admitted the truth about Adila at last. He told me that the Devil had taken hold of him, that he was carried away by his lust. He cried and asked for my forgiveness. 'It was God's test for the genuineness of my relenting in prison.'

'I have forgiven you,' I said.

'Come back to me then,' he said instantly.

I realized how easy it had always been for him to erase the mess he had created. It was a pattern: apologize, be forgiven and begin again with a clean slate. But his crimes were heaped in my heart and there was no room for more. 'I will never return,' I vowed. 'No matter what.'

His next line of attack was against my character. He visited my family and friends and proclaimed that I left him because I wanted to be a 'free' woman. He repeated the canard that I had made up the Adila story as a pretext

367

to walk out on him. Coming, as it did, after his private confession to me, this regression snatched away the final few scraps of respect I might have still held for the man.

But I was sinking swiftly and deeply into the confusion that my family and Mustafa had created. Until one day they *all* ceased to be relevant, and I found an inner strength to fight for myself. It was clear that nobody else would.

On *Ashura* (the tenth day of the tragedy of Karballa, when the Prophet's grandson Imam Husain and his family were brutally slain by the tyrant caliph Yazid) I called my mother and said, 'I want to inform you that I have left this battle to God. Islam does not give the sole responsibility of love and duty to the children of parents who do severe injustice to them. Islam fights injustice. If you are right, you will come out clean. If not, I shall rise from the grave that you have dug for me. I curse all those people who have wronged me and I shall pray to God to avenge me, as He did Yazid against Imam Husain.' I told my parents that I did not want to know them any longer.

I phoned Mustafa and declared, 'The commitment given to you by my father stands revoked. I do not know Mr Durrani any more. I have disowned my family. Any transactions that you may have had with them concerning me are null and void.'

A cousin lent me his empty flat for a month as he travelled, so I moved again, feeling much like a vagabond. There was no telephone and no transport.

Shugufta had witnessed the intrigues and injustices against me at my mother's and Adila's hands; it was at this time that she took a train, leaving behind all her belongings, to return to me and Hamza. The doorbell rang and Hamza and I went to open it. We stood in stunned silence for a moment before we hugged each other and cried. Hamza found new vitality and I realized how, sometimes, your own let you down, while even a poor servant takes a stand and rejects comfort for justice.

Zarmina's father-in-law, Uncle Sadiq, was shocked to hear of my financial situation and sent me 10,000 rupees (about £225). I sat on my prayer mat, crying and offering thanks for his compassion like a beggar.

I was told that Matloob was abusing me for creating problems for his innocent wife, who was apparently throwing tantrums because of the scandal. My entire family distanced itself from what they termed as 'too explosive and expensive a relationship'. My mother was furious with me and the rest of my family had to obey her emotion automatically.

I was stressed out but could not afford to rest yet. It was still the thick of battle, one that had been raging for many years – perhaps all of my life.

Two months of this waiting period since my divorce had passed when, through Uncle Sadiq, I ordered Mustafa to vacate my house in Lahore. Mustafa knew that his position was now weak, that I could successfully contest the deal my father had arranged, so he attempted to bargain. He said that he would give me the house in Lahore only in return for our properties in England. But I had learned much from Mustafa over the years and I played his game; I signed a power of attorney agreeing to hand over the British properties to Mustafa, but since there was not enough time to have it attested to by the British Embassy, and since it would not stand up in an English court without that, he asked Uncle Sadiq to stand as guarantor for my commitment. 'She has let her father's commitment down,' he said suspiciously. 'She will never honour yours.'

I explained, 'I will not put Zarmina in an embarrassing position – you know that. If I were not certain of honouring my commitment I would never have involved Zarmina's in-laws.'

If I were to renege again, Uncle Sadiq promised Mustafa his total support. 'This time I'm involved,' he said. 'I won't allow her to embarrass me.' Zarmina and Riaz also confirmed Uncle Sadiq's careful guarantee, until finally Mustafa was convinced and he agreed.

Mustafa moved into our large old house on the canal in Lahore and I had my home back.

When I walked through the door I realized how much I loved the Bohemian, ethnic décor. I felt the security of a roof over my head again. Hamza, Zarmina, Shugufta and I looked about with ecstatic expressions on our faces.

But although Mustafa was no longer visible in this home, his presence was still strong. I missed Dai Ayesha and my other children.

The *Idat* (the three-month waiting period before divorce) was over. The divorce was final.

Living with their father, my children became increasingly unhappy. Mustafa tried to make them resent me for breaking up their home and for maligning him, and, by extension, them. He placed impossible restrictions upon our time together. When the children were visiting me in my home, a guard stood outside the gate, preventing any visitor from entering. One of Mustafa's maids was delegated to remain with us at all times to report our conversations.

The children showed visible signs of strain and it broke my heart to see them still trapped in the prison from which I had fled. Mustafa kept me shackled by way of the children. I felt the desperate need to cut off this continuous control. But how? I could not yet fathom the answer.

There was also very little money, and that was needed for food. Shugufta worked for many months without any salary; in fact, when we were in need, she borrowed money from her working relatives.

Through various friends I tried to convince Mustafa that the children needed their mother and that we must try to provide a more normal environment for them. I pointed out that some of his children from other marriages were maladjusted. 'Please give them a chance for a better life,' I pleaded. But Mustafa remained steadfast. He had just given up authority over me, but would not give up his authority over them.

Spurred on by his wife's suspicious behaviour, Matloob tapped his own telephone line and taped hours of explicit and incriminating conversations between Mustafa and Adila. Matloob then drove around Karachi in tears, listening to the tapes on his car cassette-player. He waited for our mother to return from London and, as he and Adila drove her home from the airport, to their utter shock he played the tapes once more. Finally, armed with the evidence of adultery, he came to Lahore and played the tapes for me and several other relatives. Here, at last, was proof of my sanity.

Matloob was a feudal lord himself, and custom dictated that he commit some horrendous crime of passion in order to restore his honour. Instead, he took a progressive stand, filing the first-ever court case in Pakistan wherein one influential feudal lord formally accused another of adultery. Such an affair was an everyday occurrence in our society – everyone knew that – but no-one ever brought it into the open. Adila was despatched by our parents to their London home to ride out the storm of publicity and to avoid arrest!

Unfortunately, the timing was poor. Mustafa's supporters claimed that the criminal charge was a cheap and dirty ploy to malign the Lion of the Punjab in the midst of his 'get Nawaz' campaign. They openly wondered how large a bribe Matloob had received from Mustafa's political opponents. Mustafa issued a statement declaring, 'Now I will fight my opponent like a wounded lion. I am more dangerous than before.' Any judge would have cast a poor man into prison for a crime of this nature, but Mustafa was granted bail, a circumstance that, in Pakistan, is considered an acquittal. Mustafa, the hero, was carried from the courtroom on the shoulders of slogan-shouting People's Party leaders and workers.

*　　*　　*

The People's Party won the by-election and Mustafa was accorded complete credit for the victory. His next step was to resign his National Assembly seat and fight for a vacated Provincial seat, so that he could enter the Punjab Assembly and 'get Nawaz'. He was aiming to become Chief Minister under a People's Party government.

On the other hand, I was a social and political outcast. People whom I formerly respected turned their backs on me. I shuddered at the realization of the position that a woman falls into after divorce – especially if her ex-husband is an important person. Increasingly I understood why women dare not break away. Increasingly I experienced a humiliating lack of confidence and self-esteem. But, although I cried often in bed at night, I held on during the day with a determined strength.

At the height of his political life, when he was practically and almost unanimously acclaimed as the only alternative to the strongly entrenched Chief Minister, Mustafa suddenly announced his seventh marriage, to a twenty-two-year-old divorcée whom he had known for only a month. Taking the public relations offensive, he had the audacity to compare his many marriages with those of the Prophet.

I shook my head in disbelief when he said to me, 'She loves me more than you did.' His superficiality stung me, for I had loved him in spite of what he was. She did not even know him.

I assessed his political philanderings: he had abandoned Bhutto, escaped into exile, reneged on his deal with the generals, flirted with Indian intelligence, plotted the defeat of his own country's armed forces – then, later, compromised with them – sulked at Benazir's prominence, and committed a plethora of additional political backstabbings. He covered everything with empty rhetoric and charisma. What passed as intelligence and insight was nothing but guile and cunning. If he had remained in exile or prison without compromising his principles, perhaps I would still be with him. But I had seen his all-too-eager short cuts to power. His ideals were merely bait for the gullible.

I began to realize that the Mustafa Khar I had championed existed only in my perception. I had made him into the man that fitted my own ideals. He never existed in any real form.

Mustafa asked me to come over for lunch, to discuss how his new marriage would affect our children. As I passed through the gates of his expensive house, situated on a large plot in an exclusive area of Lahore, I thought of all our dreams for this residence. After we went into exile the military confiscated it and it had fallen into disrepair. I had it restored upon Mustafa's release. Now I remembered the promise we had made to one another to continue living in our small home. He had broken that vow, too, as he had so many others.

Mustafa was free and powerful. He had sixteen servants. He had regained his wealth and his political position was stronger than ever. I had lost everything – even the children. I walked through the corridors of my former home and realized how completely he had stripped me. This was the difference between man and woman.

He was on the telephone when I arrived, talking to Benazir's husband Asif Zardari. He was cracking a joke, laughing. When he finished his conversation he ordered lunch. For a time we settled into political small talk.

I asked, 'Mustafa, do you realize that you have taken away everything from me – thirteen years, my family, my children, my youth and everything I believed in? I have to start anew.' He listened carefully as I continued, 'I don't know what to do. Maybe I can start working somewhere, get involved in social welfare. I don't want to waste what I've learned and felt.'

He stretched, took a deep breath, breathed out and addressed me coolly and contemptuously: 'Tehmina, you are nothing any more. Once you were Begum

Tehmina Mustafa Khar. Now you are just Tehmina Durrani. When you ring up people you have to introduce yourself as my ex-wife. You have no identity of your own. Nobody knows you. People meet you because you have something interesting to say about *me*. You will exhaust your stock of stories very soon, then you'll have nothing to say. After that, you'll lose all your so-called friends. They'll be bored with you. Women won't let you come to their homes because you're a threat to their marriage. Even if you think that you can work politically, you'll be made to wait outside offices for hours, because you've removed your name from mine.'

I gulped back tears, pretending to be unaffected. The poet Ghalib's verse flitted through my mind:

> Your taunts chip away at my identity.
> No-one speaks of me with such audacity.

That evening at home alone, Mustafa's words stung me. I rethought my life, trying to define my reality. I was no longer Mrs Mustafa Khar. I had been discarded and spat out like sugar-cane chaff. He had done everything he could to destroy me and he had very nearly succeeded. A few more doses of Mustafa and my spirit would have died for ever.

Many people had suggested that I keep his surname, as it was the name by which I was known. I was repelled by that, and in any case I did not want to lean on a pillar that had fallen upon me instead of supporting me. But if I was not Mrs Mustafa Khar, who was I? The Tehmina Durrani of my childhood was an alien to me, a confused little girl whom I had outgrown. I could not relate to her. Was there a new Tehmina Durrani inside me, older and sadder, but also wiser?

Sitting alone with my scattered thoughts, I conjectured that fate had placed me on this torturous path for a purpose. Our closed society considered it obscene for a woman to reveal her intimate secrets, but would not silence be a greater crime? Silence condones injustice, breeds subservience and fosters a malignant hypocrisy. Mustafa Khar and other feudal lords thrive and multiply on silence. Muslim women must learn to raise their voices against injustice. For me, conventional politics was no longer the answer. In Pakistan, the system is merely used to hoodwink further those who are already exploited. I realized that I could do no greater service for my country and our people than to expose the camouflage.

I was determined not to waste thirteen years of my life.

I decided to cast a stone at hypocrisy.

I decided to write this book and break the traditional silence.

Epilogue

Having failed to hold Mustafa accountable under law Matloob, in true feudal fashion, reverted back to the life he knew. He flew to London, made up with Adila and denied the existence of the incriminating tapes. My parents forgave him. They and Adila pointed to Matloob's return as proof of her innocence.

Mother finally mustered the courage to confide to her children that our father was plagued by a constitutional reaction to alcohol. She said that this was why she had been forced to monitor his behaviour in such a domineering manner. She had to become hard and ruthless in order to save him from self-destruction. If this was true, we could understand the sacrifice she had made for family honour, but it was made at too high a cost. By the time she lost my father to another woman, she was sixty years old and it was far too late for her to correct the havoc.

My father now maintains two homes in Karachi and attempts to spend equal time with each of his wives.

The People's Party was disgusted with Mustafa's decision to get married rather than 'get Nawaz'. His political star fell, and for a time he disappeared from public view.

Benazir Bhutto's elected government was dissolved on 8 August 1990 by Zia's protégé, President Ghulam Ishaq Khan. Mustafa Jatoi was sworn in as the caretaker Prime Minister of Pakistan. I watched television coverage, saddened by the death of democracy at the hands of a civilian coup. As the camera panned to take in the faces of the new Cabinet members, it paused ominously on one face. I froze. Mustafa Khar was sworn in as federal Minister for Water and Power. This time he had stabbed the People's Party in the back and somersaulted back to Jatoi and the IJI.

He phoned me later and chided, 'Tehmina, you didn't congratulate me.'

I replied, 'Mustafa, if this is all you wanted, why did you not compromise with General Zia in the first place? Nine years in exile and two in prison were too high a price to pay for a silly little ministry in a caretaker government. You lost your most important asset – the People's Party worker. You lost your support and your credibility. It's time to offer you condolences. You just died a political death.'

The process of disintegration had begun. Mustafa committed one political blunder after another. New elections returned him to Parliament, but the results made Nawaz Sharif Prime Minister instead of Jatoi. Within the year, both Mustafa Jatoi and Mustafa Khar were again seen amidst cheering crowds as they teamed with Benazir, leading the long march to Islamabad in a successful attempt to topple the government and 'get Nawaz'.

Of the Bhutto boys, during his lifetime General Zia pursued his designs to ensure that these two had no political future in Pakistan, and to damage their reputations on the international scene. His propaganda campaign against them involved numerous slurs against Shah Nawaz before his mysterious death in 1985. Mir was to face even more charges after democratic order was established. Currently (1994) he is imprisoned facing charges of treason, having been tried by special courts that his sister once called Kangaroo courts. The irony is that Mir still has to clear his name while his sister has risen to the office of Prime Minister by struggling against the same dictator.

*　　*　　*

Finally, after Mustafa's new son was born, I decided to take another bold step. I called a press conference and proclaimed that Mustafa was an irresponsible father, incapable of bringing up four children without their mother. I stated that I had tried to negotiate the return of my children privately, but my attempts to handle the matter quietly had only served to allow Mustafa to implement the laws of his jungle. Now I was confronting him head on, and was prepared to fight, under public scrutiny, for custody of the children. In fact, I declared, I now had custody.

I secured the children in the house, locked the gates, called Mustafa and said, 'If you disturb us again I shall fight you with my life. By now you must know that I stand by the commitment to my beliefs at all and *any* cost.' He listened in silence as I warned, 'There will be a great imbalance in our strengths if we fight, because I am prepared to die and you are desperate to live.'

Mustafa backed away from the battlefield. We did not hear from him for six months. Then he telephoned and quietly accepted visitation rights. The children resumed cordial relations with their father. Mustafa now has two young sons, still cared for by poor Dai Ayesha, who is not permitted to visit us.

I refused to honour my commitment to Uncle Sadiq, who understood the difficulties I was facing in bringing up the children with no child support and no income. Mustafa found no option when my solicitor from London offered an out-of-court settlement. He quietly transferred the London apartment to my name as I transferred the country house to his. However the papers he signed were not sufficient; he did not pay service charges or rates and neglected the properties to the extent that rats romped through them. I could not sell without him; he would not sign. He told the children that he would rather let the managing agents have the properties. I would not get a penny, just years of mental torture trying to persuade a man who didn't mind the loss, whereas I had no money to save the flat by at least paying the charges. The court ordered its forteiture. I am now trying to retrieve it from the agents as well as from Mustafa. Haslemere stands in ruins; it has not been visited since 1986.

My oldest daughter Tanya graduated from high school in America and returned to Pakistan. Finally I was able to welcome her into my home. She has now settled with us as if she had never been away. A talented artist, she would like to pursue a career in graphic design.

Naseeba is an aspiring politician. She plans a future run for a seat in Parliament, from Mustafa's constituency, in order to fulfil the promises that her father made to the people of Kot Addu.

Nisha speaks of studying criminal law and working to help the poor.

Ali, 'my little feudal lord', shows a great inclination toward mathematics and 'shooting'.

Hamza is the gentle one, the baby who remembers little of life with Mustafa.

All five children have become firm supporters of my cause.

Nuscie and J.J., along with their children Nadia and O.J., are with us constantly, members of our extended family, helping us in our attempt to fashion a new type of home in an anachronistic society. They have been my strongest pillars.

Shugufta has learned to drive and is very much a part of our family.

The first edition of this book was published in Pakistan in 1990. The initial reviews were extremely negative. Many said that it was scandalous, publicity-seeking rubbish. Some called it obscene and pornographic. No-one in Pakistan, however, doubted its accuracy.

Some reviewers speculated that I had accepted a bribe

from Mustafa's political rival, Nawaz Sharif. In a country where the loyalty of Parliament is frequently bartered to the highest bidder, I could not blame anyone for believing this.

My father gave written notice to the press disowning and disinheriting me. He ordered me to refrain from using his name.

I answered that statement with a press release of my own, accepting his disinheritance as the natural outcome of unconventional behaviour. Such isolation is the cause of a woman's silence in our society. But I refused to give up my name. My parents have neither seen nor spoken to me since. In fact, most of my family has disappeared from my life. The only ones who have remained steadfast during my time of adversity are my sisters Zarmina and Minoo, their husbands Riaz and Ali, and my cousin Bina and her husband Aslam Quraishi.

Following publication, two criminal charges were registered against me. One charged me with treason for the assistance I had given Mustafa in his dealings with Indian intelligence agents. This occasioned much drawing-room discussion, but no action. I was not even questioned by government investigators and Mustafa, whose involvement was far more severe, remains a Member of Parliament. The other charged me with adultery. This is an offence punishable with death by stoning under the Hadood ordinance; as yet, no-one has been willing to cast the first stone.

Gradually the negative publicity decreased and my account began to be received in its intended spirit, as an insight into the socio-political disorder of our country. Although I remained a curiosity, I became acceptable. My name is now a household word in Pakistan; feudal husbands took to chiding their rebellious wives: 'Don't try to be Tehmina.'

I announced 'Jehad' – a movement to represent the silent majority to raise controversial issues that most people feel afraid to speak about. It liberated me from the corrupt politics that I had witnessed. I decided to stand apart and away from the mainstream of the rotting political system and the deficient and self-serving politicians that consumed our national wealth and exploited our people.

My movement spoke the forgotten language of truth:

– I demanded accountability, I demanded a referendum, and went on hungerstrike.

– I took up Mir's issue and extended him support against selective justice, demanding a definition of Zia's role against the violation of the Constitution and a clearer sense of justice, and humanity.

– I demanded from Benazir an explanation for using her position to install Mustafa Khar in a sensitive ministry despite serious anti-state allegations uncleared and undenied by MI or ISI. I also declared our properties in London in an attempt to put into focus Mueen Quraishis law whereby parliamentarians had to declare their assets or else lose their seats – Mustafa had not done so, nor had most others, I am sure.

As was expected nothing happened and Mustafa remains a minister despite, amongst other things, a broken law.

When a news item appeared announcing the pending international publication of *My Feudal Lord*, Mustafa called me. He was furious but controlled when he asked, 'What is this nonsense I hear about the book?'

I could not resist reminding him of our lunch conversation, when he said that I had no identity of my own and would have to introduce myself as Mustafa Khar's ex-wife. I said, 'Well, Mustafa, now the world will soon know you only as Tehmina Durrani's ex-husband.'

DAUGHTER OF PERSIA
by Sattareh Farman Farmaian

'Once upon a time, long before fatwas and ayatollahs, the daughter of a *shazdeh*, or prince, grew up in a Tehran harem. Sattareh lived with numerous mothers, more than 30 siblings and some thousand servants . . . Sattareh's father may have been autocratic, infuriatingly stingy and over 60 at the time of her birth, but he was also unusually enlightened. His motto "education is everything" applied as much to daughters as to sons. It paid off, for Sattareh provides an accomplished portrait of a childhood enriched by nightingales and bazaars, politics and family romances. More impressively, she broke with tradition to study in California, returned to found the Tehran School of Social Work and, after the Shah's downfall, survived execution by a whisker'
She Magazine

'This enthralling account . . . confirms my conviction, learned from experience, that idealism does not die. Indeed, the human spirit can still triumph, however brutal the tyranny under which so many are destined to live out their lives'
Christabel Bielenberg

'A wonderful book to read and own; a treasury of human experience'
Fay Weldon

'Her memories of her childhood . . . are lyrical and enchanting . . . beautifully written'
New York Times Book Review

0 552 13928 9

A SELECTED LIST OF NON-FICTION TITLES AVAILABLE FROM CORGI BOOKS

THE PRICES SHOWN BELOW WERE CORRECT AT THE TIME OF GOING TO PRESS. HOWEVER TRANSWORLD PUBLISHERS RESERVE THE RIGHT TO SHOW NEW RETAIL PRICES ON COVERS WHICH MAY DIFFER FROM THOSE PREVIOUSLY ADVERTISED IN THE TEXT OR ELSEWHERE.

All Transworld titles are available by post from:

Bookpost, P.O. Box 29, Douglas, Isle of Man IM99 1BQ

Credit cards accepted. Please telephone 01624 836000, fax 01624 837033, Internet http://www.bookpost.co.uk or e-mail: bookshop@enterprise.net for details.

Free postage and packing in the UK. Overseas customers allow £2 per book (paperbacks) and £3 per book (hardbacks).